"This book speaks faithfully, compellingly, and earnestly into the current crises of politically divided Christians in the US today, providing brilliant re-framings of core Christian commitments to offer sacred spaces of generative engagement and the possibilities of transforming 'high conflict into good conflict.' Carr and Helmer deliver multiple hopeful avenues through which Christians from radically opposing positions might prioritize revolutionary listening, transformative love, and practices of Beloved Community."

—G. Sujin Pak, *Dean of the School of Theology, Boston University*

"Carr and Helmer argue that the task of justice-seeking needs to be grounded theologically, specifically in justification, through which Christians receive their primary identity and belonging. Their approach to navigating diverse and often opposing views of justice is compelling and refreshing. No topic is off-limits, as they illustrate with chapters on the contentious issues of abortion and Christian participation in politics. This much-needed volume should be read by Christian leaders everywhere."

—Cheryl Peterson, *Academic Dean, Wartburg Theological Seminary*

"Carr and Helmer tackle the difficult, some might say impossible, task of addressing polarization and entrenched divisions in the Christian community over hot-button issues. Theirs is a grace-oriented approach that seeks common ground in a shared baptism in Christ in order to explore how justification can establish a renewed way of being in the world. Though readers will find aspects with which to agree and disagree, I applaud their efforts to build bridges across divides, to generate justice-seeking conversation that takes theology seriously, and to root discourse and relationships across camps by appealing first and foremost to the undeserved grace that Christ offers believers."

—Jennifer Powell McNutt, FRHistS, *Franklin S. Dyrness Chair, Associate Professor of Theology and History of Christianity, Wheaton College*

"Amy Carr and Christine Helmer make a valuable Lutheran contribution to the ongoing ecumenical gift exchange in theology and ethics. In recalling us to a shared, 'ordinary' Christian identity founded in justification through faith by Christ, they invite fresh and careful reconsideration of the connection between that identity and the work of seeking justice. This crucial endeavor involves giving a properly theological account of the possibility and importance of patient encounter, reflection, and dialogue in our fractious and polarized cultural moment. What emerges is an attractive vision of the *practice* of justification which serves the life of the Beloved Community, the hope of the world."

—Philip G. Ziegler, *Chair of Christian Dogmatics, University of Aberdeen*

"By beginning with 'ordinary faith'—the conviction that our identity is secured by grace rather than by any ethical or political performance—Carr and Helmer provide a framework for moral discernment in an ecclesial context where there often seems little on offer except silence or shouting. Addressing some of the most deeply divisive issues in the contemporary landscape, they evoke a refreshing vision of the Beloved Community, in which 'living into the spacious grace of God' entails a commitment to hear and engage the insights of all members of Christ's body—especially those with whom we disagree."

    —Ian A. McFarland, *Robert W. Woodruff Professor of Theology, Candler School of Theology, Emory University*

Ordinary Faith *in* Polarized Times

Justification and the Pursuit of Justice

Amy Carr and Christine Helmer

BAYLOR UNIVERSITY PRESS

Unless otherwise stated, Scripture quotations are from the New Revised Standard Version Bible, copyright 1989, Division of Christian Education of the National Council of the Churches of Christ in the United States of America. Used by permission. All rights reserved.

Cover design by *the*BookDesigners
Cover art by Wendy Michelle Davis, wendymichelledavis.com

Book design by Baylor University Press
Book typeset by Scribe Inc.

Library of Congress Cataloging-in-Publication Data

Names: Carr, Amy, author. | Helmer, Christine, author.
Title: Ordinary faith in polarized times : justification and the pursuit of justice / Amy Carr, Christine Helmer.
Description: Waco : Baylor University Press, 2023. | Includes bibliographical references and index. | Summary: "Addresses the contemporary problem of Christian polarization by offering a theological framing to Christian justice-seeking and proposing concrete spiritual-political practices for negotiating contested positions"-- Provided by publisher.
Identifiers: LCCN 2023018356 (print) | LCCN 2023018357 (ebook) | ISBN 9781481319317 (hardcover) | ISBN 9781481319348 (adobe pdf) | ISBN 9781481319331 (epub)
Subjects: LCSH: Conflict management--Religious aspects--Christianity. | Dialogue--Religious aspects--Christianity. | Justification (Christian theology)
Classification: LCC BV4597.53.C58 C375 2023 (print) | LCC BV4597.53.C58 (ebook) | DDC 234/.7--dc23/eng/20230629
LC record available at https://lccn.loc.gov/2023018356
LC ebook record available at https://lccn.loc.gov/2023018357

For [Christ] is our peace; in his flesh he has made both groups into one and has broken down the dividing wall, that is, the hostility between us.

Ephesians 2:14

Contents

Acknowledgments

We started writing together, motivated by the urgency of a Christianity that was rupturing. On one hand, we had a shared worry about the ways that Christian discourse in the public sphere so often seems one-sided in its portrayal of what counts as "the" Christian perspective on various matters of ethics and justice (often with views with which we ourselves disagree). On the other hand, as we began to write together, we found ourselves responding to a pull to address something else besides the "other" points of view on matters of justice—however keenly we feel about our own particular pictures of social justice. Our work crystallized around the topic of polarization: why do we so often witness such irreconcilable differences within the body of Christ? Family members cannot talk to each other anymore; friendships are broken, and different groups within Christianity, even within the same denomination, have grown so far apart that there seems that nothing can hold them in the ecclesial unity professed under the third article of the Apostles' Creed. Christianity is a dynamic religion and has been since its origins in the conflict between Peter's version of Jewish Christianity and Paul's idea of Gentile Christianity. Yet contemporary conflict so often seems less fruitful, less able to generate new ideas or ways of looking at reality or ways of Christian being-in-the-world. Often our experience of conflict today prohibits interaction and multiplies antagonisms. We have lost the sense for a dialogical dialectics that comes from listening to others. Can theology offer a model to alleviate such conflict so that conversation can begin between those who disagree? This book is our answer to this question.

A note regarding the version of the English translation of the Christian Bible that we are using: unless otherwise indicated, we cite the New Revised

Standard Version (NRSV), available as Bible Study Tools, "The New Revised Standard," *Salem Web Network*, https://www.biblestudytools.com/nrs/.

We thank institutions that supported this collaborative project: the Martin Marty Center for the Public Understanding of Religion at the University of Chicago Divinity School and Northwestern University's Office of the Dean of Weinberg College of Arts and Sciences for making possible Christine's research leave during the academic year 2021–2022; and Western Illinois University, which provided Amy with a sabbatical during fall 2021. Our anonymous readers offered helpful suggestions and earnest applause. Molly Van Gorp gave us generous feedback and helped us iron out the wrinkles. Dave Nelson, editor at Baylor University Press, enthusiastically supported this project and shepherded it through to publication. Jenny Hunt and the entire Baylor University Press team were patient, pastoral, and collegial in the process of accompanying us through revisions. We are grateful to them all. Because this theological project is a synthetic one, our interlocutors are too vast to list, stretching from mentors and colleagues we have known in the flesh to those in the communion of saints whose written works have fed our theological understanding and imagination. Most of all we are grateful to each other for the "dialogical dialectics" that resulted in the creation of a "third," the joint result of work together.

Amy Carr and Christine Helmer
Christmas 2022

1

Ordinary Faith in Times of Conflict

In August 2009 the Evangelical Lutheran Church of America (ELCA) met for its eleventh biennial Churchwide Assembly in Minneapolis. Up for discussion was a social statement, "Human Sexuality: Gift and Trust," that included, among other issues, the topic of the ordination of gay and lesbian clergy and congregational affirmation of same-sex marriages.[1] These issues had been addressed once before, at the previous synod in 2007, with no definitive resolution. In the interim, local congregations had taken up discussions regarding the statement and surveyed parishioner responses as multi-year task forces wrapped up their studies of human sexuality. On August 19, the Assembly came to its decision: a precise two-thirds majority of 676–338 voted to adopt the Social Statement, which permits congregations and synods to choose whether or not to bless same-sex marriages and to ordain clergy in gay or lesbian relationships. The landmark decision coincided with the arrival that afternoon of the first significant tornado to strike Minneapolis since 1981. The tornado dissipated near the Minneapolis Convention Center where the Assembly was being held.[2] The one-third minority interpreted this natural disaster as a sign of judgment. The majority perceived the Spirit at work in the decision, guiding the church into a deeper understanding of what it means to love our neighbors as ourselves within the body of Christ. "The Decision" has continued to guide ELCA polity.

---

[1]   Evangelical Lutheran Church in America, "A Social Statement on Human Sexuality: Gift and Trust," 2009, https://download.elca.org/ELCA%20Resource%20Repository/SexualitySS.pdf.

[2]   Ted Olson, "ELCA Assembly: Was God in Either Whirlwind?" *Christianity Today*, August 20, 2009, https://www.christianitytoday.com/news/2009/august/133.41.0.html.

In the years following, individuals, pastors, and congregations disagreeing with the new social position left the ELCA and aligned themselves with new institutions highlighting their preferences in the "culture wars." Many church denominations, such as Anglicans/Episcopalians, United Methodists, and Presbyterians, have analogous stories about their church fracturing over such issues. Some Roman Catholics are distressed about Pope Francis' pastoral recommendations for gay persons. US Eastern Orthodox leaders censor those who even voice support for normalizing queer identities (or ordaining women). A new movement called "Progressive Christianity" and led by evangelical-raised entrepreneurs riles many in the evangelical world. The fissures from these debates leave Christians reeling today. Our current situation is one in which hot-button issues, like human sexuality, are taking front and center stage in church life. Politics in the sense of culture wars implicates the church, and vice versa, with churches taking positions on either side of this battle.

The thread running through these debates regards the question, What is Christian identity? In the contemporary climate, Christian identity has taken on the different sides of political issues, with the battle for the correct Christian identity carried by the correct politics. Yet church splintering along these lines is battering the body of Christ. How do we recognize one another as fellow Christians, across earnest divisions within and across our various ecclesial contexts? In turn, how does our baptismal belonging to one another in Christ direct us into caring so very much about the precise moral shape of our lives together before God?

Indeed, who among us does not have dreams for a just society? Christians of all kinds bring their hopes and dreams to the political table. Some march together for peace and #BlackLivesMatter. Some run for school boards and state legislatures. Christians argue their cases before the judiciary and wield the power that punishes criminals. Yet we are also divided in our visions of justice. Some are convinced that those who kill must be punished by the death penalty while others think that even the most hardened criminal can be rehabilitated when given a chance. Some think that abortion is the murder of an unborn child; others think that women should be trusted to make the best decisions about their lives in the context of a pregnancy. Some think that the clergy must be male; others think that God also speaks the divine word through women. In his "I Have a Dream" speech, Martin Luther King Jr. imagined racial and economic justice,[3] yet Christians today remain divided about what that dream actually looks like. And they are in some cases so divided that their dreams are polar opposites of one another.

Even in these intractable divisions, Christian dreamers and political activists all understand themselves to be Christians. Each believes they are faithfully following Christ in trying to establish visions of justice in the world. And they might even identify their side of the moral and political debate to be the kind of justice that Jesus himself would advocate. Christian identity, in other words, gets conflated with the moral and political position one holds. Those Christians who do not hold that position are charged with being anti-Christian. How can one be a Christian and participate in justice-seeking in the world in a way that may put one at odds with other Christians? How can we understand Christian identity in ways that allow other Christians to dream just as much as we ourselves do?

Where Can We Start?

This is a book about ordinary faith—about Christians who live out their faith in a politically charged church and world. It is ordinary because it assents to living out the spirit of Christ in the world with all its mundane challenges and conflicts; it is Christian because it insists on being grounded in Christ. Ordinary faith is also communal because it requires collaborating to edify and transform our shared world.

If things were as easy in real life as these preliminary definitions suggest, then we would not be pulled into writing this book. Ordinary faith is hard to live out when we come up against competing interests. It is difficult to discern how Christians down the street, in other states and lands, share the same commitment to belonging to Christ when our opinions differ so extraordinarily from theirs. It is a challenge to see how Christians who live elsewhere can edify our own faith when their moral and political leanings are radically different from our own. It is easier to dismiss and vilify them—they are not really Christian: they are "right wing" or "radical left" or "crazy" or "woke" and thus do not belong to the same Christian faith as we do.

---

[3]   Martin Luther King Jr., "Read Martin Luther King Jr.'s 'I Have a Dream' Speech [Washington, D.C., August 28, 1963] in Its Entirety," NPR, updated January 16, 2023, https://www.npr.org/2010/01/18/122701268/i-have-a-dream-speech-in -its-entirety.

Is a conversation among such disagreeing Christians even possible? Can we even recognize one another as Christians united in the body of Christ? Can a theology of ordinary faith expand an understanding of faith in Christ so that it can be perceived to encompass even Christians with whom we vehemently disagree? In this book we address our own context in the United States. We are aware that divisions and polemics have a global reach, and are even analogous in different countries; yet we write from our observations about Christianity in the United States, focusing on particular debates currently virulent (and hope that other Christians around the world will be sparked to develop our ideas in their own contexts). There are, admittedly, many bones of contention. Here Lutherans pit themselves against other Lutherans on questions of women's ordination, whether abortion should be legal, and whether queer folk can get married. Methodists, Presbyterians, and Episcopalians too disagree among themselves—often splitting their churches into different denominational factions. Evangelical and progressive Christians disagree on the clarity with which God speaks in Scripture, the role that Christians must play in bringing about the kingdom of God on earth, and whether trans girls can play sports. Protestants and Roman Catholics disagree on Christ's presence in the Eucharist; they even disagree on the name of this sacrament—is it the Lord's Supper or the Eucharist?—and on the role of the pope in the church. Some Protestants agree with Roman Catholics on issues they disagree about with other Protestants, such as women's ordination, queer identities, and the reach of the church into the political realm. Everywhere one looks at Christians, there is disagreement.

Disagreement today, particularly about the issues of abortion and the role of Christianity in politics, seems insurmountable. We are in a situation of what Amanda Ripley calls "high conflict."[4] We are so divided that those on either side of an issue are convinced that no conversation is possible. Serious conflict is what ordinary Christians assume is the condition of Christian faith today. Is it best then to retreat into one's enclave of like-minded companions, because conversation is only possible when preaching to the choir? Should we continue to indulge our own feelings of personal rectitude by denouncing those on the other side with various terms of

---

[4]   Amanda Ripley, *High Conflict: Why We Get Trapped and How We Get Out* (New York: Simon & Schuster, 2021); see also Ezra Klein, *Why We're Polarized* (Lakewood, Calif.: Avid Reader Press, 2021).

reprobation? A high conflict expression of Christian faith finds perverse comfort in identifying who is right and wrong on moral and political issues. Such a posture of faith assumes that one's own position on a contested issue identifies who can be called a Christian, or anti-Christian.

We write this book with the conviction that a state of high conflict among Christians does not need to be so prevalent. Indeed, there are important theological reasons why high conflict indicates a sickness in the body of Christ. We use theological tools to diagnose this sickness and work out a theological model for turning high conflict into productive discussion about justice-seeking that can generate new insights and transform the body of Christ into one that reflects what we are calling an ordinary faith—a faith that proclaims and expresses our baptismal being in Christ, even within the messy dynamics at play in both the church and the world.

By Christ Alone

We need to agree on a starting point: to figure out what holds us together so that we can acknowledge each other as Christians and thus begin a conversation, even with those with whom we disagree. In fact we recognize that disagreement is a feature of conversation. Disagreement might even be the glue that holds us in conversation in the first place. If we think we agree with each other all the time, we can nod in agreement without ever entering into conversation about what really matters. Disagreement might actually be a good place to start a conversation! At the very least, our disagreement is something to talk about. Or disagreements might emerge through the course of a conversation. But can we start a conversation at all when we equate earnest differences about the shape of justice-seeking with a difference in Christian identity itself?

At heart what we intend is to take the talk of Christian identity away from moral and political positionings and move it into a theological discussion. What happens when we begin with a theology presupposed by those who take their bearings from the rhythms of an ordinary life in Christian faith, rather than with a theology that associates faith with an often adamant declaration of a certain moral or political identity? What if we took a shared identity in Christ as the common starting point among Christians of different denominations, different factions within denominations, and different groupings of Christian "identities"? What if we used theology to make sense of this identity shared by all Christians of ordinary faith?

Our perception of Christian unity—the one that anchors this book—is based on the New Testament writer Paul's idea of justification by faith. This idea was claimed with a distinctive clarity, so clear that it ended up dividing the Western church in the early sixteenth century into its Roman Catholic and Protestant confessions. Martin Luther, Augustinian friar and ordained Catholic priest, is heralded as the sixteenth-century reformer who insisted on the doctrine of justification by faith. He came to this conviction after a lengthy period of intense anguish over the passages in Paul's works having to do with God's justice. A passage such as Romans 1:17 terrified him: "For in it the righteousness of God is revealed through faith for faith; as it is written [Habakkuk 2:4], 'The one who is righteous will live by faith.'" If God's justice was revealed in the gospel, then nobody could stand blameless before Christ the judge. This question of justification—who or what makes the sinner just before God?—drove Luther's deep anxiety. He had thought with the theologians of his day that the way a sinner is justified by God has to do with the combination of divine favor and one's own good works. Luther struggled with his own recognition that all good works are somehow shot through with bad intentions and inherited sin. If even good works were tainted, then the combination of God's grace and human effort would not work out, and sinners would be condemned to the eternity of hellfire.

Luther finally found a way out of his theological and spiritual distress. His discovery set a foundation for Christian identity ever since—a way with roots in the apostolic era of the early church. Luther arrived at the insight that being Christian is not a human work; rather, it identifies a conviction that is independent of works, a belief in the God in Christ who is source and sole agent in rescuing humans from their self-inflicted miserable state. Luther's insight about justification as a divine action is a statement about the reality of God who makes sinners just through the gospel, not a God who demands justice as judge. The justifying God is the one who does all the work of salvation. God works by revealing the gospel in Christ who justifies sinners on account of his life and death on the cross. Christ rescues those destroyed by sin so that we can enjoy being in God's presence and conversely, that God enjoys our presence. Justification by faith summarizes Luther's discovery of the gospel, God's saving work that is attributed to sinners without their worth or merit. The denominations associated with Luther—Lutherans—have traditionally been committed to the centrality of the doctrine of justification by faith not as one doctrine among many, but as the doctrine that holds all others together.

The doctrine of justification by faith in Christ means precisely that we are not justified by our own efforts, but by Christ alone.

While all doctrines are special, there is something primary about justification. Amy uses the analogy of the spinning top.[5] There is the part of the top that is always on the ground; this grounding is precisely what enables the top to whirl out in many directions as it spins. Justification by faith in Christ can be understood as the part of Christian doctrine that holds the top to the floor. From there, the top can spin in different directions—toward the doctrine of the Trinity, toward formation of the Christian life, toward political activism—but there is something about the doctrine that is quite literally grounding, that centers Christian life and prevents it from falling over and thereby losing its spin.

Luther articulated justification by faith as an idea that grounds the ordinary faith of all Christians. In his time and place, most Western Christians were Catholic. The unfortunate fact through Luther's conflicts with the Catholic hierarchy was that this doctrine became more associated with Protestantism rather than Roman Catholicism. Yet Luther intended to reform Catholicism—not abandon it—and although historical contingency enabled the eruption of new denominations, he insisted that justification by faith grounds Christian identity for *all* Christians.[6]

We take Luther's understanding of the Pauline idea of justification by faith in Christ as a gift to the church, and invoke it as *the* shared identity of Christians. Justification by ordinary faith! We acknowledge that even for Christians, this idea might take some getting used to. The phrase might sound strange in North American Christianity, which is propped up by the American myth of the self-made, self-determining individual. Rugged individualism is the *homo faber* (the human who makes) in a capitalist system in which works alone matter. Hence the concern, perhaps even obsession, with determining whether one is among the God-chosen people. In the face of this North American affinity for works, for action,

5   The spinning top as an analogy for being grounded, yet nimbly able to turn in every direction, was shared with Amy decades ago in conversation with one of her former professors at Carleton College, Bardwell Smith.

6   In the decades after Vatican II, Roman Catholics and Lutherans have identified more common ground about the doctrine of justification by faith. See the "Joint Declaration on the Doctrine of Justification" by the Lutheran World Federation and the Roman Catholic Church, October 31, 1999, https://www.lutheranworld.org/sites/default/files/Joint%20Declaration%20on%20the%20Doctrine%20of%20Justification.pdf.

for liberty, for self-determination, the Lutheran idea of justification by faith provides a shocking theological alternative. The Lutheran tradition offers to Christian North American society a compelling understanding of what it means to be human from God's perspective, without the need to empirically verify one's standing before God. According to the Lutheran insistence on the centrality of justification by faith, it is Christ—not the solo self as the subject of good works—who is the center of human personhood for a Christian. Belonging to Christ is what justification by faith means. And on this basis, any concern with belonging to the elect becomes unimportant or cast aside.

But this is only part of the story. While Luther averred that justification by faith in Christ is the center of Christian identity, he did not do so to denigrate good works. He did so in order to assign good works to an important place: not as a precursor to or condition of justification, but as the natural expression of having been freed by Christ. If justification by faith is the tree, then good works are the fruit; if justification is the gift of faith in Christ, then works of justice are gifts of love to neighbor.[7] "The only thing that counts," as the apostle Paul wrote, "is faith working through love" (Gal 5:6).

How justification is related to good works of justice-seeking is this work's core theme. We have in mind those Christians who want to think about this relation, especially for those interested in diminishing the high conflict currently swirling around hot-button ethical issues, like abortion, such that they can promote generative theological thinking among those who vehemently disagree with one another. Christian good works are vital, including the good work of pursuing a more just and flourishing world. But what *kinds* of good works and what particular vision of the common good are deemed to support Christian belonging? It is precisely this question that determines so much religious and political animosity in the contemporary body of Christ. Our aim is to provide a theological account of the relation between justification by faith and justice-seeking that we hope will reduce the temperature of animosity between Christians of different moral convictions, so that real mutual conversation can transpire, and conflict be transformed from "high" to "constructive." We

---

[7]   Luther refers to the "good tree, good fruit" analogy in part 2 of his treatise on Christian freedom: Martin Luther, *The Freedom of a Christian, 1520*, trans. W. A. Lambert and Harold J. Grimm, rev. trans. Mark Tranvik, newly rev. Timothy J. Wengert, The Annotated Luther Study Edition, ed. Timothy J. Wengert (Minneapolis: Fortress, 2016), 514–15.

believe that by framing religious and political differences within a theological perspective informed by justification by faith, we can ease into a shared space in which Christians begin to talk to each other with the conviction that another person and their perspective is worth getting to know. How can theology provide resources for talking about an ordinary faith that is grounded in Christ and that does not necessarily anathematize another Christian for their vision of justice? How can we meet one another in disagreement, all the while recognizing a place of mutual belonging in the same body of Christ? How can we reflect on our own contributions to the rupture that inflicts pain upon the body of Christ, and how might we ease this pain?

The Practice of Ordinary Faith

Our starting note is that faith's mode of being is always "by Christ alone." This is Luther's Reformation insight: that participation in Christ is the ground, source, and goal of faith. We orient ourselves theologically from within this particular take on faith. When we are justified by faith in Christ, our faith is not a work of our own, not even the work of believing in Christ or assenting to Christian propositions. Faith is the gift of Christ—the unmerited gift of freedom in Christ. Faith is Christ's work in us, when the Spirit breathes Christ in us as the center of our identity.

We dub such Christ-borne faith "ordinary." Faith by Christ alone initiates us into a posture of ongoing, lifelong conversion into the ways and vision of God. For those who have had a dramatic experience of conversion, ordinary faith is what may settle in afterward. A constant companion, faith perpetually refocuses how we view the world as we find ourselves formed in the image of Christ in loving response to the world. To be sure, *feeling* faith may seem like something each of us moves in and out of depending on life circumstances. We might say we have a strong faith when we feel secure; but the minute we experience a loss or a tragedy, our faith might weaken. Why did God permit this to happen to me? "You of little faith" (Matt 8:26) is a phrase Jesus often used to address his friends. He seemed puzzled by his disciples who were not living from the fuller trust in God that Jesus wanted to impress upon them. Ordinary faith follows such rhythms of life's anxieties, frustrations, disappointments, and injustices. It is a living into daily repentance of our temptations, myopia, and whatever draws us away from a Christ-centered existence; and a daily rebirth into the remembrance of our baptism into Jesus' own dying and rising.

Ordinary faith has to do, then, with living into the spacious grace of God in Christ who heals the sick, finds the lost, and calls persons together into community. This grace precedes and follows the honest concern we each have with our individual selves, our looking within to discern our personal failures to live out this graced life, as well as to gaze at the wounds inflicted by those who have been careless with or cruel to us. While grace informs how we discern our broken connections to self and world, grace is also attuned to *divine* concern, and lures us into remembering God's gifts. Grace is gifted freedom that empowers us to love God and our neighbors as ourselves (and to dare to trust that others can love us as themselves in turn). Cast thus as a grace-filled dwelling space, such faith is more than just a set of beliefs that we assert to be true. It is a way of life that moves us and moves *with* us. An ordinary faith orders the whole of our lives and also catches and accompanies us when we fall. It informs who we are; hence we "are being transformed into the [Lord's] image from one degree of glory to another" (2 Cor 3:18). In the process, faith orients the way we think and live with ourselves and others, and situates everyday occurrences and challenges within a larger horizon of God's love for us in Christ. We can get better at living out our faith; we also fail along the way. This too is part of the life of ordinary faith: knowing the persistence of sin, we are not surprised to find that we continue to participate in destructive ways of ordering our lives. We can show receptivity to others; we can also shut them down. We can be drawn to presumption about our own virtue, and despair of our ability to effect any meaningful change to avert individual or collective vice, perhaps most notably today the vices that generate the human-induced climate catastrophe. Grace helps us discern our vulner-abilities, particularly when we presume to know what the other "side" is thinking, or despair that the other will not come to the table that Christ has set. A life of ordinary faith teaches us that we can love our neighbors as ourselves, listening to the voices of those who might themselves seem unwilling to hear, without losing touch with our own embodied histories and wounds. Such mutual listening does not preclude our each speaking the truth of things as we see them.

Justification by faith in Christ is one early Christian (Pauline) entry point for a vision of a redeemed existence: for a radical reckoning with the interior and communal forces that pressure us into hardness of heart, smallness of vision, and an inability to love God above all and our neighbors as ourselves. Remembering our baptism into Christ Jesus means remembering that narcissistic, small-minded, self-preserving forces do not have the last word; the patterns of sin are not forever fixed. We can begin ever anew to see ourselves and one another with more clarity and charity, and our world with eyes open to ongoing repentance. Claimed in and by the body of Christ, we can embark upon the effort of listening to our neighbors not only when they live next door, but when their collective voices coalesce into a movement for social change, for the naming and addressing of a particular pattern of sin that circulates in our shared world.

Ordinary faith is humble yet far-reaching. It is the faith Jesus speaks about in his parable of the mustard seed (Mark 4:30–32): it is here and now and under our feet, not far off in the heavens (Deut 30:11–14), imperceptible yet growing to surprising heights. *Such faith assumes that the resources we need to work with those with whom we disagree are already present in our midst.* We can cultivate and grow the kingdom of God, the Beloved Community, because it is present among us now, if we have eyes to see and ears to hear.

The practice of ordinary faith thus conjures a picture of justice-seeking in which doing is grounded in listening for all at work within us and within those around us—our doings embedded always within the redemptive doings of God in Christ under the gusts of the Holy Spirit. Indeed, Jesus always asked his disciples to *do* when he asked them to *listen*: to have ears to hear (cf. Mark 4:9), which is more than a literal hearing. It is being infused by the word that God speaks in Scripture and life, as faith sets up in us a second nature, one made in conformity to Christ.

This sort of attentive listening has shaped the perspectives on faith of diverse Christians across the centuries. Saint Benedict opens his famous rule for monastic living with the imperative: "Listen, carefully, my child, to my instructions, and attend to them with the ear of your heart."[8] Listening precedes doing. Benedictines speak of obedience as an act of "listening toward" God and one's community, discerning the word of God for one's time.[9] Benedict's imperative runs down the ages into the poorest areas of Latin America. Contemporary Catholic Christians living in base communities (*comunidades de base*) are invited to listen by noticing their material needs and then analyzing the barriers or conditions that prevent

[8]   From the Preface of the Rule of Benedict as translated in Joan Chittister, *The Rule of Benedict: Insights for the Ages* (New York: Crossroad, 2004), 19.
[9]   Conference of Benedictine Prioresses, *Wisdom from the Tradition: A Statement of North American Benedictine Women in Response to Our Times* (Atchinson, Kans.: Mount St. Scholastica, 2006); Chittister, *Rule of Benedict*, 19–20.

their needs from being met, like having enough water in their community. In this way, they make use of listening in order to explicitly connect neighbor-love to justice. Love requires such listening to our neighbors' account of their needs. This is one example of the rhythm of ordinary faith's movement toward pursuing justice by first naming what that justice might look like in the reality of mundane life. "Let anyone with ears to hear listen!" (Mark 4:9) is a call to keep looking for deeper understanding and more effective means ("skillful means," to draw upon a Buddhist phrase) for responding to what we hear. The exercise of ordinary faith is not about drawing attention to oneself as one who does good in the world, but about being part of the process of hearing what God is calling us to notice and respond to together.

This is not to suggest that we are made right with God *by* our listening-informed doings. This is the subtle paradox of Christian faith. Our receptive listening is twofold. Through our baptism, we tune into our justification by faith in creation's Healer and Justice-Maker, Christ Jesus. Listening to creation's needs for justice follows like a river from its source, finding its way across a rocky landscape scarred by sin. Ordinary faith paradoxically holds together a recognition of our being centered in Christ *and* our efforts to discern and pursue justice as we listen to our neighbors and ourselves. Ordinary faith risks the disorienting and reorienting process of justifying our respective beliefs about the shape of justice, precisely because we find our footing as Christians not in our particular visions of a just world *per se*, but in the One who has entered the world's brokenness to redeem and reorient each of us, singly and together.

Faith and Works, Justification and Justice

When we speak of ordinary faith as a Christ-given gift, we address an acknowledged touchstone for all Christians, especially those who identify with the Protestant Reformation, namely: justification by faith. This "doctrine" has come to be the mascot for Lutherans because it was Martin Luther who first drew attention to this Christian concept in a particularly provocative way that led to the break with Rome in the sixteenth century. Yet justification by faith is a doctrine held by all Christians who recognize the centrality of Christ's work in setting persons free *from* sin and *for* living into the vision of flourishing that God has for persons and creation.

But the question of works in relation to justification by faith asked by followers of Luther in the post-Reformation period brings Christians back to the Pauline question of the relation between faith and justice (or in biblical terms, the relation between Romans 1–11 that addresses, broadly, justification by faith, and Romans 12–15, considering good works). The theme of good works directed to neighbor presses into justice-related questions of community, society, and politics. Christians today might be more familiar with the terminology of justification by faith and good works because of its biblical inheritances. But the term "justice-seeking" that we introduce in place of good works gestures toward a relationship between justification and justice-seeking while also distinguishing between them. Certainly Paul framed justification by faith in Christ in critical relation to good works, emphasizing that our individual good works cannot earn us favor with God (even as Paul's original concern was primarily to insist that Gentiles did not need to follow the Jewish ritual laws, like circumcision and keeping kosher, to become followers of Christ Jesus). Yet as we explore, the larger picture for Paul (and Luther) is that good works are works that are "good" because they serve the neighbor's justice. The good of the neighbor can occur when they (and we) reside in relations of justice: hence our attention to the root of "justice" (*dikaiosune* in Greek) present in both justification by faith and justice-seeking.

Whenever we speak of justice-seeking, we move beyond the notion of individual good works into the terrain of social justice. The two are intertwined, often simultaneous. When Lutherans make Lutheran World Relief kits, they recognize the fundamental truth of their interrelationship with global neighbors. When we begin to ask *why* our neighbors have need of personal care items, the answers move us beyond the framework of the "good works" of direct service to others and into a more complicated narrative about the distribution of resources and of relative degrees of economic, social, and political power. The realm of the political—where we make local, state, and national laws that determine public policies—is one realm in which we formulate or alter those larger patterns of relations among one another. This is the realm where we practice collective justice-seeking and identify what *counts* as justice for policy purposes in a way that stretches us beyond the direct service realm of "good works" one neighbor enacts for another.

So the relationship between good works and justice-seeking is one between an individual moral action that benefits another human being, and a collective process of ethical discernment and advocacy, often (though not only) by attempting to influence political decision-making. Put differently, justice-seeking is often at play when we are debating the nature of the moral law itself: what counts as right and wrong, not only interpersonally, but with regard to what is permitted or forbidden, encouraged or discouraged, enabled or disabled by laws and public policies. For example, Christians who debate the ethics of abortion and of abortion access are engaged in a debate about the shape of justice whose answer finds expression not merely at the individual level, but at the level of state or national law. So too for Christian debates in the past about slavery, or today about the acceptability (or not) of same-sex marriage and gender queer identities. Here we are not speaking of good works, but of what the nature of the good *is* on various matters of human behavior or ways of being.

At heart this book is about recognizing how one Christian tradition—stressed by Lutherans as an offering to all others—offers resources for perceiving the lines of connection between justification and justice. It is also about how recalling our baptismal identity in Christ frees us to risk justice-seeking in a way that resists the polarization and demonization of political opponents in the process of collaborating toward better policies and more accurate ways of seeing one another interpersonally. Justice-seeking occurs at many levels: from knowing one another's stories to thinking about how we can move from those stories to sketching together what kinds of local, state, national, and international policies might best support flourishing for all.

To glimpse some of the diverse ways that justification by faith has been connected to justice-seeking (not only to good works), we need look no further than the ways that Luther has become iconic of *individual* resistance to any perceived unjust order of things. Doing so also draws us into the nucleus of concern that motivates our discourse of "ordinary" faith: a worry that too often today, Christian identity in the public sphere is expressed as something extraordinary, as dramatically oppositional to a perceived threat to Christian existence, if not also to the very possibility of a just world itself.

Individual Hero or Workers in the Vineyard?

This pull to moral heroism requires some disentangling, prompting the questions: Who does the works? Who is the agent in the pursuit of justice? The story of Luther, the Protestant reformer, has captured the imagination of the modern justice-seeking "agent." Here is the Augustinian friar on the outskirts of the Holy Roman Empire, in the Saxon town of Wittenberg, who spoke truth to the most powerful men of the times: Pope Leo X and the Emperor Charles V. The message to the pope was one about the freedom of ordinary Christians, which means being released by Christ from the tyranny of Rome.[10] The phrase Luther is said to have spoken in front of Charles V in April 1521 when Luther was required to recant his works (many of them on justification by faith) has come to symbolize the courage of the individual conscience: "Here I stand, I can do no other, so help me God." (These words, however, were not ever spoken. They seeped into the myth of Luther as a modern hero.[11])

This dramatic image of Luther forever captured the modern imagination. *The Freedom of a Christian*, Luther's famous text from 1520, has been troped as a spark plug for the freedom of the modern Western individual. This declaration of freedom unfortunately was translated all too often into the individual marked white and privileged and male. The "freedom" pronounced by philosophers for some was accompanied by the enslavement of many others, especially in the colonized and missionized Global South. All the same, this popular image of Luther the reformer is an icon of the modern freedom to think for oneself, apart from a group, and to disparage the sins of that group against which one bravely stands. Luther becomes the avatar of the existentialist posture, "here I stand," the leap into faith seen here as the position from which one's own truth becomes the exemplar of truth *per se*, and the reason for speaking truth to power. Not Luther's thoughts but his person is seen to embody the power of the individual to speak one's own truth.

Speaking one's truth has become a trope for the beginnings of justice in contemporary society. While speaking publicly has been a prerogative of white men who express what they deem is true, and thereby generate laws and government and culture on the terms of their own speech, the tide in recent years has turned to enable the speaking of those who have been silenced. Speaking one's own truth, one's individual truth—be it of a discerned personal identity, or testimony to experiences of exploitation, harassment, police brutality, or false condemnation—this has been the opening of the public space for individuals speaking as a token of an entire group. Our era has highlighted this phenomenon because of the ways in which society treats those who are grouped together in particular ways, through race, class, and gendered identities. The person speaking his or her truth to power is naming not just that person's truth, but the truth of experiences that are representative of that person's socio-political identity because society treats

10   See Luther's dedication to Pope Leo X of his freedom treatise in Luther, *Freedom of a Christian*, 474–81.

11   See Christine Helmer, *How Luther Became the Reformer* (Louisville: Westminster John Knox, 2019), 6.

those belonging to a particular group with similar regimes and technologies of oppression, marginalization, incarceration, and abuse.

This new sense of speaking one's truth as representative of a group in some respects exemplifies and in other respects challenges the popular Luther-inspired idea that the rugged individual alone has the prophetic insight to speak prophetic truth. The act of "coming out" and of "bearing witness" (e.g., to trauma) recapitulates the "here I stand" positioning. But when this testimony is spoken in recognition of a marginalized or oppressed group, it challenges the idea that only a rugged individual has the requisite prophetic insight. Indeed, the exceptionalist model, emerging from the modern Western sense of autonomy and freedom, has rendered the solo truth-to-power speaker an icon for modernity. It represents a model of modernity that dovetails with a biblical strand of the individual prophet perched in that uncomfortable place between God and the group, seeing God's perspective with human eyes and appointed to speak this truth to the group. But this is only the beginning of a lengthier process of joining the solo articulation of justice with the community, and then navigating the hard work of bringing different voices together as oriented to a common goal.

The "here I stand" icon is very different from the reality of communal justice-seeking. The vineyard of God's Beloved Community requires all sorts of workers with many tools and talents. Lucas Cranach the Younger's painting of the Workers in the Vineyard from 1573–1574 shows just this insight. The work in tending to the vineyard—the representation of the parable from Matthew 20:1–16—is assigned to the Lutheran Reformers. Each Reformer is given a different tool and job. Luther, recognizable in black Augustinian habit around a sturdy body, rakes the ground. Melanchthon, ever gaunt with smart goatee and a Cheshire cat smile, pulls up water from the well. Johannes Bugenhagen, preacher at St. Mary's City Church where Luther often substituted when Bugenhagen was carrying out reforms in his native Pomerania, is immediately recognizable with a gray chin-length bob and jaunty pink robe, digging out stones with his shovel. There is no one prophet, crying alone in this wilderness, but a group of workers, each important in their assigned task. Collectively their labor reverses the effects of the workers on the other side of the vineyard, the representatives of the Roman curia, who pull out the plants, throw rocks onto the ground, and set fire to the harvest.

We need to let go of—or at least be wary about—the icon of the "here I stand" celebrity. Faith is not extraordinary, but ordinary. Its real work

Cranach, Lucas the Younger (1515–1586) / German, *The Vineyard of the Lord*, 1569 (oil on panel), Bridgeman Images

for justice is done in community, together with other Christians likewise dedicated to the everyday work of justice-seeking. Advocacy is always communal; it takes various workers to tend the vineyard. For example, those who dare to break silence about sexual abuse or domestic violence have needed the accompaniment of those who listened, who named patterns of controlling behavior, who organized to create shelters, child protection services, and new policies that recognize power dynamics in abusive relationships. And even in these examples, disputes abound about all manner of policy positions (such as the value of restorative justice rather than a punitive approach with domestic abusers). Likewise, when Rosa Parks refused to move to the back of a racially segregated bus in Montgomery, Alabama in 1955, a seemingly simple act that prompted a bus boycott to end legal segregation, she was not making this choice out of the blue. When she said, "People always say that I didn't give up my seat because I was tired, but that isn't true. . . . No, the only tired I was,

was tired of giving in," she expressed a justice-seeking tiredness that was informed by years of participating in efforts to plan and organize.[12] In the movements to address domestic violence and racial segregation, as in any given vineyard working to produce the grapes of justice, moments of individual moral heroism work only when they are embedded in an organized communal process of reflection and action together.

To those vineyards, too, workers bring differences in personalities and job descriptions, and there is always a likelihood of disagreement and working at cross-purposes in some key area. The individual who works alone does not have to agree or disagree with anyone. But addressing a sinful world out of brave solitude is not really how most Christians operate. They are placed in the church; they are also members of communities of work and play. Humans are social animals, as is often stated; and in theological terms, there are many members in the one body of Christ (cf. 1 Cor 12:12).

Our Extraordinary Times: Apocalyptic Polarization

But ordinary faith is practiced today in times that are rather extraordinary. We are living in a particular moment of what Amanda Ripley (as noted above) calls "high conflict." There are two sides, and each side has built up so many walls of defense and offense that the positions themselves have become rallying cries for membership. High conflict dehumanizes one's opponents, creating a binary world of "us" versus "them"; this opposition is often framed in apocalyptic terms. One's opponents seem utterly incomprehensible and immoral; our position alone has true value. We see this heightened conflict all around us: parents yelling at each other about the curriculum at school board meetings; Christians unable to address other Christians who have different views on abortion; some who think that their faith is significant to their politics while others believe strongly that they must check their faith at the door of the public square. Our times are structured by deep polarizations on issues of faith and politics. Many fear that the center of a democratic society will not hold.

There is another way of conceptualizing conflict that Ripley calls "good conflict." Disagreement about an issue can be productive; it does not have to be a rallying cry around an identity marker. Instead, disagreement about an issue can nudge us toward curiosity about why someone else

---

[12]   Rosa Parks, with Jim Haskins, *My Story* (New York: Puffin Books, 1992), 116.

holds a belief that differs from our own, can push the dialectical process of coming to deeper insights into the truth of an issue through conversation and listening to each other's stories, and can actually end up articulating a tentative agreement that represents a diversity of beliefs in a larger amalgamation. Good conflict involves genuine disagreement that, when engaged with honesty and mutual respect, can generate an outcome more responsive to everyone's needs and concerns.

This process of migrating toward agreement or some sort of consensus (albeit partially and eschatologically) through good conflict is the challenge we undertake in this work. And our commitment to this is based on a Christian idea (as old as the church in Paul's day) that community is essentially a most untidy undertaking, one that involves acknowledging and engaging rather than fearing our differences, one that invites cultivating our dispositions around listening and conversational styles that are oriented to staying with good conflict. Regardless of our discomfort, we can enter a chaotic process of looking for ideas that generate solutions to whatever divisions plague us.

The idea of a pure Christian church is one of the fictions that has appealing purchase for some, especially in modernity. The idea of a decline from a perfect origin—the fall—has been reproduced in another dimension: a fall from an imagined earlier purity (of Christian times). We can see this in various theological appraisals that cast the modern world as "secular" and Christ as the principle of truth against that secular world. There is resistance to any mixing between Christ and the secular that might taint the Christian gospel by secular values. This idea often finds an ally in twentieth-century Protestant thought initiated by the Reformed theologian Karl Barth. Barth framed his theology around the opposition of God's word to human history, culture, religion, and politics. It was in the context of National Socialism that he did this; he needed a critical principle that could theologically call to account any subservience to a fascist regime that replaced God with a nationalistic idol.[13]

The idea of a fallen world, inevitably under divine judgment, is one that haunts the contemporary theological distinction between Christ and culture that is the title of a famous book by H. Richard Niebuhr. Here the world is perceived to be divided into an ecclesial community

---

[13]   On the theological position pitting the church in opposition to the secular world, see Christine Helmer, *Theology and the End of Doctrine* (Louisville: Westminster John Knox, 2014), 88–107.

of the gospel and the larger world under the law.[14] "Gospel" is conflated with the Christian community as an imagined space offering a worldview of theological and moral purity that is opposed to and in conflict with a secular world seen as sullied. This distinction creates a separation between church and world, an intrinsic and ontological conflict, and the fiction that the Christian identity marker of moral purity is set against the secular for theological reasons.

What is interesting is that this sort of theological distinction between Christ and culture is analogous to the polarizations we see today, each contrasting purity with toxicity, stain, or pollution. On one hand, the conservative-identified "Christ" camp considers itself in opposition to a clueless or insidious "secular" world. This opposition is characterized as the "culture wars," primarily around issues of gender and sexuality, but now also (at least in the United States) around critical race theory. Such Christians prioritize preserving what they perceive to be the purity of the gospel, which they believe unambiguously stipulates the moral order. Any deviation from this order is considered antithetical to the gospel, and denounced.

On the other hand, the "woke" culture privileges social and political awareness of the systems of racism, capitalism, colonialism, heterosexism, and patriarchy that are constitutive of the modern world. Public assertions of wokeness place one within a privileged moral vantage point that regards the systems we inhabit in the contemporary world as inherently corrupt. Even when overt theological language is not used, the world (or the hegemonic social order) is portrayed as ontologically fallen, and anyone who deviates from assent to this judgment is called out (or, as opponents feel, "canceled").

The "woke" camp, like the "Christ versus the world" camp, claims the vantage point of purity. Each camp perceives itself as capable of being untainted by the faults each applies to the other. Interestingly, we encounter here parallel appeals to purity. As each side claims purity for itself, each depicts the contemporary world as out of order. The "Christ" camp does so on the basis of a purity/secular divide, while the "woke" Christian camp structures its polemics on the basis of insight into the original sins of racism, capitalism, and patriarchy. The result is a "culture war"—the high conflict of two antithetical sides who fight each other for more political power to organize social institutions, each portraying the other as if it represented a monolithic, static point of view.

[14]   This is one type of Christ-culture relation in H. Richard Niebuhr's typology in *Christ and Culture*, 50th anniversary ed., foreword by Martin E. Marty and preface by James M. Gustafson (New York: HarperCollins, 2001).

One dynamic in contemporary US culture wars is a temptation to make moral purity for oneself *the* focus of concern, even more than the end goal of the common good that is envisioned in one's picture of a just world. Pursuit of one's own moral purity can be expressed in an obsession with naming the sins of those who do not seem to share one's own vision of the common good. Here both "right" and "left" can participate in what is often (if too simplistically) called a US legacy of Puritanism: seeking to purify the nation of its errors. Some perceive "woke liberals" as "the Democrats' new Puritans" who, through seeking the firing or canceling of persons for past bigoted statements, can seem "more focused on purity and atonement within the liberal tribe . . . than making society less discriminatory."[15] Likewise, the Holy Synod of the Orthodox Church of America (OCA) issued a statement that seeks to silence all Orthodox Christians who dissent from the OCA's official teachings on the sinfulness of same-sex attraction or queer gender identities:

> We call upon all clergy, theologians, teachers, and lay persons within the Orthodox Church in America never to contradict these teachings by preaching or teaching against the Church's clear moral position; by publishing books, magazines, and articles which do the same; or producing or publishing similar content online. We reject any attempt to create a theological framework which would normalize same-sex erotic relationships or distort humanity's God-given sexual identity. . . . Consequently, those who teach these errors become participants in the sin of those whom they have tempted or whom they have failed to correct, and thus should seek remission of this sin in the mystery of holy confession. Those who refuse correction open themselves to ecclesiastical discipline.[16]

As these examples suggest, equating moral purity with conformity to a particular sort of proper thinking and speaking is something we can see

[15]   "Religious Fervour Is Migrating into Politics," *The Economist*, March 25, 2021, https://www.economist.com/united-states/2021/03/25/religious-fervour-is -migrating-into-politics. See also Anne Applebaum, "The New Puritans," *The Atlantic*, August 31, 2021, https://www.theatlantic.com/magazine/archive/2021/10/new -puritans-mob-justice-canceled/619818/?utm_source=newsletter&utm_medium =email&utm_campaign=atlantic-daily-newsletter&utm_content=20210831& silverid=%25%25RECIPIENT_ID%25%25&utm_term=The%20Atlantic%20Daily.

[16]   Holy Synod of the Orthodox Church in America, "Statement on Same-Sex Relationships and Sexual Identity," July 21, 2022, https://www.oca.org/holy-synod/ statements/holy-synod/holy-synod-issues-statement-on-same-sex-relationships -and-sexual-identity.

done by some on both the progressive and conservative side of issues around race and gender (among others). But punitive disciplining of our own or another's speech shuts down serious ethical and theological reflection. A single-minded pursuit of idealizing oneself and one's justice-seeking projects (and related group identities) can be accompanied by demonizing one's opponents. Seeking absolute moral purity in these ways is one mark of high conflict.

A pillar of Western Christianity, the fourth-century bishop and saint Augustine, had a very different idea about life in the world, one that is arguably much more productive theologically and practically. He advocated the idea that the city of God dwells together with the city of the "human" in ways that cannot be so clearly separated by a divisive worldview. Augustine's reasoning was thoroughly theological. He referred to Jesus' parable of the wheat and the weeds in Matthew 13:24–30 to illustrate his point.[17] Let both grow together in the same field, the owner instructs his workers. Only at harvest time can the wheat be distinguished from the weeds, and then be separated. Augustine's interpretation of this parable serves as guide for themes we address in this book, namely, that because we are Christians who cannot clearly distinguish between wheat and weeds with our limited intellectual resources and finite perspectives, we should better practice an ordinary faith that transforms high conflict into good conflict in order that together a better vision of justice might be worked toward.

As we think about Augustine's use of the parable to warn those who might tend to prematurely uproot the weeds, we might add here a caveat about our own possible denunciation of those who denounce others in the name of moral purity. A subtext throughout our extended theological reflection on justice-seeking is the ever-pertinent value of mutual listening. That includes listening to fathom why we are sometimes drawn to polarized discourse that seeks to position ourselves on the side of goodness, and our opponents on the side of all that is evil and misguided. In the chapters ahead, we dip in and out of attention to this level of listening—beneath overt arguments to the affective needs being expressed.

[17] Saint Augustine, *Sermons on the New Testament: Sermon 23* (on Matt 13:19), trans. R. G. MacMullen, in *A Select Library of the Nicene and Post-Nicene Fathers of the Christian Church*, 1st series, vol. 6, ed. Philip Schaff (Buffalo, N.Y.: Christian Literature Publishing, 1888), rev. and ed. for New Advent by Kevin Knight, http://www.newadvent.org/fathers/160323.htm.

One human need triggering polarization we might mention here is the hunger for a sense of safety amid trauma. In her classic *Trauma and Recovery*, contemporary psychiatrist Judith Herman synthesizes clinical studies of those who have experienced trauma due to war, sexual abuse, domestic violence, rape, torture, or other intense interpersonal violations of trust.[18] These studies suggest that at the initial stages of healing, survivors often find themselves less tolerant of ambiguity, more in need of a clear sense of where the safe spaces and the dangerous spaces might lie. Later, or intermittently, there is time for remembrance and mourning, and of beginning to connect one's own suffering to that of others. Those who research the trauma of collective oppression, like systemic racism or homophobia, note that stages of trauma and recovery occur in reaction to these chronic conditions as well.[19] So part of our mutual listening amid high conflict might involve recognition of how any of us might feel an urgent desire to identify with moral purity (and denounce the impurity of others) when we grapple with traumatic spaces triggered by violation, ongoing oppression, or profound alienation. While feeling unsafe does not exempt us from responsibility for our own moral decision-making,[20] we might heed the spirit of Jesus' parable about the wheat and the weeds. This parable encourages us to cultivate a patience even within those intense "here I stand" moments. As we orient our justice-seeking by an ordinary faith characterized by patience, we remember, mourn, and find perspective through our belonging to the One who endured trauma before and now with us.

Ordinary Christian faith in extraordinary times can steady us into creative ways to move past high conflict, within ourselves as well as between us. In our time and place, high conflict comes in shades of red and blue, of right and left, of good and bad drawn along ideological lines, binaries that erase others in the too-easy self-interest of one's own assertions and

---

[18]   Judith Lewis Herman, *Trauma and Recovery: From Domestic Abuse to Political Terror* (New York: Basic Books, 1992).

[19]   Among others, see Shoshana Ringel and Jerrold Brandell, eds., *Trauma: Contemporary Directions in Trauma Theory, Research, and Practice*, 2nd ed. (New York: Columbia University Press, 2019); Alisha Moreland-Capuia, *The Trauma of Racism: Exploring the Systems and People Fear Built* (Cham, Switzerland: Springer, 2021); Beverly J. Stoute and Michael Slevin, eds., *The Trauma of Racism: Lessons from the Therapeutic Encounter* (London: Routledge, 2022).

[20]   "Though the survivor is not responsible for the injury that was done to her, she is responsible for her recovery." Herman, *Trauma and Recovery*, 192.

beliefs. High conflict can become good conflict when we begin to hear how the other side's narratives make sense (or in the case of a conspiracy theory, identify something that is at stake for someone that drives them to a narrative that may be out of touch with empirical facts) and insist, along with Augustine, that the condition of the life of the church on earth is precisely to wait for the harvest. We wait while yet engaging with both wheat and weeds, not ultimately distinguishing between them (but letting God alone judge), and humbly acknowledging that we ourselves might be weeds at this or that moment in our pursuit of justice in church and world.

Beloved Community, Church and World

Ordinary faith is a practice in these extraordinary times of polarization. There is a prophetic dimension to this practice to be sure, for Christian faith is a call to justice-seeking. Like the biblical prophets, Christians can agonize about injustice and seek ways to alleviate it. Just as Jesus wandered around Galilee establishing justice by healing the sick, exorcizing the demons, feeding the hungry, and offering new life possibilities for those at the margins, so too Christians heed Jesus' prophetic call to work for those issues we feel most passionate about.

But we have underscored that this faithful practice of justice-seeking is not the kind of engagement exemplified by the presumed heroism of the prophetic individual who insists on speaking truth to power, apart from participation in one's community. Ordinary faith is not extraordinary heroism. Ordinary faith does not center one's own moral heroism in the face of implacable systemic sin and all those deemed to uphold it. Ordinary faith neither shirks nor valorizes the prophetic voice, but is open to sitting down to talk about what in fact is worthy of prophetic attention. It assumes engagement within communities. Ordinary faith is communal faith. Work in the vineyards from which we press grapes for the wine of justice requires an attitude that resists the polarization fostered by vociferous prophetic heroes keen on distinguishing between wheat and weeds (or, here, between grapevines and weeds!). The faith that refuses to insist on the moral purity of one's own position is a faith that humbly, steadily participates in a community that reminds each of us to recollect our baptism in Christ. In this community we are perpetually reminded of the need to die to our sins (and our woundedness by sin) in Christ, and then to rise with the new possibilities of living together given by Christ Jesus.

What kind of communal living also *engages* the prophetic call for justice? How can we make sense of a community that is grounded in Christ yet is also oriented to seeking justice, as a community, in the world? At this point, we seem to be invoking an idea of community that has two dimensions: one having to do with a Christian's reception of justification by faith and another that advances good works. This question of community with two aspects is necessary as we hold on to the theological distinction between justification and justice-seeking. Such a distinction, as we will reiterate in various ways, is necessary for subverting any illusions that Christian identity is to be equated with a position on the kind of justice commitment to pursue. Christian identity is based on Christ as justifying, well-making gift. And this idea of justification by faith is correlated to a community that makes this its central message. The justice-seeking that emerges as a consequence of this primary message is correlated to a community that is oriented to the world.

Here we invoke another theological distinction that has been deployed since Augustine in order to make sense of how a community based on justification by faith can be related to but distinct from its orientation to justice, namely, the church/world distinction. Many Christians usually think about the church as the community in which the gospel is communicated and the world as the realm in which justice is sought. But how are the two related? Some theologians think of the church in antithesis to the world. On the basis of the gospel's revelation in the church, the church is opposed to all values in a world that is incapable of solving its own problems. Some desire a clear church/world distinction to insist on purity, or liturgical integrity, or that there is something unique about the church having to do with divine revelation in Christ and the distribution of that revelation in ways that empower Christians to serve the world and to work toward its transformation.

But on close inspection, this opposition between church and world blurs. Even while insisting on its unique gospel message, the church is infused in some ways by culture, economics, and politics. Church members tithe in the currency of the state; printed bulletins for Sunday service are made possible by worldly inventions of the printing press and paper, and recently the large picture screen. Even values such as what justice projects are sought out have to do with broader cultural shifts in technology, gender/sexuality, and how religious freedom can be guaranteed by and exercised in the state. Hence it is helpful to think of the boundary between church and world as semipermeable. The church engages with and in the world in all sorts of ways, absorbing some of its dimensions while also projecting its own visions of justice-seeking into it. Augustine's wheat and weeds coexist both in church and world.

Yet what distinguishes the church from the world? Justification by faith in Christ is the characteristic mark of the church itself, the reality that sets it apart from the world. Justification by faith imprints Christians forever with the cross of Christ. It is the place of baptismal identity, where we receive grace in the reception of the Lord's Supper, and where we are renewed again and again in the hearing of the gospel. It is, as Martin Luther King Jr. termed it, the Beloved Community, the place in which the divine attribute of love (1 John 4:18) is active in transforming sinners into beloved citizens of the kingdom of God.[21]

The Beloved Community's integrity rests in its creation by Christ. But that Beloved Community becomes concretized for us in local, national, and global churches. Within these contexts, we bring to bear diverse attitudes and obligations. We might be a leader or just sit in the pew, an active member of the church council or a lapsed churchgoer. Yet some form of interpersonal ecclesial belonging is key because it invokes, in a Christian key, the social constitution of what it means to be human. As social beings, we engage with others through belonging and its various registers of affect, reason, and connection. Central to our book is this idea of belonging, whether one names it a church, or community of faith, a congregation, or the *basileia tou Theou* (kingdom of God). This place of belonging nurtures our core identity in Christ through the gospel message proclaimed in word, sacrament, deed, and fellowship. This reliable, multi-textured sense of belonging to and in Christ—in and through particular communities—dissuades our fears of loss of belonging.

One key part of our work in this book is to describe theologically the ecclesial community that sustains the integrity of justification by faith. This is our primary place of belonging as Christians: the place that creates our shared identity in Christ. Here forgiveness and grace are presented as touchstone realities amid life's changing circumstances. This stability is central to the repetitions invoked in churches—the liturgy, the preaching of the gospel, even the finite Bible with its infinite interpretations—a place that anchors and reanchors, the rock on which our faith is built. It is from this point of stability that Christians can stretch to imagine justice that

---

[21]   "The aftermath of nonviolence is reconciliation and the creation of a beloved community." Martin Luther King Jr., "The Power of Nonviolence (1958)," in *A Testament of Hope: The Essential Writings and Speeches of Martin Luther King, Jr.*, ed. James M. Washington (New York: HarperOne, 1991), 12.

they seek to embody in their own communities, as well as project into the world. And importantly, we will suggest, the paradox of ecclesial belonging to one another in Christ is that it is a fact that can secure us even in seasons when we feel betrayed by particular churches and their leaders. This is because the gift of belonging to the covenant in Christ is based on God's own initiative, on the creative wiliness of the Holy Spirit in tracking our lives toward the faithful renewal of the covenantal body of Christ, not on humans who can be prone to justifying our harming of one another, even in the name of God and church.

We conclude these opening remarks on the distinction and relation between church and world with two notes. First, we write mindful that some of our Christian readers might have sharper and others fuzzier distinctions between church and world, between all God's creation and the Beloved Community as that which opens redemption in Christ to all persons, indeed to the cosmos as a whole. Martin Luther King Jr.'s own evocation of the Beloved Community issues from the center of Christian imagination to address the whole of the United States, and ultimately the entire human race. Christian philosopher Marilyn McCord Adams does something similar in her distinctions among what we might call wider and narrower dimensions of the church. She describes "the Church universal" as "the whole human race, all those human beings for whom Christ" had defeated horror. She notes, "Membership in the Church universal is independent of whether or not the individual human beings believe that God exists, that God was in Christ, or that God in Christ has established" a path to the defeat of the horrors of sin and evil.[22] She depicts the gathered "congregating Church" as the conscious, self-aware expression of the church, where Christians "get together to articulate and to celebrate and to reinforce one another's confidence in Christ's Stage-I horror-defeat. The congregating Church also gives itself over to the study of Scripture and tradition, and to their practical application."[23] McCord Adams' distinction suggests something akin to Karl Rahner's "anonymous Christians,"[24] a kind of inclusivist vision in which all persons (and the cosmos) are

[22] Marilyn McCord Adams, *Christ and Horrors: The Coherence of Christology*, Current Issues in Theology (Cambridge: Cambridge University Press, 2006), 201.

[23] McCord Adams, *Christ and Horrors*, 201. McCord Adams also writes of the wrestling church and the missionary church on 200–202.

[24] Paul Imhof and Hubert Biallowons, eds., *Karl Rahner in Dialogue: Conversations and Interviews, 1965–1982*, trans. Harvey D. Egan (New York: Crossroad, 1986), 207.

affected in salutary ways by God's redemption in Christ, whether or not they know or appeal to the name of Christ Jesus.

In our own working out of a relation between justification by faith in Christ and justice-seeking, we do not presuppose that fellow Christians hold to such an inclusivist view of metaphysical truth and salvation. We trust that our theological reflection on Paul's teaching about justification can speak meaningfully to Christians who have different assessments of how their Christian and non-Christian neighbors might belong to the Beloved Community. When we speak here of the Beloved Community, we are leaning out to behold the whole of existence from within the light of what we hold most sacred, what catches us up in our own baptism into the crucified and risen Christ.

A second note is less about conceptualizing and more about actually navigating church and world simultaneously. The great temptation to reduce justice-seeking to upholding the idea of one's own or one's group's moral purity (or at least the purity of our own moral imagination) may be associated in part with a fear of making moral mistakes, or of being perceived by others as being in the wrong in our moral or justice-seeking judgments. For some Christians, that temptation takes the form of acting politically from within a nostalgia for an imagined time of the church's own past purity, to re-establish a world more in tune with days of perceived (if relative) church-state harmony. For other Christians, political action in both church and world is accompanied instead with the chronic pain of knowing the church's long history of systemic sins, from anti-Judaism to misogyny, racism, and imperialism. Yet whether we tend toward nostalgia or toward a sense of damnation about the church's complicity in sins within itself and in the larger world, we can navigate our risked political participation in both church and world with a frank awareness that not only disagreement, but disagreeable sin arises from within the church—not only in the world. In Marilyn McCord Adams' words:

> The Church is headed by Christ and led by the Spirit of Christ, but the Church is human as well as Divine. The fact that we human beings are both social and socially challenged means that any human institution is apt to spawn horrors. However hard we work to improve our institutions, it is precisely their systemic character that makes them veer out of our control to produce effects beyond our powers to anticipate or prevent. History proves that the Church is no exception. The Church

has been a horror-perpetrator. . . . This means that the Body of Christ (whether Church or cosmos) is uncoordinated and dysfunctional, both headed by Christ and directed by the Spirit of Christ, and yet riddled with systemic evils and productive of horrors. This ambivalence should keep members from turning their ecclesial institutions into idols. It should make us humble and vigilant, starkly self-critical, ready to repent and to seek God's help. We will all have to live in this tension until God acts to bring horrors definitively to an end.[25]

We extend McCord Adams' call to engage with repentant self-awareness in justice-seeking—or, as she puts it here, horror-reduction—to other worries or insecurities we might have about navigating church/world relations in the political realm. We might freeze at the idea of the conflict of political engagement and prefer to focus on being healers and pastoral caregivers. There may be fear involved in learning to practice advocacy and finding ourselves having a different temperament than that of the most vocal, strident organizers of a group (or, conversely, frustration in feeling prepared to go further than others in naming and speaking truth to power on a particular issue). There can be fear involved in moving from a space in graduate school where one has learned to speak and think in a certain language of social justice, into a rural congregation that allows concealed carry of firearms in the sanctuary and opposes same-sex marriage. But to our anxiety about conflict with others, or about making mistakes along the way, we can be aware that the church's mojo has been to invite a spirit of repentance within the framework of belonging to the Beloved Community on the basis of Christ's gifting us there, not our own moral perfection. We can speak back to our fears with the words of our baptism: *I belong here; so do you; we belong together by virtue of our faith in Christ. Our corporate identity in the body of Christ is primary.*

However we conceptualize a church/world distinction, and whatever our challenges in navigating justice-seeking in both spheres, those justified by faith in Christ participate in the Beloved Community—the communion of the saints across time and place—as our stable place of Christian belonging, even when we or our local congregation or the global church errs. The Beloved Community is the space in which we can stay with all the varied affective expressions within ourselves and others as we experience, name, and work through conflict (including conflict about the shape justice takes). Grace speaks a transcendent word into our contemporary

---

25   McCord Adams, *Christ and Horrors*, 203–4.

polarization and reminds Christians that God's team is much more capacious and immense than the insistence by any of us on being right. The Beloved Community carries the trust in the Spirit's promise to lead us into truth even though we admit that we are not fully there yet.

Invitation to Dialogue

While readers will likely notice that we lean toward the progressive side politically, we do so with theological commitments to thinking with and from the creedal orthodox traditions in Christian thought as well as the theological-ethical obligations to think with those with whom we disagree— because even in disagreement we are bound together by a more fundamental identity. We understand our constructive theological contributions here to resonate across the spectrum of theological and political sensibilities, trusting that our fellow Christians—progressive, conservative, and somewhere in the middle—belong to these same traditions.

Indeed, we offer this book up with the hope that readers of every stripe would find themselves filling in the gaps of our theological vision here, contributing from their knowledge of their own theological conversation partners and social locations of every sort. We have written in a way that synthesizes theological resources that have spoken to us or that are well-worn through use by one or both of us. But we trust that our readers will bring to bear their own theological sources and spiritual traditions as they think about our central thesis about justification by faith in relation to justice-seeking. We hope this book will serve as a seed crystal for more Christians to reclaim and develop anew the classic Christian doctrine first articulated by the apostle Paul.

2

Justification by Faith

What It Is and Why It Matters Today

Why Does Justification Matter to a Divided Church?

Different groups of Christians today have different ways of noting their identities. Roman Catholics talk about their commitment to the sacraments; in ecumenical contexts, Eastern Orthodox highlight *theosis*, deification; Wesleyans refer to the holiness tradition; Episcopalians their global allegiance to Canterbury; and Lutherans—an unapologetic insistence that Christ justifies the sinner without any human worth or merit. Each one of these Christian branches or denominations, not to mention each non-denominational church or evangelical association, charts out different ways to live out these identities in personal, social, and political ways. How a particular church understands itself in a plurally religious world has to do with how that church expresses its central commitments in the world.

Our current church and political divisions have to do with precisely this issue, namely, how particular commitments to church identity are worked out in the social and political spheres. What it means to be a "Christian"—an evangelical, Lutheran, Pentecostal, Orthodox, Roman Catholic, or Reformed Christian—is all too often evaluated by whether one adheres to one or another side of a moral or political issue. Christians battle each other on the political landscape. Christian identity is demarcated by one's position on a hot-button political topic, like abortion, race, or government control. Christians embody their church identities in the world by advocating particular justice issues.

We, like many others, are concerned about the entrenched divisions in what we are broadly calling "justice-seeking" initiatives. How can it be that the "body of Christ," the church, is so deeply divided that the most basic conversation is impossible? How can it be that Christians accuse each other of "wokeness" or "traditionalism" or "insanity" without even trying to understand where the other is coming from or what the other has been through? And to express the central question of this book: *How can we reframe our approaches to these serious divisions on justice issues so that a more grace-filled orientation to abundant life together is possible?*

The aim of this chapter is to recalibrate our basic intuitions about Christian identity. We begin our discussion of justice-seeking by describing an identity marker that is most theologically fundamental to Christian faith, namely, justification by faith. Our theological revision to the question of justice-seeking is to focus on the justification that Christ works in personal lives and in the church. Christ is the One who heals all divisions, forgives sins of hostility to one another, and creates a new community in which belonging is based on grace. Grace is more fundamental than human action; it is the condition upon which all justice-seeking takes place. Divine justice—in other words, grace—is the foundation of the Beloved Community. Our work in this chapter consists of outlining this basis for belonging: justification by faith in Christ.

This is not the first time that theologians have taken justification seriously as central to reconstituting Christian identity. In the early sixteenth century, Martin Luther called out the divisions in the body of Christ. Luther criticized how the monks, nuns, and priests deemed themselves morally superior to regular churchgoing persons because of the type of dress they wore, vows they took, and most importantly, the church power they took for themselves. Luther struggled with how the bishops established on their terms what it meant to be approved by God, and how they identified the miter and cope, the fancy palace, and the close association with dukes and emperor as matters of importance in the church. Luther criticized the power they exerted, much of it unjust. He turned what the priests and bishops identified as the identity markers of the church upside down. Rather than robes and property, the identity of the church is Christ's work of forgiving sins and inviting sinners into a new community. Luther identified the community of justified sinners as Christ's body. He revised its identity by grounding it in God's justice. Divine justice meant the freedom Christ gave to sinners so that they could be freed from terrified consciences and free to serve their neighbors in love. Christ, not the priests, was the church's foundation.

The question for the church today, particularly a body that is so deeply divided, has to do with revisiting once more our assumptions about Christian identity. How can the notion of Christian identity be construed so that Christian faith is oriented by a more basic sense of belonging to one another in Christ? This is the question of what justification by faith means today for a divided church. How can a focus on justification orient Christians toward a belonging that is rehearsed again and again amid attempts to work out approaches to contentious justice-seeking issues? Justification matters for justice. Justification, not justice, is the central identity marker for Christians. Justification means belonging to the body of Christ, regardless of one's type of commitment to justice-seeking work. Justification by faith, as we claim in this chapter, is a place to return to again and again. In the lifelong conversion that comes with living into our baptisms, we take our bearings from justification by faith in Christ that frees us for and moves us toward justice-seeking love of our neighbors and ourselves. To be sure, from Paul's day to our own, there has not been consensus about every feature of what constitutes right ways to identify justice or how to pursue it. It is into the expressions of division around justice-seeking today that we hope to stir a reminder of the power and wisdom of grounding Christian identity in justification by faith in Christ.

How does the Christian doctrine of justification by faith offer a starting point for reflecting on the facets of our lives together as Christians? This question brings us back to the story of Martin Luther, how he rediscovered the gospel as justification by faith, and launched the Protestant Reformation. In fact Martin Luther inspired us to use questions to structure our journey through this chapter. Luther wrote the *Small Catechism* in 1529 after discovering that many Christians of his time lacked even the most basic knowledge of what it meant to be a Christian. What we appreciate about the *Small Catechism* is its format of question-and-answer. There is something about this format that helps in learning the basics of faith. Hence we imitate this format as we formulate the basic questions about justification by faith that guide each section of this particular chapter—which is formative for all that follows.

Why Does Doctrine Matter for the Gospel?

Theologians work with concepts. They try to make sense of terms like "love" and "freedom" as these words say something about human beings, the world, and God. These words have come to mean particular things in the present. Theologians thus study the ways these terms have changed, depending on their use in particular churches and communities, while also holding on to a common element in their meanings. Terms are used with different connotations in different settings. The term "word of God," for example, can be taken in a number of ways. When theologians speak about the Christian doctrine of the Trinity, they take "word of God" to refer to Christ, or the second person of the Trinity. When liturgists announce "word of God" after reading the lesson, they take the term to refer to the Bible. Theologians have as their job to make sense of how different people use the same terms. They try to identify what is true about these terms, even when they are misused.

"Justification" has come to be one of the more important terms for theologians. Particularly since the religious reformations that took place in sixteenth-century Europe, justification has become central to the way theologians make sense of God's actions in personal lives and in the church. Martin Luther drew particular attention to "justification" in identifying something central to God's action in Christ. In fact, Luther is credited with a reorientation to this term that challenged the dominant Catholic theology of his day. While Luther's insistence set him and his followers on a path separated from Rome, he did not identify something entirely new in the history of Christianity. Luther intended to show what Christianity had always had as its central message: the Christian belief in Christ's action of the forgiveness of sinners that is motivated by God's compassion for the human condition. Twentieth-century German American theologian Paul Tillich insightfully called justification "the Protestant principle." For a world that had witnessed the horrors of World War II and the genocide of six million Jews, Tillich thought that the "Protestant principle" could relativize all claims to absolute authority (or, we could say, identity). All identity markers, all political positions, have the potential to be elevated to absolute claims of identity. Christian faith rejects any claims that are touted as absolute because of its commitment to a more basic claim: justification by faith in Christ. In this world, justification is the only reality that has the power to resist worldly tendencies to arrogate power to its particular forms of justice, however unjust they might be. Justification identifies what Christians understand about how God transforms persons into an existence that is unprecedented, unworldly, and unpowerful. In Christ, as the apostle Paul writes, there is a new creation (2 Cor 5:17) that we witness in the Spirit, even as its fuller emergence is ever ahead of us.

Theologians use many words to point out God's action in Christ. Biblical words such as grace, redemption, and reconciliation have made their way into the theological vocabulary. Each of these terms has its own connotations and uses. But justification has become central to the way Lutheran theologians speak about God in Christ. The significance of this term in the Lutheran vocabulary is due to the way in which particular German theologians at the turn of the twentieth century sought to make sense of Luther's experience of God. Until that time, theologians had been preoccupied with doctrines rather than experience. But this early twentieth-century group of church historians and theologians had become interested in how Luther's experience became the basis for his ideas about God that ended up with his excommunication from Rome in 1521. In his book from 1917, *What Did Luther Understand by Religion?*, Karl Holl shows how Luther's experience of God consisted of a dramatic shift from the fear of the all-encompassing ought—the demand of the divine law—to faith in God's love that fulfills the law.[1] Luther identified a new meaning of "justification" by experiencing the dramatic change from sin to salvation. Luther's legacy for Protestant churches, as well as for Roman Catholicism, lies in the central idea of justification.

The churches emerging from the sixteenth-century reformations, particularly the Lutheran churches, insist on the centrality of justification for Christian identity. This centrality is captured by the phrase, "justification is the article by which the church stands or falls." The Christian church is grounded in Christ and is established by his work of creating a community of justified sinners. The unique witness of Christianity is directed to Christ whose incarnation, crucifixion, and resurrection redeems sinners from the consequences of sin and offers a new life together with him. Discerning and explaining how Christians understand and preach the meaning of new life is a vital theological exercise for Christians.

Justification is the unique work of the Christian God who takes action on behalf of sinners in order to forgive them of their sins. This doctrine has been historically central to Protestants—again, the "Protestant principle," which is the particular criterion that establishes how Christian preaching and teaching can be true. The truth of the Christian message in all its forms is based on the idea of the gospel that justifies sinners and sinned-against without their contribution, sacrifice, or deserving. God acts in Christ to save us from the destructive power of sin; God works to generate abundant life. Justification by faith in Christ is the gospel witness to God's action in redeeming the world from the catastrophes of human making by reorienting us amid their very swirling.

---

[1]   Karl Holl, *What Did Luther Understand by Religion?* trans. Fred W. Meuser and Walter R. Wietzke, ed. James Luther Adams and Walter F. Bense (Philadelphia: Fortress, 1977).

Why does this doctrine of justification matter today? What does this "Protestant principle" have to say in a world whose existence is fraught with insurmountable catastrophes that have only intensified to a planetary scale in the two thousand years since Jesus' earthly life? Human actions have precipitated disasters of climate change. Humans are complicit in systems that actively destroy minds and bodies because of differences like race, class, gender, place of origin, and ability. In this world as it is, how can the message of God's justifying activity be understood to be true, to be weighty in a world shaped by social media memes and conjured communal identifications of sundry sorts?

As theologians, we try to make sense of justification as the unique Christian witness to a God who works in Christ to benefit creation. The implications are countercultural insofar as we still dwell in a society based on the competition for wealth and status acquisition, with its own sins of greed, punching down, and elbowing others out. Some thinkers see our contemporary world in terms of a secular rejection of religion, while others see post-secular opportunities for a variety of religious formations that are emerging today. As theologians, we take the contemporary social and political context seriously, especially the work of those seeking justice for persons and our planet in various, sometimes competing, ways. As theologians we have something to contribute to our secular justice-seeking companions but from a particular perspective—one that is grounded in justification by faith.

How does justification establish a renewed way of being in the world as it is?—that is the theme of this entire book. The Protestant Reformation's gift to Christianity has been the truth of justification as central to the Christian message. God's action in Christ has to do with who God is and how God is invested in the salvation of sinners. Justification is a message that creates a communal witness to who God is in the world as it is. It is an unapologetic insistence on a God who thinks that the project of creation is too important to be left to its own devices, and a God who risks the death of the Son to ensure that life has the final word. Justification establishes a particular relation between God and the world engulfed by sin—between God and the sin-struck in this world. Its emphasis on divine action is the starting point for all theological reflection. Justification, in other words, is a space that points to divine possibilities within human impossibilities. As such, ever new possibilities are created—including justice-seeking possibilities in our common life together.

How Is Justification by Faith More than a Cliché?

Justification by faith is the doctrine that Lutherans, who otherwise disagree among themselves on many issues, agree on. They all stand on the "doctrine by which the church stands or falls." "Here I stand," Martin Luther boldly announced (so the story goes) as he stood before Emperor Charles V at the Diet of Worms in April 1521. What he meant was precisely that he stood on the idea of justification in Christ that had taken him years of struggle in the monastery to articulate. No one could convince him that justification was anything other than both the sole cause of forgiveness and ground of the church. In other words, justification by faith without works is the essential basis for all Christian identity: Protestant, Roman Catholic, and Orthodox.

The entire Christian religion is founded on the work and person of Jesus Christ. Jesus is God's chosen one, the incarnate Word, the baby in the manger, the Crucified Christ, the Prince of Peace, who forgives sins, heals divisions, and orients persons to life in and with him. Lutherans, on the whole, can be rather carefree and sometimes even nonchalant about works that follow from Christ's justifying action. This attitude of nonchalance emerges from a fundamental theological sense that justification by faith is the primary reason for Christian existence. Christ sets sinners free, as Lutherans echo Galatians 5:1. It is not human intentions, or efforts, or good works, but Christ who creates the "freedom of the Christian"—to refer to the title of an important work by Luther that sparked the Protestant Reformation.

Justification by faith in Christ is central to the identity of the Christian church. What this means, however, is up for discussion. One common understanding of justification is that it is "forensic." The term "forensic" in contemporary speech has to do with evidence, particularly around a crime. Forensics today is a field in criminal science. Yet the English term is derived from a Latin root, "forum," referring to the forum or marketplace in an ancient Roman town. The Latin presupposed by "forensic" can thus be translated "of the marketplace." When the Latin sense of "public"—associated with a public space, such as the marketplace—entered into English, the term "forensic" ("of the marketplace") became connected to the public space of the legal courts or a public debate. "Forensic" then came to mean the arguments and also the rhetoric advanced in a public debate or legal context.[2] This sense of a public declaration gets at the

---

[2] "Forensic," *Merriam-Webster Dictionary*, https://www.merriam-webster.com/dictionary/forensic.

theological meaning assigned to justification. Justification is a public "speech act" by which God declares a sinner's forgiveness. The church is the public space in which this speech act is proclaimed. After the sinners and sinned-against in the pew have announced their inability to free themselves from the forces that keep them captive to themselves—sin, death, and the demonic—they hear the words that the pastor speaks to them: "In the name of Christ, I forgive you all your sins." The word of God is the declaration of forgiveness. This word of forgiveness is spoken; it is eaten in the bread and wine. It is a word that acts when it is spoken and eaten. It creates the reality of new life in Christ. The forensic word of justification "does what it says."

"Forensic justification" has its roots in the theology of Philip Melanchthon, Luther's friend and colleague at the University of Wittenberg. Philip Melanchthon wrote about forensic justification in his theological interpretation of Paul's Letter to the Romans, the *Loci Communes*, or in English, *Commonplaces*.[3] Melanchthon was trained as a humanist whose expertise was Greek. He was particularly attentive to rhetoric. He identified "forensic" early on as the sense of justification that he thought Luther had in mind. This sense of a "declarative speech act" has come to dominate the current Lutheran understanding of justification. Lutheran theologians, like Oswald Bayer and George A. Lindbeck,[4] are convinced that words matter. Words do things; they have the power to convince people of truth and to shape one's perception of reality. The word of the gospel also "does" things that are amazing and miraculous. The gospel creates life. The living God speaks the word of the gospel that creates a life free from the effects of sin done by or to us. Lutheran theologians identified justification as God's "speech act" that is communicated in the public context of the church. The "word alone" accomplishes the forgiveness of sins.

Yet "forensic" is just one meaning of justification by faith. Doctrines come to mean something different in new contexts when they are explained and clarified. When someone tries to make sense of the important truths of faith, they use language and arguments. They

3   Philip Melanchthon, *Commonplaces: Loci Communes 1521*, trans. with intro. and notes by Christian Preus (St. Louis: Concordia, 2014).

4   Oswald Bayer, *Living by Faith: Justification and Sanctification*, trans. Geoffrey W. Bromiley, Lutheran Quarterly Books (Minneapolis: Fortress, 2017); George A. Lindbeck, *The Nature of Doctrine: Religion and Theology in a Postliberal Age*, 2nd ed., intro. by Bruce D. Marshall (Louisville: Westminster John Knox, 2009 [1984]).

interpret doctrines in order to better understand them in the present context. Through attempts to make sense of, better understand, and interpret them, doctrines take on new nuances, meanings, and connotations. What this implies for "justification" is that its "forensic" meaning—by word alone—is the result of an interpretation that became dominant in the second half of the twentieth century. Bayer and Lindbeck wanted to better understand "justification" at a time of interest in language, particularly the question of how words matter. Our present interest in the question of why justification matters today has to do with our desire to make sense of this doctrine *today*, as we face polarization around religious identities and the causes we support while simultaneously submerged by challenges of ecological devastation, rampant capitalism, grotesque inequality, and the threat of social collapse due to climate change. Justification needs an updating—how to make sense of God's restorative word of life in the context of devastation, death, and disputes about how to name and address injustice.

Theology that is meaningful requires getting back to ways in which people actually experience a particular reality. To ferret forth words that adequately explain a doctrine so that it makes sense involves getting back to stories in which those experiences are embedded. Justification, at its basis, is not a doctrine compressed into a formula but an experience told as a story. Recollecting this, we draw in additional sources, stories, images, and language in hopes that the doctrine of justification's explication is not reduced to a cliché but becomes alive in understanding. The resource we draw on in the next section has become foundational to our contemporary understanding of justification. It is, as we underscore, just one way of describing what justification means, although it is this story that is foundational to the history of Protestantism: it is the story of how Martin Luther experienced justification.

How Did the Protestant Story of Justification by Faith Begin?

Justification has a distinctive *story* in the history of Protestant thought. The story of how Luther came to experience divine grace is one that is paradigmatic in the Protestant imagination, if not in the history of the modern West. Luther gives one account in the preface he wrote for the complete edition of his Latin writings. At this point in his life, he is an old man, looking back at his early years. The year is 1545, one year before his death.[5] This particular version of Luther's story of justification has been embellished through the ages in order to highlight its drama. Although recently some historians have called these details into question, Luther deliberately invoked the language of conversion—Luther was after all a

5   Martin Luther, "Preface to the Complete Edition of Luther's Latin Writings, 1545," trans. Lewis W. Spitz Sr., in *Luther's Works*, 55 vols., vol. 34, *Career of the Reformer IV* (Philadelphia: Fortress, 1960 [1545]), 336–37 (hereafter cited as LW). The entire story is translated from the Latin as follows:

> Meanwhile, I had already during that year returned to interpret the Psalter anew. I had confidence in the fact that I was more skillful, after I had lectured in the university on St. Paul's epistles to the Romans, to the Galatians, and the one to the Hebrews. I had indeed been captivated with an extraordinary ardor for understanding Paul in the Epistle to the Romans. But up till then it was not the cold blood about the heart, but a single word in Chapter 1[:17], "In it the righteousness of God is revealed," that had stood in my way. For I hated that word "righteousness of God," which, according to the use and custom of all the teachers, I had been taught to understand philosophically regarding the formal or active righteousness, as they called it, with which God is righteous and punishes the unrighteous sinner. Though I lived as a monk without reproach, I felt that I was a sinner before God with an extremely disturbed conscience. I could not believe that he was placated by my satisfaction. I did not love, yes, I hated the righteous God who punishes sinners, and secretly, if not blasphemously, certainly murmuring greatly, I was angry with God, and said, "As if, indeed, it is not enough, that miserable sinners, eternally lost through original sin, are crushed by every kind of calamity by the law of the decalogue, without having God add pain to pain by the gospel and also by the gospel threatening us with his righteousness and wrath!" Thus I raged with a fierce and troubled conscience. Nevertheless, I beat importunately upon Paul at that place, most ardently desiring to know what St. Paul wanted. At last, by the mercy of God, meditating day and night, I gave heed to the context of the words, namely, "In it the righteousness of God is revealed, as it is written, 'He who through faith is righteous shall live.'" There I began to understand that the righteousness of God is that by which the righteous lives by a gift of God, namely by faith. And this is the meaning: the righteousness of God is revealed by the gospel, namely, the passive righteousness with which merciful God justifies us by faith, as it is written, and "He who through faith is righteous shall live." Here I felt that I was altogether born again and had entered paradise itself through open gates. There a totally other face of the entire Scripture showed itself to me. Thereupon I ran through the Scripture from memory. I also found in other terms an analogy, as, the work of God, that is, what God does in us, the power of God, with which he makes us strong, the strength of God, the salvation of God, the glory of God.

friar in an Observant Augustinian order, which was named after the great pillar of the Western church, himself a convert to Christianity upon reading Paul's Letter to the Romans. The Protestant story of justification is paradigmatically framed on the template of the conversion of Augustine, and before him, the conversion of apostle Paul (Acts 9:1–19).

Luther focuses his recollections on a particular passage in Paul's Letter to the Romans: Romans 1:17, "For in [the gospel] the righteousness of God is revealed." The key term that caused Luther much anxiety was the meaning of "divine justice," in Latin *iustitia dei*, also translated into English as divine righteousness. Luther's struggles to understand this passage were not abstract and intellectual; they were existential. As Luther had been schooled to understand it, divine justice was the demand God makes on all humans. This demand is the law, every single bit of it. To the law is attached the consequence of obedience, namely, eternal reward, or disobedience, specifically eternal punishment. The fear of hell precipitated Luther's anxieties, more precisely, his terror. It was impossible for a mere mortal to fulfill the divine demand. Even a saint, who had the best of intentions and did the most good works, had a teeny bit of self-interest somewhere in their hearts. Any bit of self-interest disqualifies heartfelt obedience to the divine demand. Luther was angry at God for having created creatures who sinned, thereby setting them up for failure. The entire system was stacked against obeying the inexorable demand. Luther, never known to mince words, announces: "I did not love, yes, I hated the righteous God who punishes sinners, and secretly, if not blasphemously, certainly murmuring greatly, I was angry with God."[6] For any medieval Christian this admission of hating God was tantamount to being eternally damned. Anyone who hated God could never fulfill the divine demand to love God with one's whole heart.

Then Luther abruptly writes in a new register: "Here I felt that I was altogether born again and had entered paradise itself through open gates. There a totally other face of the entire Scripture showed itself to me."[7] Luther notes a spatial shift. He is transported from hell to heaven. Entry to paradise is a new birth that signals an epiphanic reorientation. Luther's entire existence is now based on an entirely different reality than the one experienced under the divine demand in his earthly hell. He is converted to a quite different understanding of divine justice. The meaning of divine justice that is revealed in the gospel is now the good news

[6] LW 34:336.
[7] LW 34:337.

of Christ. *Christ* is the sinner's justification. Divine justice is seen not as a standard, but as the gift of God's righteousness given in Christ. The divine justice revealed in the gospel is the divine act of justifying the sinner.

Luther explains his new perception of "divine justice" in the terminology with which he, as a trained medieval theologian, was familiar. "Justice" is a divine attribute, meaning a characteristic that is predicated of God, and taken as an identifying quality of God's nature. Whenever a medieval theologian uses the language of "attributes," they appeal to a branch of philosophy called metaphysics. Metaphysics is the study of being, or the ways in which different natures have "being" and the ways they are differentiated from each other according to qualities of being. With regard to God, then, the attribute of justice is a particular characteristic of God's being. Of course, because justice is divine, it is taken in an absolute sense, rather than in any human sense of "justice." God's attribute of justice is absolute, all-demanding, all-encompassing, and final. When this attribute is understood as something humans are expected to embody as Luther did, then it means a demand that humans are obligated to obey. This sense precipitated Luther's terror. He knew that given God's absolute being, there was no way any human could fulfill the divine law of justice, let alone a tiny bit of it.

Luther's conversion to a new meaning of "divine justice" had to do with a new kind of metaphysics, one based on what it means to be God outside of any human determination. God's nature is to give healing life in Christ. The gospel of Christ reverses Luther's former sense of divine "demand." Instead of a divine justice that demands full-fledged obedience, the divine justice in Christ is the gift of obedience, of rightly aligning with God. Rather than justifying oneself before God, one is justified with God *by* God. The new understanding is given with Luther's shift in perspective. In his earthly hell, Luther (mis)understands the divine attribute of justice as an absolute standard of justice that human beings must meet. In paradise, Luther understands God's nature according to a metaphysics of gift. God's being is just in that God acts to assign justice to those needing it most. The sin-afflicted on earth are the beneficiaries of this gift. The gospel of Christ discloses this grace-bearing way of understanding the divine nature. Gift, not demand, characterizes God's being in Christ. Through this gift, sinners are made just.

Luther tells the story of his conversion in terms of a dramatic translocation from hell to heaven. The story is layered with a new understanding of the key verse at the beginning of Paul's Letter to the Romans. The shift in interpreting the Bible is a key detail in this story of justification. And another important detail is a shift in philosophical meaning. Luther now understands justification in terms of a new theory of God's nature. This metaphysics sees the divine attributes as gifts that God gives to beloved creatures. God's nature is to give life, not to damn for all eternity. God's nature does not entail God's possessing of attributes for the divine life; but the divine life consists of giving the attributes to sinners in order to translocate them from hell into the divine presence. Here the paradox for which Luther's thought is famous has its determination. In Christ, a new metaphysics is made real: death is exchanged for life; damnation for eternal blessedness; trauma for healing. The revelation of the divine nature in the gospel opens eyes to Christ "given for you."

Other Christian justification stories, like Luther's, add different and important dimensions to the doctrine. They introduce metaphors to describe shifts in experience and affect. Luther's account highlights the spatial metaphor. His new understanding is an existential shift from hell to heaven. His hate turns into joy.

These stories, like Luther's, also point out challenges, aspects that are messy and difficult. Luther expresses an existential struggle with Scripture and the discovery of a more profound insight into its meaning. The story of justification includes wrestling with the word of God itself. It is about struggle, difficult emotions, and the pursuit of understanding amid sometimes very troubling experiences. These onerous dimensions become part of the story of justification, for Luther and for us.

How Can We Practice Justification by Faith?

Justification is a story, including Luther's story. It is many stories of how we became more attuned to the divine presence in our lives, of how we have experienced the divine presence in others, and how we had a change of heart, sometimes dramatically, sometimes through slow imperceptible changes. The point is that justification is a reality from which one lives. Yes, it is a doctrine that compresses many stories into a formula; it is a church teaching and the "grammar" of worship and Christian language. But it is also the reality out of which the Beloved Community lives and to which it returns in the mindfulness of faith, again and again.

How can we dwell with this doctrine so that we can understand it in this sense: as an awareness of and commitment to belonging to the Beloved Community? How can we imagine this doctrine as the reality that orients and reorients us throughout processes of justice-seeking?

We begin by pointing out that this doctrine is a reality, perceived as such through the theological lens we use in this chapter and throughout the book. Justification is a reality that grounds, sustains, preserves, and frees Christians within the Beloved Community. It is the reality from which we emerge, and into which we grow.

How can a doctrine like justification be a "practice," a daily practice? How can this doctrine be practiced as ordinary faith? This is an important question because it gets at the experience of the foundational belonging, the common identity, of all Christians, and a reality that secures this common belonging amid the messiness, challenges, and joys of justice-seeking that arise as Christians move out into the world. We describe justification as a "lived doctrine," alluding to historian of American religion Robert A. Orsi's phrase, "lived religion," in order to show how this particular doctrine orients the whole of ordinary Christian life.[8]

Understood from this perspective, justification is a potent touchstone to take our bearings from in every conflict. If we belong to God and to one another, not on the basis of our own virtues but unconditionally on the basis of the gift of God's own journeying with us in the power of the Spirit animating the body of Christ, then *recalling* the fact of our belonging to Christ can reset us amid every precarity, anxiety, failing, deep disagreement, or confrontation with the need to listen and repent. This is no small thing. It is certainly no small thing when it comes to living out our faith in a polarized time, whether or not we ourselves tend to identify with a particular political or cultural group's point of view.

We look again to Luther for inspiration, as one who drew on his monastic heritage to put justification into practice for all Christians in their everyday lives and callings. He invited Christians into intentional devotional practices that would reorient them into seeing themselves and the world through eyes of faith. The texts he used for this purpose were traditional. The church used catechesis from its earliest years to instruct Christians in the reality and words of faith. Luther was even more familiar with catechesis because he preached on the elements—Decalogue, Creed, Lord's Prayer—twice a year, as was the requirement of the medieval Catholic lectionary for the two seasons of penance, namely, Lent and Advent. Luther thus made use of the catechism to explore the dynamics of justification by faith for Christian life.

---

[8]   Robert Orsi, "Everyday Miracles: The Study of Lived Religion," in *Lived Religion in America: Toward a History of Practice*, ed. David D. Hall (Princeton: Princeton University Press, 1998), 3–21.

Baptism in particular is one of the catechetical elements that Luther thinks is central to the practice of justification. Luther advocates the daily remembrance of baptism as an important way of experiencing and thinking about one's justification. Of course, for those like Luther, who advocate infant baptism, such a recollection can seem rather odd. If one is baptized as an infant, as is the practice in Roman Catholic and some Protestant churches, a daily recollection of the historical event of one's baptism is not possible. One can hardly remember what one had last Wednesday for lunch, let alone something that happened before one's earliest memories! Yet, Luther insists that the daily practice of remembering one's baptism is a "living into" one's justification. What could Luther mean?

Let us connect with Luther's words in his *Large Catechism*, written like his *Small Catechism* in 1529. In his explication of baptism, Luther instructs Christians:

> In baptism . . . every Christian has enough to study and practice all his or her life. Christians always have enough to do to believe firmly what baptism promises and brings—victory over death and the devil, forgiveness of sin, God's grace, the entire Christ, and the Holy Spirit with his gifts.
>
> These two parts, being dipped under the water and emerging from it, point to the power and effect of baptism, which is nothing else than the slaying of the old Adam and the resurrection of the new creature, both of which must continue in us our whole life long. Thus a Christian life is nothing else than a daily baptism, begun once and continuing ever after.
>
> Therefore let all Christians regard their baptism as the daily garment that they are to wear all the time. Every day they should be found in faith and with its fruits, suppressing the old creature and growing up in the new.[9]

When Luther writes about baptismal remembrance, he is not thinking about historical memory. Rather what he means is to meditate on the fact that we always already belong to the body of Christ, the Beloved Community. We recall the fact of justification as living reality. Our belonging is based not on our embodying certain feelings or virtues, but on the basis of God's claiming us through our baptism into Jesus' own life, death, and

---

[9] Martin Luther, "The Large Catechism (1529)," in *The Book of Concord: The Confessions of the Evangelical Lutheran Church*, trans. Charles Arand et al., ed. Robert Kolb and Timothy J. Wengert (Minneapolis: Fortress, 2000), 461, 465, 466.

resurrection. To remember our baptism as Christians functions for us as touching the ground did for Siddhartha Gautama during his enlightenment: it is a way of speaking back to the voices that tell us to give up on ourselves or on one another.[10] This is a daily exercise—an exercise of our spiritual muscles in the profound yet ordinary recognition that the fact of faith is something we need to rediscover afresh as we face each day's inner temptations to despair, numbness, or distractions. To remember our baptism is to reorient us to the gospel truth expressed in the doctrine of justification by faith: whatever our nearsighted ways and failings, we belong to God and to one another as the constant ground of our shared journeys in faith toward a renewed creation.

If the daily rehearsal of one's spiritual muscles in the practice of justification is not enough, Luther suggests a second, long-familiar Christian practice. This one—the ingesting of the body and blood of Christ—is not a memory lost in the recesses of infant experience but one that can be experienced in the life of ordinary faith. Like baptism, the Lord's Supper is to be practiced as often as possible. Luther insists on a daily exercise program! Likewise, the sacrament of communion or the Lord's Supper ritually reminds us of the at-once near and eschatological promises of God in Christ that are present for us at all times, but that we can see, taste, and touch in the bread and wine shared in the company of others. Like many sacred rituals, the Lord's Supper draws us into a space where time past, present, and future come together at once in an event that is both recollection, in the now, and a "foretaste of the feast to come": "On the night in which he was betrayed, Jesus took bread, blessed, and broke it. . . . 'Do this in remembrance of me.'" "Christ has died, Christ has risen, Christ will come again."[11] These words of the liturgy, repeated by Lutheran ministers every time the Lord's Supper is told, bring the story of Jesus as origin and ground of justification into the present. The ordinary practice of faith is the experience of justification through taste and touch.

George Lindbeck described such participation in the church's sacraments as part of the process of being initiated and socialized into a Christian worldview until we are fluent in it.[12] But rather than assuming progressive fluency in the Christian life (without denying growth in

---

[10]   Neuroscientifically, we could say remembering our baptism is one way of using our prefrontal cortex to practice metacognition in relation to fear, flight, or freeze responses from our brains' limbic system.

[11]   These are phrases associated with Lutheran communion liturgy.

[12]   See Lindbeck, *Nature of Doctrine.*

Christ), Luther emphasizes our fragility, our unsteadiness, our vulnerability to losing touch with a worldview that roots us in justification by faith. The gospel must be preached and internalized over and over. So he depicts spiritual practices like reciting the Lord's Prayer or partaking of the Lord's Supper as a way to *remind us* of what our shifting kaleidoscope of fears and feelings might whirl us into, like forgetting the real presence of Christ in our midst. These sacraments remind us of a vision of a reconciled and reconciling community that persists even amid our sinful failings of one another and our own open or scarred-over wounds.

It is not only, then, that the doctrine of justification by faith is the title of a born-again conversion story about Paul or Luther. It might include our personal initial discovery that our being rightly aligned with God and one another depends first and foremost on our being borne by grace in Christ, not our own impeccability. But through ordinary enactments in ritual, we are drawn into Jesus' own story. This story grounds our justification with God and one another, connecting what happened on Calvary to our own lives in the present. When we recall our baptism and share in communion, we practice being integrated into a worldview that centers our lives and our well-being upon the gifts of God's renewing love for the world. This practice roots our present hope in truths of reconciled belonging that are at once mysteriously here and still to come to pass.

For Luther, ordinary faith is the daily exercise of spiritual muscles in recalling baptism and experiencing Christ's body and blood. Yet there is another dimension Luther wants us to consider. The practice of ordinary faith is an invitation into a worldview that is eschatological. What this means is that our daily practice initiates us into God's act of justification that will be completed by God. The promise of justification is that all things will be made well. It might not look like things are well at all. In fact, our contemporary crises—capitalist excess, violence at local and global levels, climate catastrophe—indicate that nothing is well. Why then does justification's promise of all-things-being-made-well-in-Christ matter for the work of justice-seeking, which is all about striving for a state of affairs that is still to be brought into the world? When recollected, when held in our gaze, justification's promise shapes the way we go about pursuing a more just world while reckoning with our individual and collective failings to live up to our own ideals of right relations with one another and our planet. If we perceive that we always already belong to one another in Christ, if we behold the whole world as Julian of Norwich did when she saw the entire world held like a hazelnut in the palm of God,[13] then we can resist the voices that condition one's belonging to a community upon having proved one's own sufficient wokeness, one's sufficiently correct political views (be they on what we today call the right or the left). Our belonging to the Beloved Community on the basis of justification by faith offers us something more durable and farseeing than a covenantal belonging conditioned upon the anxious securing or the aloof presumption of our own rightness or righteousness.

In this sense, seeing and living by the doctrine of justification by faith in Christ provides what Benedictines call stability of life. We can stay with the various affective states that arise as we walk through being called out on our own injustice or on daring to name it in others; as we risk transformation by seeking mutual understanding; or as we try to hold one another to account without freezing, fighting, or fleeing. We can pursue with persistence our respective callings to ways of strengthening the Beloved Community, knowing that we *all already unconditionally belong to one another in Christ.*

As we will explore in the chapters ahead, the stability of life that comes from recollecting our baptism into Christ frees us not *from* conflict itself, but *for* entering directly into the choppy waters of learning how to work together through unresolved questions and fundamental disagreements about what, exactly, our Beloved Community should look like as it manifests in this time and place.

Why Does Justification by Faith Matter for the Beloved Community?

The authors of the New Testament gospels use a distinctive term to highlight Jesus' message. Jesus preaches the coming of the *basileia tou Theou*, or the kingdom of God. In fact, Mark insists that the reason for Jesus' existence on earth is precisely to preach the imminent arrival of the kingdom

---

[13]   Julian of Norwich, *A Revelation of Love*, ed. with intro. by Elisabeth Dutton (Lanham, Md.: Rowman & Littlefield, 2008), 28: "And in this he showed me a little thing, the quantity of a hazelnut, lying in the palm of my hand, as it seemed. And it was as round as any ball. I looked upon it with the eye of my understanding, and thought, 'What may this be?' And it was answered generally thus, 'It is all that is made.' I marveled how it might last, for I thought it might suddenly have fallen to nothing for littleness. And I was answered in my understanding: It lasts and ever shall, for God loves it. And so have all things their beginning by the love of God. In this little thing I saw three properties. The first is that God made it. The second that God loves it. And the third, that God keeps it."

of God. Mark begins his gospel with the passage: "Now after John was arrested, Jesus came to Galilee, proclaiming the good news of God, and saying, 'The time is fulfilled, and the kingdom of God has come near; repent, and believe in the good news'" (Mark 1:14–15). Jesus announces the reign of God and then embodies that reality in his actions. He proclaims freedom for prisoners and sight to the blind (cf. Luke 4:18) and then enacts these words by healing the sick, freeing people from demons oppressing them, raising Jairus' daughter and his friend Lazarus to life, and turning water into wine. Jesus shows that God's reign is real by creating the Beloved Community.

The "Beloved Community" is a contemporary translation of the Greek *basileia tou Theou*. This phrase conjures a picture of the world characterized by right relations with God and neighbors—a vision of abundant shared life, made possible by the mending, life-upholding dimensions of justification by faith in Christ. The term has become familiar to contemporary US Americans because of its use during the civil rights movement. Dr. Martin Luther King Jr. explicitly referred to the Beloved Community throughout his sermons and writings to conjure up the vision of a global community of justice. In one of his earliest speeches, his April 1957 address at the Conference on Christian Faith and Human Relations in Nashville, King insisted that boycotts cannot represent the goal of the struggle, rather "the end is reconciliation; the end is redemption; the end is the creation of the beloved community."[14] This community is founded on *agape*, the transformative love characterizing God most of all, and persons who nonviolently resist injustice and thereby infuse toxic situations with redemptive love. Transformative love is the central attribute of the Beloved Community. Love transforms injustice into justice, inequality into equality, and violence into peace. It is one contemporary analogue to Jesus' proclamation of the reign of God, a vision that encompasses Christians and non-Christians alike, in the creation of a new community inspired by transformative love.

[14] Martin Luther King Jr., "'The Role of the Church in Facing the Nation's Chief Moral Dilemma,' Address Delivered on 25 April 1957 at the Conference on Christian Faith and Human Relations in Nashville," in *The Papers of Martin Luther King, Jr.*, vol. 4, *Symbol of the Movement, January 1957–December 1958* (Berkeley: University of California Press, 2000), available online through the website of the Martin Luther King, Jr. Research and Education Institute at Stanford University, https://kinginstitute.stanford.edu/king-papers/documents/role-church-facing-nation-s-chief-moral-dilemma-address-delivered-25-april.

For King, the *basileia tou Theou* is a vision guiding contemporary action. It evokes what the Spirit today persuades many to be the shape of the world as it looks when guided by God's governance. As such, this vision inspires persons to resist in nonviolent ways the monarchical world and to work toward establishing what feminist biblical scholar Elisabeth Schüssler Fiorenza calls a non-kyriarchical or non-hierarchical society.[15] To be sure, even progressive Christians typically assume some form of hierarchical authority in homes, churches, and society; most are not committed anarchists. Indeed, the idea of the Beloved Community can resonate with diverse forms of governing a just society in which all experience due process and equality before the law, as well as with the non-anthropocentric translation of the *basileia tou Theou* coined by Cuban American theologian Ada María Isasi-Díaz: "kin-dom" of God.[16] But, the image of abundant rather than oppressed life—of flourishing—circulates in all of the eschatological depictions of life together carried by terms like the kingdom of God or Beloved Community. Even a New Testament writer as obsessed with justification by faith in Christ as Paul concedes that justification is Spirit-empowered participation in Christ. This Spirit-filled community shares in the abundant life displayed in the forgiveness-practicing, meal-sharing, and healing community that Jesus called the kingdom of God.

In the context of Jesus' kingdom of God teachings, we can more clearly perceive how justification by faith in Christ works as both gift and norm. As gift, justification creates the Beloved Community into which we are invited. As norm, justification empowers our living in and by the kin-dom of God. This norm-bearing gift has implications for appreciating how necessary community is for ordinary faith. Justification by faith is communal and ecclesial, never merely individual. Christian life is communal, which implies that the idea of an autonomous decision-making individual is called into question by the very idea of justification by faith. Living in Christ means living together out of a shared source of "individual" existence. Belonging to the body of Christ is an ecstatic existence; the self is

---

[15]   Although the term dates to the early 1990s, for one definition, see "kyriarchy" in the glossary section of Elisabeth Schüssler Fiorenza, *Wisdom Ways: Introducing Feminist Biblical Interpretation* (Maryknoll, N.Y.: Orbis Books, 2001).

[16]   Ada María Isasi-Díaz, *Mujerista Theology: A Theology for the Twenty-First Century* (Maryknoll, N.Y.: Orbis Books, 1996): "I use 'kin-dom' to avoid using the sexist and elitist word 'kingdom.' Also, the sense of family of God that 'kin-dom' represents is much in line with the centrality of family in our Latina culture. I am grateful to Georgene Wilson, O.S.F., from whom I learned this word" (83n14).

not the sole center of autonomous moral decision-making, for one dwells in Christ's body in community with others. This brings an ecclesial sense of living in relation to others—not as an individual apart from or prior to all relationships with other persons, but as someone who is fundamentally related to others in the body of Christ.

Far from being about only the single individual's rescue from a damned future, then, justification draws us into a world of rightly aligning creaturely relationships that extend across time, across all that is to be preserved or redeemed, holding us accountable while releasing us from bondage to sin and its wounds. As God's act of forgiveness, justification is God's act of initiating a restart for us whenever we have been contributors to (or victims of) the sin of the world, even as throughout this life we convey the inheritances of the "old Adam." As Christine tweeted on January 1, 2022, "another New Year, but that pesky old Adam followed me into it!"[17] Remembering our baptism in Christ, we witness fresh possibilities as we are drawn into the new creation now, living a paradox of being caught between old and new. Justification by faith thus means a new start in the middle of the old. We find ourselves rooted right here and now in God's Beloved Community, with its invitation to an ongoing renewal of our ways of being one with another. This is the eschatological truth that frames the whole of our lives in a dying and rising with Christ.

Reclaimed daily in the remembrance of our baptism, then, a new start in forgiveness—the power of God's "otherwise"—is not just a break with sin's dominance, but a creative living together out of the abundant life that Jesus says he has come to bring (cf. John 10:10). On one hand, justification is not less than a gift for each individual Christian, a freedom from an enervating captivity to the "I" that ends in (as Luther often put it) "sin, death and the devil."[18] In the midst of our captivity, justification is offered as a way to explore abundance, which has its most immediate outcome in the

---

[17]   Christine Helmer (@theologygurl), Twitter, January 1, 2022, 11:16 p.m., https://twitter.com/theologygurl/status/1477403366716317702?s=20.

[18]   See strophe 2 of Luther's hymn, "Dear Christians, One and All, Rejoice," that narrates the "I's" descent into sin, and the bondage to death and devil as a result: "Fast bound in Satan's chains I lay, / Death brooded darkly o'er me, / Sin was my torment night and day, / In sin my mother bore me; / Yea, deep and deeper still I fell, / Life had become a living hell, / So firmly sin possessed me." "Dear Christians, One and All, Rejoice," *The Free Lutheran Chorale-Book: Mining the Treasures of Lutheran Hymnody for the Benefit of the Church*, https://www.lutheranchoralebook.com/texts/dear-christians-one-and-all-rejoice.

breaking of the *incurvatus in se*—the curving in upon ourselves that shrinks our horizons, as both sinners and sinned-against. This in turn means that justification by faith presupposes an abundance of life that is experienced *together* with others amid a transforming existence in Christ. It is never just about each of us in our respective private relationships to Christ, but also about the possibility of new connections and relationships in the whole body of Christ. Abundance of life is not based on the self's ego as central to life, nor on the sinned-against self's radical self-protection as central to survival. Rather, abundant life presupposes that those participating in it are decentered and recentered selves—called to repentance *and* drawn into life abundant in the Beloved Community. It is a Christ-grounded (and routinely re-grounded) person who can be broken open in accompaniment of and by others in the company of the body of Christ.

Justification by faith is thus a liberating invitation to try out abundance, imagine its possibilities, and live out of the reality that it offers. What does this mean concretely? A deciphering is involved here as we live in Christ as a new creation: a practice of theological reflection that asks us to envision what to become together and how to get there as we continuously work out the paradox of old and new creation. The gospel is not simply about abstract possibilities of new life in Christ. It is the announcement of God's in-breaking reality within the "old" familiarity of our shared lives broken by sin, and an invitation to orient our lives in accordance with the gospel's Christ-enabled way. This is of course difficult, if not nigh-impossible, at least in the view of Christians who have a healthy understanding of the pervasiveness of human sin and an appreciation for the deep-seated psychological barriers to change. In spite of decades of therapy or education for some, we still tend to be socialized into ways that prohibit change. But theology admits the profound possibility of change grounded in grace. And deciphering the precise shape of the Beloved Community is itself ongoing theological work within faith communities.

Abundant life as a gift and norm of justification by faith thus directs our gaze beyond a concern with individual virtues alone to seeking together the shape of justice, of right relations. Certainly, a life of virtue or holiness is one dimension of Christian tradition. To belong to Christ is to live always within a divine pedagogy, within a process of being taught by the Spirit how to live from Christ the source—a growth into virtues, informed by what Catholic tradition has called supernatural virtues. A theology of the Christian life, the *ordo salutis* (the order of salvation), or the possibility of Christian perfection or sanctification: these describe how justification by faith establishes ever-new possibilities for being guided by the Spirit, including possibilities for change in character, perspective, or worldview. Pessimists will still chart this as a battle with the old Adam that is perennial until death. Optimists will see possibilities for embracing God's otherwise—and even requirements for signs of it—based on an understanding of how divine power forms persons and communities in the image of Christ. But whether one holds a pessimistic or optimistic account of how new life in Christ translates into personal holiness, there is a consensus in Christian theology concerning the Christian life as a dynamic process. That process interrupts deadly imprisonments to the self as sinner and as sinned-against, and empowers renewed possibilities for navigating a life sourced by Christ, open to others as we live out freedom from self-preoccupation to love our neighbors as ourselves. This includes establishing practices of virtue and right thinking as possibilities, however precarious, that reflect justification as an initiation into abundant life in Christ. But because a theology of justification is also ecclesial, being formed in and by Christ is also being formed in and by the body of Christ, the church near and far. Our participation in that formation process (God's work in process, so to speak) involves reciprocity: shared dialogue as well as shared ritual. It entails practicing being human in the vulnerability and Spirit-windy space of Christ's corporate body—sometimes intentionally, sometimes intuitively, sometimes alone, sometimes together—as we navigate with others in the Beloved Community.

Thus, beyond our practices of individual virtue—and indeed shaping their precise form—abundant life in the body of Christ also involves envisioning and even debating together what a just society looks like. While Christians might agree in the abstract that the church as the kingdom of God or Beloved Community is characterized by flourishing, by a shared abundant life in which all have their needs met, a quick look at past and present Christian history reveals that agreeing on this principle does not itself generate agreement on how to implement it in practice. Christians have always debated the nitty-gritty of how we should live together as a church, much less as a world shaped by a commitment to loving God first and loving our neighbors as ourselves. The early churches that Paul and other epistle writers addressed disagreed about whether or not to eat meat that had been sacrificed to idols (1 Cor 8–10), whether or not Gentiles should adopt the circumcision and kosher dietary practices of Jesus' own Jewish community (Galatians), what kinds of apostolic and prophetic authority were open to women as well as to men (1 Cor 11:3–16;

1 Tim 2:9–15, among others), and even how old a widow should be before she qualified to live off the welfare of the church (1 Tim 5:3–16). Later the church divided over how best to understand Jesus' relationship to God and how best to construe the relationship between the divine and human in Jesus (the latter debate especially involving divisions related in part to whether one lived within or beyond the Roman Empire, with the lurking question being whether, say, a Persian Christian who affirmed the Council of Chalcedon was really a close ally of the Roman Empire). In North America, Christians have debated whether people of indigenous and African descent could become Christian (and with what acceptable cultural practices). Christians divided denominationally over whether slavery was acceptable, then spent a century working out whether equality meant racial segregation or integration. Today we divide over questions of gender, dividing denominationally over whether or not women may be ordained as pastors, and now also over whether or not to accept same-sex marriage and to ordain queer Christians as clergy. We also disagree about whether or not to name and engage what many of us perceive as systemic injustices—like racism, sexism, heteronormativity, or environmental crisis—and whether or not the Beloved Community involves gender complementarity or egalitarianism (or gender fluidity). We are sure many more disagreements could be added to this list, from differences about infant baptism and the nature of biblical authority to any host of differences about doctrine and ecclesial authority—not to mention diverse theological approaches to religious pluralism.

Even if the vision of a reconciled community in Christ carries all of us, such disagreements about the shape of the community to which we belong unconditionally can tempt us to collective forms of *incurvatus*—a turning inward to some particular groupthink. Here the doctrine of justification by faith reminds us to take our bearings from our baptismal belonging to the body of Christ, and not from our own efforts to justify contested particular shapes of the Beloved Community. Justification by faith draws us into those earnest efforts to limn our collective flourishing in particular ways, and it is to efforts at justifying contested views of justice-seeking that we turn in the next chapter. But justification by faith calls us into the mission of justice-seeking precisely by illuminating that our Christian identity is marked first and foremost by our always-already belonging together to God in the body of Christ.

What Is Justification by Ordinary Faith?

We cannot fathom the link between justification by faith and justice-seeking unless we recognize that justification by faith, rather than being understood solely in terms of an individual's relation to Christ, is from the get-go communal in nature. Baptism is into the corporate body of Christ, the church, or communion of saints. The person set free by Christ is thereby bound up with, as well as freed for, life with others. Beheld within a Christian imagination, then, the Beloved Community is the space created by justification in Christ. By using the language of Beloved Community, we emphasize in contemporary terms a communal perspective on the life of faith. The Christian life transpires through our practices of being in relation to each other within the body of Christ. Justification *by faith* in concrete terms means living together in Christ and with the guidance of the Spirit ever stirring us, as we are learning wiser ways of being together.

By emphasizing the significance of justification as the point of orientation for Christian life (and for this book), we disclose a theological commitment to the primacy of divine agency and its possibilities for redemptive transformation. *How* that transformation takes place, how the divine word creates a new reality amid a sin-broken world, begins for Christians with the gospel of justification by faith. Lutheran theologians have long associated justification by faith's power with the "word of God" which, when spoken, creates a new reality of forgiveness. So we began by investigating how the gospel of justification takes hold in the lives of those baptized in Christ, including how it orients attitudes and dispositions for justice-seeking in church and world. The doctrine of justification is the witness to the "otherwise" in the world as it is. Justification is not just a word pronounced, but a reality altered as we—a bundle of sinner and sinned-against—are realigned in and with God at work in Christ Jesus.

In short, justification by faith in Christ offers a way of naming the life-benefiting reality of God. That reality is necessarily communal. By emphasizing that Christian belonging is something we receive rather than achieve, we emphasize justification not as an extraordinary human accomplishment, but as ordinary faith, lived out as a practice of life together. We are ruled not by our efforts to secure our standing before God and others, but by the everyday rule or daily ordering of faith in Christ, in whose life our lives are borne. When we turn in subsequent chapters to reflect on justice-seeking, we continue to hold in view that Christian justice-seeking is based on Christ's foundation of justified life together. An identity as Christian is thus not made by our moral decision-making or moral enunciations, though it includes these. It is created by justification by faith that is ordinary faith—the commonplace rule of faith that so often stands in the background rather than the foreground of Christian proclamations in the public square. We aim throughout what follows to repeatedly foreground it.

3

Justification by Faith and Justifications amid Justice-Seeking

Introduction

Contemporary British author Francis Spufford describes how his mind changed about same-sex marriage. Writing for the column How My Mind Has Changed in a recent issue of *Christian Century*, Spufford claims that he once held the position that marriage was to be solely between one man and one woman, but now affirms that marriage should be expanded to include same-sex couples.[1] What is significant about his account is that he refuses to vilify the persons who share his starting-point. Even after his shift, he is committed to regarding those people with whom he disagrees as persons with whom he wants to continue to dialogue.

Spufford documents how he came to hold his current position. He reasons with Scripture. The New Testament Book of Acts, Spufford claims, is a good place to show how changes in theology and practice took place as Gentile Christians historically began to separate themselves in the first century from Jewish Christians living in Jerusalem. These Gentile Christians, living in the cities that Paul and others were missionizing, decided to give up the rules for kosher and circumcision that Jewish Christians had stipulated for the Christian community. They reasoned along with Paul that their freedom to adhere or not to particular practices was based on the principle of "justification by faith." In other words, they introduced into their thinking the idea that justification by faith is *itself* the principle of Christian identity. This basis allowed them, so they argued, to adapt their practices to serve the interests of the community that extended beyond Jerusalem. Justification by faith served as the theological foundation for Christian practice. Peter, the leader of the Jewish Christians in

---

[1]   Francis Spufford, "How I Changed My Mind about Same-Sex Marriage," How My Mind Has Changed, *Christian Century* 138, no. 15 (July 28, 2021): 26–31.

Jerusalem, agreed: "We believe that we will be saved through the grace of the Lord Jesus, just as they will" (Acts 15:11).

Spufford finds inspiration in this early church record for understanding his own shift. He adapts what he sees to be the process of preferring principle—justification by faith—to a traditional rule about the impermissibility of same-sex marriage. The conflict is, as he describes it, "between the rule distinguishing pure from impure sexual acts and the principle that all of God's adopted children are called, on the little scale of their lives, to live in love." Rather than the rule, we should prefer the principle of the kind of love that in marriage is "made exclusive by patient attention to one soul."[2]

But importantly, on the basis of this same principle, Spufford warns against demonizing those who disagree with him:

> I'm suspicious of the tendency among liberal Christians now to try to deal with remaining opposition just by glaring at it and bombarding it with our moral disapproval. Wedge strategies for achieving change can be very effective. First you ask for compassion for those an existing moral rule condemns; then you convert compassion into tolerance, tolerance into acceptance, acceptance into a new normal; and then, when 51 percent of people perceive the situation the new way, you pivot promptly and suggest that disagreement is now intolerable, illegitimate.[3]

Spufford shows how the shift in moral position is quite naturally connected to a condemnation of others. Just as holding a position from the outset is connected to the simultaneity of superiority and approbation of others, so too a shift can elicit the same disposition. Does holding a moral position necessarily lead the holder to despise the other, the other also a Christian? Spufford draws our attention to the larger point, which is also the main question of this chapter: can Christians engage in disagreement that is both earnest and refuses to vilify?

How can Christians contest different moral positions while being committed to a shared abundant life before God? Is it possible for Christians to work out the shape of justice in the Beloved Community without demonizing or shaming their opponents? How can Christians nevertheless persist in discerning and advocating for the kind of justice they sense the Spirit is calling them to create?

---

2   Spufford, "From Rules to Principles," 30.
3   Spufford, "From Rules to Principles," 27.

In the previous chapter we described justification by faith as the divine action that creates the shared ground of belonging for all Christians. In this chapter, we consider the process of forming our positions within Christian debates. We want to hold on to the theological idea that the process of forming moral beliefs—sometimes strengthening and sometimes shifting a position—is grounded in a prior reality: that of justification by faith. Yet this grounding can, as we pointed out in the Spufford anecdote, free us from particular "rules" that might restrict our capacity to earnestly engage with others across differences. This process of forming moral beliefs involves a second form of justification: the justification of beliefs.

Here we adapt a term—"justification of belief"—popular among philosophers who study how people give reasons for what they hold to be true. To be sure, we adhere to beliefs through different aspects of the self, including unconscious habits, nonrational preferences, and internalized communal influences. But we also have a human capacity to provide conscious reasons for our beliefs. This step involves community: one offers reasons to others, just as others offer reasons for their own beliefs. As theologians we nuance the term "justification of beliefs" to include a theological accounting for beliefs within the Christian community. We consider how the practices of being formed in (or experiencing a shift of) a particular belief integrate different aspects of the self, including reason, in order to elicit the "justification" of those beliefs within the Beloved Community.

A sidenote is in order here: our double use of the term "justification" in both justification by faith and justification of belief is intentional. This doubling invites our readers to ponder how we use the word "justification" in two contexts: our *own* being justified or aligned with God through our faith in Christ; and the justifications or supporting reasons for our respective beliefs about the shape of justice (or a moral view) on this or that matter. Our justice-seeking flows out of the justification by faith that draws us into the Beloved Community; but because we are sorting out a sense of what justice entails, we justify to ourselves and one another why we hold the beliefs about justice or ethics that we do. So there are two senses of "justification" at play: one that accounts for *how we ourselves as persons are aligned with God* and one another through an empowering grace from beyond our own individual efforts and failings; another that accounts for *how we, as persons within the body of Christ, come to align or "line up" with the particular beliefs about justice that we hold*. We ask readers to bear in mind and to ponder the different connotations of "justification" (of ourselves before God vs. of our ethical beliefs).

We are alert, then, to how beliefs or positions about justice are formed through a multifaceted process of justifying them. When we delve into the reasons for holding on to particular beliefs and positions, we do so in the presence of others. This process can be seen as the effort to make sense of one's beliefs and positions for both oneself and for others. Particular passages in Scripture are invoked to lend authority to one's belief. Some might offer anecdotes from tradition in order to bolster their position. Sometimes different scriptural passages and anecdotes are exchanged as Christians appeal to the more common elements in the Christian community, such as prayer and liturgical formulas.

We also evoke other dimensions that play significant roles in the process of justifying beliefs in relation to others. For instance, we lift up the presence of stories—our own and those of others—throughout this chapter as central to the belief-justifying process. As we navigate relations to our own and one another's stories, dimensions of affective experiences and empathetic imagination come into play. These aspects can combine with exchanges about Scripture and tradition and coalesce in different ways. Housed within the grace of Christ that conjures us into the Beloved Community, we seek to espy the Spirit-led shape of justice within that community and beyond it. Justified by faith in Christ, we participate in building up the body of Christ by sharing with one another our justifications for our respective notions of just or right relations. We reckon that *how* we do so matters as much as the conclusions we dare to share with one another.

Our chapter begins with a sketch of elements that we think are important in the process of justifying particular beliefs about justice. We explore ways to better understand the relation between justification by faith and justification of beliefs, considering this relation from a theological perspective. There are, of course, different ways of configuring the relation between justification by faith and justification of beliefs. Various fields are also concerned with the question of how motivation leads to action. Philosophy, anthropology, ethics, and psychology are fields interested in the relation of self to community and the kinds of moral decisions humans make that facilitate the community's flourishing, or its demise. Yet the particular theological tools that we invoke explicitly focus on grounding in Christ, faith in whom is the key mark of Christian identity.

Perhaps ironically, to promote capaciousness in mutual deliberation, we employ a doctrinal norm-testing tool that has often been used to build or demolish a particular vision of the church's teachings: the practice of declaring that a position is orthodox or heretical. The discourse of orthodoxy and heresy is typically used to define those whose views allow them to belong (or not) to the body of Christ. But here we deploy the language of orthodoxy and heresy to address the seriousness of attending well to the truth dimensions of the processes by which we justify our beliefs about justice itself. An ordinary faith is orthodox because it heeds Jesus' refrain, "Let anyone with ears to hear listen!" (Mark 4:23). Heresies historically involve selectively attending to a particular truth to the exclusion of others; orthodox positions form when the soundest insights of competing positions can be brought together into a paradoxical acknowledgment, if not synthesis. As a heuristic for engaging in Christian contestation, we suggest that probing the orthodoxy of our justifications for beliefs entails attending to the widest range of truths—empirical, affective, doctrinal—and avoiding the heresy of standing firm on one particular truth without acknowledging the others at play, a practice feeding the mutual refusal to listen that characterizes polarization. An ordinary faith is one that pulls back from taking a heroic stand in a way that blinds us to seeing any legitimacy in a fellow Christian's concerns, but instead, routinely attends to our neighbors' perspectives, sifting for the truths that can form a common good. In later chapters, we will explore how mutual, critical attention to our processes of justifying beliefs might bear fruit (or at least illumination) in some of the most contested debates among Christians today.

Justification by Faith and Justice-Seeking

Justification by faith in Christ is the central identity marker of a Christian. This is our book's theological and ecclesiological starting point. The Nicene Creed, one of the most significant documents for all of Christianity—East and West—confesses faith in the "one holy catholic and apostolic church."[4] This means the church in its entirety is already "one" based on baptismal union in Christ, as Paul notes in Ephesians 4:5: "one Lord, one faith, one baptism." Baptism is what welcomes Christians into the church's unity that is founded on justification by faith. The phrase about the church from the Nicene Creed extends unity to an expansive, generous whole: "catholic" means capacious inclusion. The next term, "apostolic," refers to the witness of the early apostles who accompanied Jesus in his Galilean travels and then experienced him after he rose from the dead. The apostolic

---

4   The Nicene Creed, https://download.elca.org/ELCA%20Resource %20Repository/Nicene_Creed_Evangelical_Lutheran_Worship_.pdf.

witness to Christ and its extension to the global church rests precisely on the message that Christ's work of justification grounds the church's unity.

This unity exists despite the church's many divisions. Christian unity is already established by the justification that Christ works in the church. The apostles whose witness to Christ is written down in the Bible form the early basis for the church in history. But it is our justification by faith in Christ across the centuries which creates the church's unity. The basis for our identity and belonging as Christians is this ongoing reality of Christ in the church. In an abiding sense, then, the unity of the many churches existing around the world today is already available through justification by faith.

From the apostolic age to our own, the challenge is: What does it mean to live out the Christian life on the ground of justification? What is the relationship between justification and the ways in which Christians live out their vision of what the church should look like in the world? In other words, *how* does justification by faith inform a life oriented to justice? It is this precise question that divides the church. If it is justification by faith, not particular positions we hold, that identify who is a Christian, then it is the questions regarding whose vision of justice and how this vision can be achieved that provoke debate and division. Paul foresaw the church's inevitable bickering about Christian identity and addressed it in his letter to the church in Corinth. Christian identity, Paul wrote, is not attached to a particular person or school but to "the cross of Christ" (1 Cor 1:17). The cross informs the Christian life of justification that is lived out in the rough and tumble and complex messiness of this world. How then can we understand the relation between justification by faith and justice-seeking in church and world?

Theologians have considered different answers to this question. Some distinguish between justification as the work Christ does for us and sanctification as the works we do in Christ. These theologians, some of them Lutheran, insist that what Christ does is salvific while what we do contributes nothing to merit salvation—instead, it serves our neighbor in need. Other theologians, including those in the Roman Catholic and Wesleyan traditions, think about Christ's work as connected to our own: faith is naturally expressed in works of love. In Paul's words, "The only thing that counts is faith working through love" (Gal 5:6). Because justification by faith establishes a new identity in Christ, a transformed self invests in our neighbors' welfare. Other theologians, especially those in the Reformed tradition, use the term "third use of the law" to explain that justification establishes a new law. This "new law" is the law of "evangelical freedom": the gospel that welcomes Christians into a new kind of obedience to the law of Christ, voiced in Jesus' Sermon on the Mount in Matthew 5–7. It is a "new law" because Jesus uses the phrase "But I say to you" to insist on his intensification of the Mosaic law: "But I say to you, 'Love your enemies and pray for those who persecute you'" (Matt 5:44). If you are a follower of Jesus, you must "be perfect, . . . as your heavenly Father is perfect" (Matt 5:48).

Such differences among ways of relating justification by faith to justice-seeking have historically triggered church conflict. The topic of faith and works rallied the Protestant Reformation; Martin Luther caused a rift within the Catholic Church when he insisted on justification by faith without works. Yet Luther *was* interested in good works, as some Protestant theologians observe.[5] He dedicated the second half of his 1520 treatise on Christian freedom to how Christians must stay vigilant as they battle the selfish desires of the flesh and how they might show love to their neighbor in need. The role of the Holy Spirit, Luther averred, is to help Christians accomplish good works in their daily lives. Theologians after Luther persisted in exploring the idea of sanctification. The founder of Methodism, John Wesley, wondered how Christians could embody a moral life that provided external evidence of their Christian convictions. Wesley, like other theologians, was concerned with how justification creates a new Christian self that can accomplish good works. Yet Wesley, like Luther, insisted on the centrality of justification by faith as the basis for Christian justice, not the other way around.

We orient the older question of good works, made acute by the Protestant Reformation, in a contemporary context in which the disputing church seems keen on co-opting the identity marker "Christian" for particular moral and political positions. Insisting with Paul that the Christian identity marker is justification by faith, we meditate on just how this

---

[5] See Antti Raunio, "Introduction: Faith as Darkness and Light Active in Love: Luther on Christian Life," in *Darkness Light and Active Love: Studies on Theory and Practice in Luther and Lutheran-Orthodox Ecumenical Theology*, ed. Antti Raunio, Schriften der Luther-Agricola Gesellschaft 74 (Helsinki: Luther-Agricola Gesellschaft, 2020), 7–38; Antti Raunio, "Luther's Social Theology in the Contemporary World: Searching for the Neighbor's Good," in *The Global Luther: A Theologian for Modern Times*, ed. Christine Helmer (Minneapolis: Fortress, 2009), 210–27; Candace L. Kohli, "The Medieval Luther on *Poenitentia*: Good Works as the Completion of Faith in the Christian Life," in *The Medieval Luther*, ed. Christine Helmer, Spätmittelalter, Humanismus, Reformation / Studies in the Late Middle Ages, Humanism, and the Reformation 117 (Tübingen: Mohr Siebeck, 2020), 127–42.

central idea forms and informs the way we think about justice-seeking. Justice-seeking—a variant on good works—is the source of conflict in the church today. Indeed, in many respects, Christians today are caught up in fervent debates about the nature of the moral law itself. The question is not whether one is saved by good works or grace, but what actually counts as a good work—what constitutes a right, ethical position. Does the moral law shelter a woman's ability to control her fertility, or does it shelter the ability and right of a fetus to develop into an infant? Is it more in keeping with the moral law to foster the conditions for free-market capitalism or for a just distribution of resources? Do we recognize the moral law as blind to questions and histories of race relations (once a norm of racial equality is assumed), or does the moral law call us to name and address a history of racial inequities? We can get so caught up in debating the nature of the moral law that we begin to slip into associating Christian identity with one side of each particular debate. But even when we remember that debates about good works and the moral law do not themselves define (even if they always haunt) Christian existence, how one justifies one's beliefs in a particular account of justice-seeking, while navigating others' different justifications, remains a theological question. Its answer is attuned to the Spirit's work in sustaining the Beloved Community. We offer below a theological account of the relationship between justification by faith and the process of navigating inevitable differences in visions of justice-seeking.

The Messy Question of Justice

We start with an empirical observation: life is messy—even more so when we add in the question of how to orient the Christian life to justice. Even saints sin, and our intended motivations for our own actions may be mixed with desires we might not want to publicly defend.

Furthermore, we pursue justice-seeking from within particular institutions. A Christian lives in diverse institutional contexts: in the church, one's work community, the family, political organizations, and in the fluid space of social media. However flawed and fallible one finds these institutions and conversational spaces, they are inevitably the places in which Christian justice-seeking occurs. In other words, justice-seeking is communal, not individual; it takes place in and through institutions—through collective reflection and action. It is not primarily about moments of individual heroic exceptionalism. Part of life's messiness, then, has to do with its multifaceted institutional shaping, in spaces both physical and virtual.

Morally messy disagreements and polarization among Christians can be mapped onto state institutions in ways that publicize picking one side of a justice issue as key to Christian identity. One sort of Christian belonging might presuppose opposition to abortion, scriptural inerrancy, and complementary gender norms that prohibit both women's ordination and transgender self-identifications. Another sort of Christian belonging might emphasize the prophetic biblical texts that lift up a social justice vision of human rights, the inclusion of women and LGBTQ+ persons in positions of authority, and an equitable distribution of resources. Given that one set of positions on the Christian life profoundly challenges the limitations or permissions of the other, in church authority or in law and public policy, it is tempting to think that the mark of a legitimate Christian is whether or not one's political allegiances are progressive or conservative.

Competing Christian justice-seeking endeavors expose how much theology is deeply interconnected, if often divisively so, with politics. Is a Christian framing of justice inevitably different from a political one, or is there an intersection or even convergence between theological commitments and political convictions? Christ makes the sinner just before God, yet justice orients the political realm. In our Pauline-inspired terminology, justification by faith grounds and activates the justice-seeking mark of the Christian life, while justice-seeking involves the unkempt collage of each Christian's social identity, the institutional commitments of the groups to which Christians belong, the truths that are circulated in these institutions, and cultural values held as truths. All this is to suggest that justice-seeking is never wholly apolitical, but instead draws on many forms of the *polis* (the Greek term is suggestive of the city-state-nation complex) in which we participate—many forms of belonging, identity, and advocacy that we inhabit and from which we develop our ideas. The many sides to the embodied forms that the body of Christ takes in the world means that justice-seeking is inevitably a tangled, challenging, and creative process.

Justification by Faith as a Freeing Communal Touchstone amid Justice-Seeking

When we Christians forget our bearings in justification by faith, we condition Christian identity and belonging on our distinctive visions of what we think a just society should be. Without remembering that we belong to one another by virtue of our baptism into the grace of Jesus Christ, we identify the true mark of a Christian with a set of beliefs we associate with the true church. Yet somehow justification by faith must have something to do with justice-seeking, if only for the theological purpose that dis-agreements in justice-seeking initiatives are not solely political but have a theological framing as well.

What kind of relation is there to envision, then, between justification by faith and justice-seeking? How does the Beloved Community into which we are baptized grow into the fullness of Christ (Eph 4:13)? In one sense this is among the oldest questions in the world: how do ideas become reality? Or, as Plato put it in the *Republic*, how does the idea of justice get conveyed as actual justice?[6] One thing is certain: justification by faith has never led to perfection or holiness in this world. Justification by faith does mean that the whole of a Christian's life participates in the crucified and risen Christ—Paul's overarching point in Romans 6:3–11. But being justified by faith in Christ does not translate into any guar-antee of virtue in this life. Paul admitted this truth, expressing it in the language of opposition between flesh and Spirit, the struggle between old and new Adam and Eve (Rom 5:12–21) that persists among those baptized (cf. Rom 7:14–25).

Likewise, we cannot assume that justification by faith directly implies one coherent vision of justice for all. Justification by faith grounds justice-seeking, which is partial, limited by our own participation in particular communities, and shaped by the language used and ideas valued by those communities. The work of imagining justice inevitably involves conflict with others who are working in different ways with dif-ferent commitments toward this goal. Our life in the present church in this world is inevitably complicated by the old Adam and Eve. That is, our justice-seeking is inflected by limited and often sinful perspectives; sectarianism haunts justice-seeking; and sometimes justice can turn out to be its opposite: injustice.

Justification by faith is—and this point is significant—communal. Indeed, the Protestant Reformation emphasized the individual. Luther insisted that grace is "for you" so that each person would perceive and believe that Christ is given as a gift to calm one's personal anxieties and fears. Although Luther insisted on the individual, he assumed that the Christian community was the place in which Christ was communicated. Christ "for you" is also "for (another) you" and "for (another) you," so that each Christian and all together enjoy justification as gift.

---

6   Plato, *The Republic*, trans. Benjamin Jowett, The Internet Classics Archive, 1994, http://classics.mit.edu/Plato/republic.html.

Justification by faith furthermore invites individual persons to be freed from their obsessions with their own self (perhaps as the mark of libertarian self-sufficiency!). Justification lifts up the theological truth that the human person is essentially personal only in Christ's community. Thus our question about the relationship of justification by faith to justice-seeking requires thinking communally. Moral actions are never heroic and solitary by definition; virtues are never solely the prerogative of the individual. Actions and virtues are embodied in relationships between persons in their communities.

When justification is considered from this perspective, namely, as a communal event of gift and creation, then the question about its relation to justice-seeking takes on communal urgency. How can one articulate a communal vision for justice-seeking that also reminds the community that its existence is created by the Spirit of Christ? Justification is necessarily social; the body of Christ, in other words, is composed of hands, a larynx, a colon, and toenails (cf. 1 Cor 12). Once real hands, colons, and toenails contribute to the voicing of a vision for justice, then the body parts must learn how to interact with one another's strengths, functions, and weaknesses. Communities become real when persons express positions and manifest behaviors while navigating one another's positions and behaviors. Justice-seeking becomes real when it navigates the sufferings, idiosyncrasies, and fences of the persons participating in it. Power is an inevitable factor, and if unchecked, becomes destructive of community. As Christians figure out with one another—and against one another—how to embody together a vision for justice, they live out ordinary faith.

All along we have been referring to justification by faith as theologically primary. But reality is complicated and theology is not only abstract. The connection between justification by faith and justice-seeking is dynamic, not a one-dimensional relationship. There is reciprocity between justification by faith and justice-seeking. Justification by faith first forms Christian identity and then inspires justice-seeking. As the community seeks justice, it is called back to justification by faith as its ground. Justice-seeking transpires under the auspices of the daily reminder that justification by faith is the gift of freedom in Christ. Justice-seeking is inspired by Christ's right-aligning of sinner and sinned against, and imperfect as it must be within the messiness of life, it witnesses a primary belonging to Christ. Although justice-seeking inevitably involves differences of opinion, Christians who hold conflicting visions of justice all belong to the same community of those justified by faith. Even through disagreement, the reminder of a more fundamental belonging can hold resources for a more capacious, communal justice-seeking.

Ordinary faith involves the rhythm of remembering our justification by faith in Christ while engaging a fallen world. Personal lives are marked by trauma; communities are permeated with gossip and violence. We are prone to delusion, the love of power, and all sorts of nastiness that cannot be eradicated by the mere call to return to justification by faith. Yet the recognition that there is power and persuasion, argument and self-deception involved in justice-seeking should not negate our efforts. Nor should cautions about identifying with one's own virtue exaggerate the significance of our capacity for self-deception. The theological relation of a regular, daily return from justice-seeking—marked by inevitable injustices—to justification by faith acknowledges that all of life—in the world as it is—is upheld by the gift of justification in Christ, even when decisions for justice are shortsighted or one-sided. Justification by faith urges justice-seeking because faith grounds the communal body of Christ. Such faith also admits this life's propensity to power in institutions that can, in spite of their fallenness, further justice in this world.

The freedom that justification creates for ordinary faith is the freedom from a preoccupation with feeble efforts at justifying *ourselves* to God and one another. Rather, this freedom orients us toward attending with curiosity and compassion to our neighbors as fellow children of God. But as every baptized Christian discovers, ordinary faith does not entail a zippy transition from self-absorption to complete freedom from the tug and twists of sinful patterns in our individual lives and in our shared world. The freedom of a Christian is to recall our baptism repeatedly, to remember over and over that in Christ we are not sovereignly subject to any other authority—including our own capacity for despair or destructiveness—and to thereby find (over and over) the perspective to do the hard work of discovering how best to be servants and stewards of our neighbors and our planet. Justice is precisely the shape of our shared world when we love God first and love our neighbors as ourselves.

How do we arrive at the shape justice takes? To journey there together, we need to attend to something that lies in between the present truth of our justification by faith, and the emergence of justice shaping the community that we share in Christ. In between justification by faith and justice, we find another expression of justification at play: the justification of our particular ways of construing what justice looks like, and how to advocate for or institutionalize that justice. In the next section we look at how justice-seeking invokes justifications of values, allegiances, and policies that mediate between our sense of Christian identity and the identities and commitments to which we are drawn as we live out our faith in the public sphere—in the interface between our individual lives and our civic engagement. The untidiness, complexity, and necessary exercise of power in justice-seeking demand our theological attention, even as justification by faith establishes a life ever energized in Christ.

Justifications of Justice-Seeking Paths

As we have reiterated, we identify one feature of Christian identity as the basis of agreement for all subsequent reflection. Our claim is that justification by faith is *the* defining Christian identity marker. All Christians, however they might think about doctrine or ethics, are grounded in the justification that Christ gives as gift.[7] It is from this foundation that the thinking about justice-seeking and the work toward achieving the goal of justice emerges. Luther thought about the relation between justification by faith and justice-seeking in his *Freedom of a Christian* treatise along the lines of the good tree that bears good fruit (cf. Matt 7:17). Matthew's image of the tree alludes to the "entrance" to the entire Psalter, with the tree symbolizing the righteous person in Psalm 1 (Ps 1:1–3).

But the question posed by the biblical imagery—What does good fruit look like?—is precisely the subject of contemporary conflict among Christians. Some Christians, for example, think that the good fruit looks like wearing a mask during a pandemic to protect oneself and others from transmitting the coronavirus; others think that the good fruit looks like refusing to wear a mask because the image of God requires asserting personal freedom against government intervention. By naming justification by faith as the good tree, we begin with a theological claim about what fundamentally constitutes Christian identity. We then turn to where the conflict really lies—in identifying the good fruit from a theological perspective.

The question concerns how justifications are formed, discussed, contested, and navigated in the Beloved Community in which Christians have different, often opposing ideas about justice-seeking. We probe these reasons, asking why or why not someone assents to a belief. For example,

---

7   Martin Luther, *The Freedom of a Christian, 1520*, trans. W. A. Lambert and Harold J. Grimm, rev. trans. Mark Tranvik, newly rev. Timothy J. Wengert, The Annotated Luther Study Edition, ed. Timothy J. Wengert (Minneapolis: Fortress, 2016).

one person might hold on to the belief that Jesus will prevent them from contracting COVID-19. Christians can take this person's belief at face value and ask why this person holds on to this belief. Perhaps this person has experienced non-medical healing in the past that they attributed to the *Christus medicus*, the medieval designation of Christ the physician. Perhaps they take the biblical passage in Mark 16:18—"they will pick up snakes in their hands, and if they drink any deadly thing, it will not hurt them; they will lay their hands on the sick, and they will recover"—as applicable to the contemporary pandemic. How a person interprets the Bible and applies a theological concept to a particular situation are ways of justifying one's beliefs.

As theologians we use the term "justification of justice-seeking" to get at why one holds a particular vision of what justice-seeking looks like, and the ways one behaves in order to achieve that aim. We assume that people have reasons for the positions they hold. They might even use their positions to impute reasons for why others hold different positions. Mask-wearers who are concerned about the science of transmission might think that the anti-maskers are crazy for endangering their lives; the anti-maskers concerned with personal liberty might be concerned that the mask-wearers are gullible to a conspiracy theory. Often the justifications of one's own position are related to imposing another rationality—even if it is to designate the other as "crazy" or "not a Christian" or a "heretic"— onto someone else. As we figure out why we hold on to one vision of justice-seeking, we must keep in mind that others too have their distinctive justifications at play. Working them out, thus, is an exercise in learning both how to articulate reasons for one's beliefs and how to listen when others do the same.

Justification of beliefs about justice-seeking is a process that is sometimes philosophical, sometimes theological, and almost always existential. The practice of justifying arguments engages others as we work out why we hold on to particular accounts of justice-seeking and reject others. This process takes place within particular communities with their own histories and traditions of thinking, acting, and feeling. It presupposes the language used by the community, its preferences for some biblical texts over others, preaching styles, pedagogies, and ways of discerning and mandating. But persons within Christian communities also participate in other communities, such as work environments, families, and social and political cultures. These communities also make use of particular vocabularies and concepts to promote specific positions and prejudices. As persons navigate their commitments to different communities, they exhibit varying degrees of porousness or imperviousness to them. For instance, one can be on top of the national news, while disinterested in the politics playing out in the state legislature that will definitely affect public school education. At some point in this living in and in between communities, one might become interested in probing the reasons for why particular positions are held.

Questions inspiring justification of beliefs might arise quite naturally out of curiosity or be provoked by negative emotional reaction; or they might be discerned spiritually. There are different entries into probing justifications of beliefs: a conversation with one's best friend, a reaction to a sermon, a political message, a gut intuition, or a deliberate attempt to reach across the aisle. Entries are always social. Asking someone questions about their belief is the starting point for relationship.

The justification of justice-seeking is, basically, a *work of process*. It is a process of finding out meanings and relating them to experience and reason and stories. It is about asking questions, of others and of oneself. It is about paying attention to the log in your own eye even as you ask for clarification about the speck in the other person's eye (Matt 7:3–5). It interrogates wokeness and normativity, both, as one pays attention to the language one is using and the prejudices one projects onto someone else's work of justifying their beliefs. It is a learning from each other, from those in one's communities and those in other places. And it is an exercise in learning to embody virtues of patience, courage, and courtesy, even if the other person's rhetoric inflames. One can choose to walk away or to participate in this process. Justification of justice-seeking thus involves an "ethic" of relationship on the foundation of the Beloved Community.

Why is justification of beliefs about justice a *process* rather than an articulation of a done deal? Because persons navigate their porous and nonporous identities in the rough and tumble of life. Life needs improvisation, even as it needs guidance. Thinking guides our approach to reality, just as questioning arises from experience. One might disagree with a friend about same-sex marriage, but when one's own child announces a "save the date" of the wedding to their queer partner, then one might begin to question one's position. Love motivates thinking in one direction, fear in another. The people we talk with, the social media we follow, and the books we read influence our thinking, acting, and feeling. When we switch channels, travel to another community, or just reflect on why we had that awful feeling in our stomach when the pastor told parishioners to vote for this particular candidate, then a process is set into motion. This process of justifying our beliefs might be formalized in explicit ways, but more often it is spontaneous. When it takes place, it requires attending to particular features of the process, to which we turn in the next section.

Discerning the Shape of Justice: Working with Stories, Imagination, and Affect

Once we admit that different proposals for justice-seeking conflict, how can we then consciously attend to—and perhaps expand—our repertoire for justifying our convictions? And how can we attend to others who advocate for their beliefs in our presence? Interestingly, community is constituted in this very act of wanting to navigate disagreements, whatever level of agreement we find. While the Christian community gathers around the sacraments of baptism and communion that center its identity and faith in Christ, it brings that identity to bear amid reflection and action in the world. Yet how we engage in shared reflection and debate matters, including whom we imagine at the table for conversation. To whose words and experiences do we give our attention? Whose do we ignore?

The question of *who* participates in exchanging justification of beliefs (and who is ignored) informs the justificatory process. This question has to do with the kind of community that is drawn up. Are the exchanges to be limited to like-minded Christians or can they be imagined to take place among those who disagree, even vehemently? If a Christian decides that only those who hold certain views on contested topics—from abortion to gender identities to a choice of political candidate—are truly in a restricted fold, then they might exclude other Christians with different views from meaningful conversation. Feelings play up decisions to exchange or not. One might be comfortable preaching to the choir. New relationships involve risk and the possibility of rejection. One might not want to move past self-satisfaction when asked to make one's inner beliefs clear to a conversation partner. The other might be feared because they hold a position that threatens one's own deeply held convictions, or because they deny the legitimacy of one's capacity to speak as a theological authority in a patriarchal church. Then one perceives that the overcoming of difference that has been underscored by one's apprehension is psychologically impossible.

Justice-seeking involves the work of navigating our sometimes very heated differences from within a commitment to justification by faith as constitutive of the Beloved Community. For that reason, we do not here offer a set of mandates (however much we ourselves do have fairly formed moral convictions on all manner of justice-related questions). Rather, what we recognize first are practices of morally discerning together, from the fullness of our respective lives—practices attuned to the untidiness of navigating questions of justice-seeking in community. Indeed, the practices we suggest involve being self-aware about the ways we are formed in our moral and justice-seeking convictions by much more than rational argument alone: we think with narratives that open up our imaginations and emotional responses.

To be sure, philosophers might use the term "justification of beliefs" to draw attention to the ways in which rational arguments are advanced in support of the beliefs that are held or that are disagreed with. As theologians, we are committed to thinking also with stories, not to the exclusion of rational arguments, but because the genre of storytelling informs the ways Christians fundamentally see themselves. The Bible is, after all, a collection of stories (in addition to other genres) that has fascinated readers for centuries. Moreover, our personal identities and group identities are constantly shaped and reshaped by the stories we hear and the stories we tell. Stories make statistics real. We know that at least one million US Americans have died of COVID-19. Yet we also personally know someone who mourns the devastating loss of a grandfather, someone who continues to suffer brain fog and debilitating fatigue. Stories can embed or nourish or complicate arguments. But stories also invoke more embodied participation in moral reflection because they jog the imagination and elicit affects. Below we draw out how embodied storytelling is central to exchanging justifications of beliefs, and how stories involve imaginative and affective dimensions that play into the articulation of one's belief in the presence of others.

Stories for Justificatory Practices

Justifications of our beliefs—our beliefs about justice—have to do with the stories we hear and tell. Stories are not just for the kids in Sunday school. Pastors illustrate sermon messages with stories. Politicians tell stories, as do teachers, union leaders, and parents to bring messages home, into the hearts and felt imaginations of people. People resonate with stories, finding in them a relatable aspect—the mother whose child was killed in a school shooting; the first-generation student who was mentored for success in college; the student who cannot pay off a mountain of student debt; the local community pulling together to install windmills and solar panels; an Asian American suffering blows in a racist attack; families caring for refugees.

Stories shape the way we see the world. The creation stories in Genesis, for example, have long shaped Jewish and Christian ideas about steward-ship of the earth and humans as made in God's image. Likewise, stories influence how we make decisions about living in the world. Think of how a WWJD (What Would Jesus Do) bracelet invites its wearers to imagine how Jesus might behave in the movie theater or treat one's intimate partner. Stories can be singularly moralistic or marvelously multivalent. They can conclude with moral advice—the turtle is singled out for stubbornly focus-ing on reaching the goal, even though it moves much more slowly than the fickle hare. Stories might tend toward a happy ending or a dystopian night-mare. Or they can be ambiguous, as when the hero embodies vice—think Samson's vanity that perpetrated his fall into enemy hands, and the villain who shows signs of repentance. Biblical stories, some have pointed out, are delightfully powerful because they do not insist on a strict moral dichot-omy. David commits adultery; Moses disobeys God; and Peter denounces Christ. Even the story of Jesus is told by different authors; there are four gospel writers: Matthew sees Jesus as fulfilling law and prophets; Mark suggests two endings to the story of Jesus; Luke insists that Jesus brings concrete liberation from oppressive forces; and John's mystical speculation is a favorite among philosophically oriented readers. And Paul, who never experienced the antemortem Jesus, nevertheless insists on Christ crucified as the quintessence of the gospel.

We also hold different—even contradictory—stories together, depend-ing on the roles we play. In a role as a political actor, we might hold a different outlook on an issue than we might on the basis of ideal Chris-tian commitments. Friedrich Schleiermacher is a case in point. As a Christian ethicist, he was against divorce; but as a member of the Prus-sian Ministry of the Interior, he adjudicated on divorce cases. Some of us might not personally choose abortion, but would advocate for legal abortion so that others might have this choice. So often the various sides to our identities converge and contradict in ways that draw us toward compartmentalizing our sundry selves, performing different versions of ourselves for different contexts.

While this might sound like hypocrisy (and can be), our own individual inhabiting of individual stories is also a resource for ongoing moral reflec-tion within ourselves and with one another. Sometimes we strive for coher-ence, but more often than not, we are plunged into thinking and feeling amid stories that muddy whatever clarity we might have thought we had obtained. We might believe same-sex relationships are wrong, but then are faced with the story of our own or a best friend's child coming out as gay; we ourselves are so anxious that the gospel message of love casting out fear is not the reality governing our lives (cf. 1 John 4:18).

Stories are sources for moral reflection not only because they remind us that we can think and interact otherwise, but also because they convey a wide register of observed or explorable truth claims. We inhabit a range of stories that confront us with varying kinds of truths, from the empirical to the eucharistic—from the news that relays what happened today, to scientifically supported truths like human evolution, to the ultimate truth of our being made in God's image and the eucharistic truth of the feast at God's table. Justification by faith in Christ Jesus is the macrostory Christians tell about our existence in the Beloved Community, even as our particular stories—the joyous, the disagreeable, the contradictory—inflect our identities, dispositions toward others, and our navigations between others in the communities we inhabit. Recalling our essential belonging to the macrostory of faith can shape our attitudes toward storytelling and story-listening in the process of pondering why we hold on to beliefs informed by various kinds of truth claims.

To be sure, stories are more touchstones for shared reflection than stand-alone arguments for particular beliefs, including those about justice. Behind every position is a story, possibly many stories. We tell a story about young, single women and their promiscuity, and then we make abortion illegal for women. We tell another story about the high school senior who was in class one day, planning her prom dress, and the next day she was gone. Someone whispers, "She died of sepsis resulting from a self-induced abortion." Her friends show up on state capitol steps, with signs demanding abortion rights for all women.

Stories embed positionalities derived from painful experience. A mask-wearer insists on a mask mandate for all because she experienced the traumatic death of a beloved child from COVID-19. Sometimes different stories are glued together in order to attempt to make sense of a belief when emotional registers conflict. One might, for example, acknowledge that Jesus is the bringer of peace among the nations, while insisting on the right to bear arms. Conversion stories are often trotted out as singular evidence for the superiority of one's new belief. Spufford, in the introduction to this chapter, draws attention to this danger that his "conversion" to the legitimacy of same-sex marriage might entail a vilification of his now opponents, those he sided with before his conversion. But even in nondramatic spaces we describe ourselves narratively; we each have stories to tell about where we grew up and how our identities took shape among peers and through education that inform how we think today about a moral position. We meet others in their own self-descriptions and try to understand their beliefs by contextualizing them in the stories we hear about their upbringing, jobs, and families. Stories can reveal relevant truths for moral reflection; they can also conceal and occlude those truths; they can break silences; they can narrate details that other narratives ignore.

Stories are powerful tools for informing beliefs because they reinforce what is thought to be real and what ought to be. A community is held together by shared stories about the world. One community thinks that science should be followed to guide actions during a pandemic; another community rallies around a shared belief that the government exceeds its jurisdiction by enforcing vaccines as a preventative measure. Each group has its own stories that generate common belief in personal freedom and the social contract, or evidence-based truth or truth based on stories with secret origins (like conspiracy theories, such as QAnon). There are stories that unsettle us by disclosing aspects of reality we have denied but can recognize—like the prevalence of domestic violence and racial discrimination. And there are narratives that are of the sort that lead us, like Jesus when he was at odds with Peter's interpretation of his own future, to say, "Get behind me, Satan!" (Mark 8:33). This is how many of us feel today about our current political climate in the United States. What some of us took for granted is now contested: that our country agreed to live by a shared, reality-oriented story with regard to democratic values such as free and fair elections and the use of vaccines to prevent life-altering diseases. Accepting or contesting values and facts is central to the stories we tell and the beliefs we hold.

Our focus on Christian debate, however, is around those justice-related issues where we have something other than a self-protective or self-promoting denial at stake in our positions. While polemics often takes the form of discrediting the character or trustworthiness of those with whom we disagree, our impulse in this book is to resist the turn to simply refusing to listen to the stories and perspectives of someone we have placed in the "other" camp on an issue that matters to us deeply. Listening does not mean keeping silent about our own stories and perspectives, but it does mean listening first for what is at stake for another—listening like a child who is open to hearing something for the first time, seeking to understand it (and to better understand the teller). In fact, this suggestion to listen is actually a biblical exhortation: "Truly I tell you, whoever does not receive the kingdom of God as a little child will never enter it" (Mark 10:15).

When debating justice-seeking visions, we inevitably take up particular positions. But positioning is not itself a listening to others; and one might not be aware of the stories embedding someone else's point of view. Hence we need a strategy that establishes a practice that recalls how positioning is grounded first and foremost in the Beloved Community. Positioning as Christians—even though it can be oppositional—takes on the valence of freedom in Christ as the reality informing the debate. Recall the original gift of Christ's freedom for being in the Beloved Community.

Freedom in Christ is real. But living with this freedom takes practice. It takes learning particular skills, learning about the power of stories to inform views about the world, and practicing the strategies that exhibit the freedom to listen to stories told by others that play into who they are and why they hold particular positions. Wisdom is needed to discern how multiple stories intersect as they embed particular positions. Different people, even those holding on to similar positions, may be moved by vastly different stories. As stories are told, listeners can probe how the new stories intersect with what they have been told.

Stories change hearts, perhaps offering unanticipated perspectives. A pagan Roman centurion acknowledges Christ and is baptized (Acts 10:1–48)? The Bible is full of such unheard-of events: the postmenopausal Sarah, pregnant? The sinless man Jesus given the death penalty? One story might be so powerful that it effects a conversion from one idea to its opposite, as Spufford recounts. More broadly, stories enlarge one's perspective. The story of the Ukrainian pregnant woman killed in a Russian bomb attack tugs at compassion and anger. The story of the Roman soldier piercing the side of the dead Jesus adds a subtle detail that plays importantly into the theological guarantee that God's death is salvific for all (John 19:34–35). Surprise, emotion, and vivid details affect the hearers, jog them out of their expectations, move them to feel, and lure them into curiosity.

We often speak of changed hearts in the language of conversion, but stories also light up our ability to see ourselves and one another more clearly along the way. Stories often rely on dramatic tension, a journey from one state to another, often a process of maturation. Narrative psychology studies the methods of autobiographical storytelling in working through the effects of traumatic events on the self by encouraging persons to narrate them as a story that does not stay static.[8] And Christian life itself involves ongoing conversion from all the stuck or sin-soaked spots in our lives, individually and together, to grace and compassion and love. A central story throughout this book is that Christians root their identity around a shared narrative of belonging to one another through baptism into Christ Jesus—whose own story encompasses not only a ministry of storytelling and healing, but also the trauma of the cross and the mystery of the resurrection. Justification by faith in Christ involves the aligning of lives within and in sync with Jesus' story. Christian storytellers who share a common grounding in Christ—the center of the story we live out together—can then swap stories that disclose the personal and communal attachments that inform our positions, those that keep us stuck in closed-mindedness and resistance to others. Amid the in-between of their exchange, stories facilitate mutual comprehension of one another through a process that demands self-restraint and recalls a shared identity that inspires a further impulse to understand, however challenging it might be.

Imagination in the Practice of Justifying Beliefs about Justice

Why do stories tug at hearers? What is it about the human capacity for listening to others that invites us into a larger world? Justification by faith itself is a story about empathy-opening freedom in Christ. We are released from preoccupation with self, or our over-ordinate preoccupation with others at the expense of self-care, and we are freed for aligning ourselves with justice-seeking. Humans are social animals, which means care for self occurs in relation to love of neighbor and in the work toward communities that establish just relations. Stories do the work of enlarging one's world—beyond the smaller world constrained by our personal and group identities. Stories appeal to dimensions of the self that are embodied; we think in and through our bodies. We daydream and imagine even as our bodies store traumas, experiences, and joys. The imagination is a powerful resource for justice-seeking. Storytelling is one way to activate the imagination. Stories become alive through the imagination.

Contemporary Nigerian author Chimamanda Ngozi Adiche talks about the danger of the single story.[9] When we allow one story to dictate our

---

[8] Michele L. Crossley, *Introducing Narrative Psychology: Self, Trauma, and the Construction of Meaning* (Philadelphia: Open University Press, 2000); János László, *The Science of Stories: An Introduction to Narrative Psychology* (New York: Routledge, 2008).

[9] Chimamanda Ngozi Adichie, "The Danger of a Single Story," *TEDGlobal*, 2009, https://www.ted.com/talks/chimamanda_ngozi_adichie_the_danger_of_a_single _story.

perspective on reality, we miss truths available in other stories. We live diminished lives, distorted by the one-sidedness of immobility in our own story. Our imaginative capacities are squelched. We are unable to empathize with others. We live unto ourselves, locked into rigid thoughts and behaviors, unable to appreciate a world that is complicated, horrifying, and enormously interesting.

Scholars who study stories insist on the creative interface between storytelling and listening. The self is interrupted by the story; the outside world offers up one of its dimensions to curiosity. At this interface, the self is confronted with a story that is not its own. And curiosity then jogs aspects of the self that facilitate how the self tiptoes into the story, reaching for aspects of sameness while engaging difference. Here the imagination is evoked—that instrument of human perception that attends to the realm of the possible.

Justice-seeking depends on the imagination. It depends on the human capacity to imagine ways of being in relationship with each other that attribute to others the social and economic benefits that are available to all. The imagination extrapolates the justice that accrues to some and entertains that justice for others. How might a just society operate? What can justice look like for all? This question gets at the realm of the possible—the way things ought to be, the hope for a future flourishing, the anticipation of a society in which unwarranted sufferings cease.

We can resist the exercise of imagination involved in listening to stories of another, but does this not go against the grain of loving our neighbors with the care we might bring to our own stories? In issues of moral decision-making, sometimes we embody the spirit of the old Adam: with a fierce focus on the abstract, with self-righteous assurance, and the swift ability to cancel when the other does not match up to our own conception of what is right. But individuals to whom we attend can disrupt concepts to which we have been clinging, as if warding off an enemy. Living in Christ invites us to soften that clinging, to decenter and destabilize our certainties when we confront the vulnerable face of another in their own story. Loving our neighbors as ourselves includes listening to their stories, and in the process becoming more generous in regarding others as subjects in relation to each other rather than as symbols of right or wrong.

Christian life is thus about becoming more attuned to the person of Christ and Christ within. It is Christomorphic, about Christ being formed in us, as Paul put it when he compared himself to a person "in the pain of childbirth until Christ is formed in you" (Gal 4:19). Within this context of a life energized by that of Christ Jesus, the Christian life is an appeal to the imagination: How might Christ best be expressed in moral decision-making? How might Christ establish just relations among persons in a society? Harnessing the imagination is just another way that Christ invites us to imbue relations with the justice of being adopted as siblings—bickering among them included—in the body of Christ.

While the imagination's work invokes the possible, it is real in the process of moral reflection. As one tells one's own story, one imagines how the hearer might receive it. One might thus change up the details, or highlight certain steps (as in virtue-signaling) and diminish others (in order to elicit a predicted reaction). Storytelling involves imaginative resourcefulness because stories are told to others—for confession, for persuasion, for empathy, for recognition of one's own truth.

Likewise listening invokes the hearer's imagination. Details, feelings, insights, and challenges all press upon one's held beliefs, opening to a new line of inquiry. Sometimes one can even project oneself into the other's story, if only for a moment, in order to take a step in their shoes, imagining what it might be like to be in a bunker that is bombed; to be a politician who is dedicated to making lives better for her constituents; a mother of three who just cannot feed another mouth; a middle-class homeowner who champions low-income housing in their neighborhood; a person of color who has been redlined out of an area where the schools are better. Imagining the world through the lens of one another's stories does not pause the process of moral reflection. Taking up positionality is a step along the way, whether or not we revise our positions. Having a position need not (and, we caution, ought not) function as a "final word on the matter" that precludes ongoing attempts—however feeble and self-centered at times—to continue to stay engaged in the intersubjectivity of Christ's body.

This is because imagining the world by taking affects and details from the stories of others into one's own is itself an ethical disposition. In *Of Women Borne: A Literary Ethics of Suffering*, literary scholar Cynthia Wallace reflects on the interplay between an "ethics of literary representation" and an "ethics of readerly attention."[10] What she means is that while there may be ethical dynamics at play within a story, readers themselves also engage in ethical reflection while thinking about the story. The ethical dynamics in a story may be complex and ambiguous,

[10] Cynthia Wallace, *Of Women Borne: A Literary Ethics of Suffering*, Gender, Theory, and Religion (New York: Columbia University Press, 2016), 195.

as in the case of novels by Toni Morrison; or a story may seem to have a specific moral position. A clear example is Jesus' parable of the Samaritan who stops by the road in order to take care of the man who was beaten up by robbers (Luke 10:25–37). The story has an imperative to be compassionate to others—even those outside your clan—who suffer because of injustice.

The moral embedded in the story, however, can be heard with different nuances by different people. One hearer might be affected by the Samaritan's lack of concern about the political divide between Samaritans and Jews. Another hearer might be moved by the generosity of the Samaritan, and the attention to detailed aid offered. Another might hear an anticlerical message against the clergy who walked by the bruised and bloody man lying in the ditch. The listener imaginatively encounters the story by querying what the story's ethical dynamic might mean in the concrete world. Stories in literature, film, social media, and neighbors talking come alive as listeners imaginatively engage the stories' moral dimensions. How do I understand the ethical dynamic here? How might this help me attend to my neighbor? What can I take away from this story?

The New Testament tells stories about how Jesus listened to others. Precisely *as* one who spoke and acted with authority, Jesus as we encounter him in the gospels engaged with others without denying their subjectivity. He stayed in conversations that were open to change. He was genuinely interested in seeing the situation from the other's point of view. "What do you want me to do for you?" he asked the blind Bartimaeus (Mark 10:51). To be sure, Jesus did not hesitate to call out those he distrusted because of their persistent sophistic misconstruals of his healing ministry as somehow enabled by Satan: "You brood of vipers! How can you speak good things, when you are evil? For out of the abundance of the heart the mouth speaks" (Matt 12:34). Jesus was an active, engaged listener; he responded to what he heard. Sometimes he spoke bitterly about his opponents in the great debate with fellow Jews about how to keep the Torah. He was shaken to the core when he listened deeply to the way some of his interlocutors viewed the world, even as he kept speaking with them throughout his life. But he also approached others with questions that drew out what was most at stake for them: "Who do you say I am?" (cf. Matt 16:13–16; Mark 8:27–29; Luke 9:18–20); "What can I do for you?" (cf. Matt 20:32; Mark 10:51; Luke 18:41). These statements reveal Jesus regarding another human being as a person with whom to be in relationship—not as a concept to be talked about or an object prescribed to. Jesus approaches others with openness, with a beginning that allows another person space to self-articulate; he responds from there. Jesus invites conversation while making space for the other to speak their own truth, desires, and expectations. The model of Christian listening can take a page from Jesus' conversations with others.

A remarkable story in the New Testament also sees Jesus changing his mind. Mark's gospel recounts how a Syro-Phoenician woman persevered in asking Jesus to make a demon leave her daughter (Mark 7:24–30). Jesus initially refused. He excused himself by noting that the woman was a Gentile, someone from an alien ethnic identity; he in effect called her a dog: "it is not fair to take the children's food and throw it to the dogs" (7:27). As she persevered in her request, Jesus insulted her. The woman came back with a zinger that turned Jesus' mind around: "Sir," she said, "even the dogs under the table eat the children's crumbs" (7:28). Jesus was moved by her quick wit and her love for her child. He responded by freeing the child from the demon that possessed it. This unusual story offers an example of how Jesus appreciated the woman's brave turning of his own words—perhaps of insult, perhaps of rhetorical jest—against him. She turned rejection into a request for healing. The interface between her imagination and Jesus became a creative encounter, and one that established justice for the daughter.

How we imagine a just world is more than just a conversation; it is an ongoing social enterprise. The Christian life is a living together with those who hold diverse visions of justice-seeking. The visions of others might be similar to our own. They might also conflict. Our contemporary American landscape is marked precisely by divisions between Christians that have to do with clashing views of a just society. Hence imagination is fundamental to the way we tell stories and listen to them. Our appeal to the imagination aims thus to initiate conversation—and persist in it—with those who hold on to beliefs that challenge one's own. It is through our capacity for imagination that we can hold the whole of a conversation within us, including dissonant points of view about the nature of justice. One might indeed learn something new at the interface of telling and listening. And an imaginative exercise together might even hold a promise of building a shared world of justice.

Affect in the Practice of Justifying Beliefs

We listen to stories and feel things—horror, joy, frustration, confusion. Affect has not often been recognized as an important element in the justification of beliefs. The term "justification" implies reasoning, and for a long time, many have thought that reasoning is cold and calculated, not touchy-feely. But recent studies in psychology and religious studies are showing that affect is vastly important in how people navigate their worlds.

Scholars who study social media are exposing how computer algorithms change human feelings and alter brain reactions to visual stimuli, and have shown just how powerful an effect the internet has on one's affective reactions. Likes on social media platforms stimulate feel-good endorphins; clickbait triggers feelings that generate page views. Moral decision-making today is particularly vulnerable to the reactive factor in news stories. We inhabit informational ecologies that are, to a large extent, dictated by algorithms derived from political information about zip codes as well as personal consumption preferences. Hence news pitches and clickbait underscore reactions to stories that reinforce one's beliefs, while eliciting outrage at views from another perspective. These algorithmic mechanisms amplify affective reactions to moral positionings. And because of their addictive ecology, they prohibit the kinds of values of Christian imagination that lend themselves to explore storytelling through imaginative and affective capacities. Indeed, one moral to our story here might be to pay attention to the out-of-proportion dimension placed on affect through our informational ecologies. We can resist affective extremes by focusing intentionally on how our reasoning is used to justify beliefs, including how our reasoning is attuned to storytelling and the imagination and feelings that are elicited.

Feelings of aversion or attraction possess moral valences. Feelings inform the ways we value or devalue one another. For instance, as we encounter (or presume to know) someone else's justified beliefs about justice, our emotional responses can prompt us to push that person away while moving us to empathize with someone else. So much that binds people together is of an affective nature, which while subtle is immensely powerful. We know how first impressions are emotionally predictive—they powerfully shape how we hear what that person might say to us. When we experience others who do not seem to affectively register our presence to them, then we are prone to a sense of grievance. The emotional register of conversations can be highly volatile depending on how we perceive the other in relation to us. On contentious moral issues, emotions run high. They can prevent an ease in intersubjectivity by blocking out what we do not want to hear. We reduce our capacity to empathize when we insist on our own sense of being right.

Indeed, too often we neglect the affective dimension when we mis-characterize the Christian life as moral decision-making according to a cold principle that is uniformly applied to real life. Righteousness, or precisely self-righteousness, often operates this way: we identify with what we have come to feel is the right position and ignore the face of a neighbor who might be or feel harmed by that position (or at least by our inattention to their experiences of it). But at its most alert, the way of the Beloved Community is such that positionality and thinking and listening involve a process of being deeply invested in the emotional registers of intersubjectivity.

The place of the emotions in navigating our experiences and in forming our beliefs is a recent theme in psychological research. Popular studies offer wisdom practices for better navigating our own and others' needs and emotions, mindful of how our cognitive and emotional processes seem to work. For instance, in *Useful Delusions: The Power and Paradox of the Self-Deceiving Brain*, Shankar Vedantam and Bill Mesler synthesize studies that suggest how self-delusions can help us to function psychologically by fostering an optimism that lets us avoid being overwhelmed by harsh realities.[11] In his Udemy online course *Master Your Brain: Neuroscience for Personal Development*, Gregory Caremans tours four brain structures—reptilian, paleolimbic, neolimbic, and prefrontal cortex—and describes how we can read our own and others' behaviors in light of them.[12] In light of such awareness, he suggests ways we can move beyond fear, flight, and freeze responses (as well as tendencies to pick teams and think from them) in order to take our bearings from the higher order space of perception and judgment provided by the prefrontal cortex. Undoubtedly, theologians have much to learn from scientific studies of human behavior, even as Christians have their rich heritage of spiritual practices that neuroscientists might, in turn, map onto their own accounts of the human.

Indeed, because the affective register connects (or disconnects) people, the Christian life is characterized in part as an *ordo salutis*, a training in the emotions of the Spirit: a healing of emotions so that emotions can facilitate intersubjectivity rather than shut it down. Paying attention to affective registers entails noticing how we are preconceptually related to the world, and how strongly these preconceptual emotions or internal

[11] Shankar Vedantam and Bill Mesler, *Useful Delusions: The Power and Paradox of the Self-Deceiving Brain* (New York: Norton, 2021).

[12] Gregory Caremans, *Master Your Brain: Neuroscience for Personal Development*, Brain Academy, Udemy, January 2022, online course.

states persist alongside (even in spite of) our intellectual engagement with conceptual arguments. We can shut down rather than listen because our emotions—cued to our immediate relations to the world and to our own reactive pathways—can be so wrought. Paying attention to someone else's storytelling involves metacognition about the aspects of the self that prohibit listening or jumping to conclusions. Intuiting and interpreting affect's cues involves a lifelong practice of coming to terms with emotions and how they are the undercurrent of the way we navigate our world. Sanctification, in other words, is also about the feelings we attach to good works.

Sanctification heals the emotions through which intersubjectivity is built up or destroyed. Jesus was particularly attuned to the emotions of people who clamored for his healing. He knew that Zacchaeus was ashamed of his height and called him to come down from the tree in order to become visible as he was (Luke 19:1–10). Jesus knew that the parents whose son was born blind felt guilty, and he freed them by claiming that their sins were not the cause of their son's blindness (John 9:1–23). He knew the devastation that Mary and Martha felt after they lost their brother Lazarus, and he called Lazarus out from the grave (John 11:38–44). These gospel stories show that healing encompasses turning guilt into joy, sorrow into joy, shame into confidence.

But just as we now have the Holy Spirit as the first fruits of the new creation (cf. Rom 8:23 and 2 Cor 5:17), so too we have the perspective-providing orientation of the gospel, even if not the fullness of healed emotions at every level of our being. As anxiety-prone Luther advised, we need to remember daily our baptism amid whatever manner of internal states we are encountering. Theologically construed, emotional healing is a lifelong process that is oriented to our baptismal identity and our identification with the crucified and risen body of Christ. We need many resources to embark on this journey. It is a practice that we come back to again and again, even as we make incremental steps toward healing, and often a few steps forward are followed by a step backward.

Spiritual Practices for Justifying Beliefs about Justice

Our thinking theologically about belief-justifying practices has led us to consider different aspects of the self that inform our justice-seeking. We all have reasons for why we hold particular beliefs and why we reject others. Yet the reasons, like the tip of an iceberg, hide the many subjective and intersubjective dimensions that percolate beneath the surface. Reasons have their own reasons, so to speak. We react or are convinced because of neural pathways, resonances of sameness, and feelings of aversive disgust. We think, but our thinking is embodied—embodied in two senses: in our own body-selves, and in the systems in which we live and were raised. Feelings are embedded in bodies and are triggered by events. The imagination is a human capacity for good or for evil. And storytelling can trigger the hearer, shut them down, put their backs up, or spark curiosity.

In addition to being aware of the roles of story, imagination, and affect, there are various ways to evaluate theologically our processes of justifying our beliefs about justice and of ethical, wise, or prudent ways to pursue it. Below we describe three theological practices that some may find helpful amid forming and debating beliefs about the shape of justice.

Attention to Presumption and Despair

Medieval monks and nuns were trained in the daily practice of introspection. Introspection was foundational to a life of penance. Each day they had to figure out which sins they had committed so that they could confess these sins to God. The process of identifying sins was facilitated by using tools, such as the Ten Commandments, that they held up as a "penance-mirror" (in German, *Beichtspiegel*) for self-analysis. Penance required deep and thorough analysis of sins; even sins hidden from surface-level conscience had to be ascertained. And penance also included the exhibition of appropriate emotions. The goal was to feel contrite, which means heartfelt sorrow for sins committed. "A broken and contrite heart, O God, you will not despise," was the famous verse from Psalm 51 (v. 17), one of the penitential Psalms that guided the hope that a penitent had sufficiently identified sins and demonstrated contriteness.

Monks and nuns were taught to identify two particular sins: the sins of presumption and despair. In fact, Martin Luther was interested in making these two sins the focus of his own introspection, and by extension, his theological writing. In his introduction to the Psalms, Luther notes that the human heart is tossed between these two opposing emotions.[13] The heart is either arrogantly presumptuous in its own actions and thoughts. Or it despairs of all its capacities for any good action or thought. Furthermore, Luther thinks that God's law condemns presumption; the divine law judges all human attempts to justify their own actions as presumptuous. Humans engage in self-deception of all sorts, including that of

---

[13]   Martin Luther, "Preface to the Book of Psalms," 17–23 in *Martin Luther's Manual on the Book of Psalms*, trans. Henry Cole (London: R. B. Seeley and W. Burnside, 1837), https://www.lutheranlibrary.org/pdf/367-luther-psalms-cole.pdf.

self-righteousness. God exposes this for what it is—a self-delusion that the human can earn their own salvation by good works. Yet God's law for Luther is so targeted at exposing self-righteousness that its work ends up affecting the sinner at a fundamental level. The law deprives the human of any comfort in one's own good works to the point that the human despairs of all actions as in any way being acceptable before God's throne. For Luther, presumption and despair characterize how the self attempts to justify itself before God and how God exposes those attempts as delusional.[14] The life of penance includes paying attention to how we might veer from presumption to despair and back again.

Presumption is a useful concept to capture our attempts to justify our justice-seeking beliefs. It names sinful forms of being self-righteous about our beliefs. "Virtue signaling" is a common way that we show to others how we are in the right. We can be smug about commitments to a particular justice movement, such that we reject all others. Or we can persist in presumption by emphasizing our own moral purity (be it "wokeness" about racism or considering someone Christian only if they oppose legal abortion). Likewise, we risk presuming our social-media-advertised and friendship-circle-defined political identity—whether labeled conservative or liberal—as the mark of righteousness. Just because we think we are righteous, or we perform it for others, does not mean that we really are. Indeed, presumption subtly shifts the focus from justice-seeking to our own moral self-justification.

Despair is presumption's opposite. In fact, despair might even be more significant given our contemporary world marked by so many crises. The perception that the system seems too big to change and the self too small elicits despair, anxiety, and hopelessness. Despair deprives justice-seeking of any hope that it is a worthwhile collaborative project. It fosters cynicism about the worthwhileness of justice-seeking, or any effort to seriously engage with those holding seemingly opposing notions of justice.

Luther describes the heart as tossed between presumption and despair, and here we note this tossing in relation to our processes of justifying our beliefs about the shape of justice. Both presumption and despair distract us from sharing stories and empathically swapping arguments. Presumption shapes us into focusing on our own moral standing as if that suffices

---

14   Luther, "Preface to the Book of Psalms," 20.

for justice; despair casts us into a space of withdrawing or of bitter resignation. Both presumption and despair are emotive states that resist forward motion. They render us inert, preventing us from doing the ongoing soul work of engaging the individual and collective dimensions at play in interpersonal and systemic injustices. Thus spiritual work is needed to identify emotional states in our lives, how they render us unable to engage with others, especially with those with whom we disagree, and how they prevent us from the very work of justice-seeking that is so badly needed in our communities today.

Distinction-Making as a Bridge-Building Practice in Justifying Beliefs

Another familiar theological tool for taking stock of how we justify our beliefs is the philosophical art of distinction-making. This way of thinking goes back to ancient Greek philosophy and was expertly employed by medieval Christian theologians such as Thomas Aquinas. Distinction-making has to do with asking: in what respect can we affirm (say "yes" to) and in what respect do we disagree with (say "no" to) a particular judgment about justice-seeking?

Doing so prompts us to provide reasons for affirmation or negation. It can also help in trying to understand someone else's position. If we can describe in what sense we might agree with someone whose overall beliefs about justice we do not share, we demonstrate that we are listening to their own convictions, hearing what is at stake in them. In the process, we can find common ground. Distinction-making is an exercise that widens our empathy even as it hones and nuances our arguments for our ethical convictions and the policies that could support them.

Attention to Structural Justice

As a third tool for self-reflection about our own moral convictions, we might ask ourselves when we are focusing too much on an individualistic virtue ethics—on taking our bearings primarily from James' admonition to keep our own selves "unstained by the world" (James 1:27) or from Jesus' saying "You always have the poor with you" (John 12:8), rather than from Mary's prophetic song and Jesus' Isaiah-based announcement of the low being raised high, the prisoners released, and the deaf and blind healed (Luke 1:46–55). Such biblical visions of a made-just world challenge us to identify and seek to transform structures, instead of focusing only on what we can control personally about our own habits of virtue—as if they could be isolated from our web of relations to one another. In this sense, being unstained by the world means not hiding from the contention of public debates and social change movements, but instead avoiding the worldly temptation to think only of ourselves. We must be willing to make mistakes, not avoid conflict because we prefer preserving the image of our own moral perfection.

Attending to structural sin and not only individual virtue, incorporating a way of saying "yes" to an opponent's point of view, noticing our temptations to presumption and despair: these are all spiritual practices that foster forming and holding our beliefs in a way that keeps us attentive to our neighbors—including our neighbors who perceive the shape of justice differently. They are also the kinds of practices that have historically been used to build consensus toward orthodox doctrine. In fact, these practices facilitated the ways that theologians and bishops in the early church synthesized the insights of competing parties to form and articulate doctrine. We turn next to describing why and how the historical formation of orthodox doctrine about the Trinity can be a heuristic lens for evaluating Christian processes of justifying beliefs about justice.

Orthodoxy and Heresy: Ordinary Faith as a Non-Polarizing Process of Justice-Seeking

We have addressed the processes by which we form our beliefs, processes that involve implicitly or explicitly thinking from our particular stories and affective experiences in relation to our identity as baptized Christians. We have argued that those beliefs that translate into this or that side in public policy debates do not *themselves* mark our identity as Christians; our belonging to Christ in faith does that. But those beliefs reflect our intuitions about the shape justice should take. How do we guard against the temptation to identify fiercely around those beliefs in ways that eclipse our identity rooted in justification by faith in Christ?

We have advocated for the virtue of mutual listening in how we justify our particular convictions about just flourishing (and the pathways to it). Self-awareness about a penchant for self-righteous presumption, making careful distinctions, and remembering to notice structural as well as individual sin—these can inspire our mutual listening as we contemplate our own beliefs about justice. Now we retrieve a perhaps surprising lens of analysis from Christian theological tradition, a lens with which to perceive and assess *ways* that we justify our beliefs about issues that divide us. We turn to the notion of orthodoxy and its opposite: heresy.

Historically, language of orthodoxy and heresy has applied to doc-trines of Christ and salvation. Theologians debate which attributes can be truly predicated of the God-man or whether or not to exclude works from justification by faith. Appeals to orthodoxy and heresy are usually part of the serious questions of doctrine, not the nitty-gritty of how we live out our daily Christian faith. Yet it is not uncommon today to hear Christians using the term "heretical" for feminist or progressive Christian views.[15] Here we suggest that it is precisely *this* kind of heresy shout-out that is *itself* heretical, for it conditions Christian belonging upon a partic-ular vision of the moral life. Indeed, the very history of determining what counts as doctrinal orthodoxy may offer more insight for ordinary rather than polemical practices of justifying beliefs about justice—practices that reflect the generosity of an orthodoxy that shows it can hear what's at stake for both sides in a conflict. Such practices can convert high conflict to good, productive conflict.

Indeed, recall once more that Paul helped develop the doctrine of jus-tification of faith precisely by rejecting a praxis-oriented marker of eccle-sial identity. His first Letter to the Corinthians documents his rejection of Jewish kosher dietary and circumcision laws as identity markers of the Christian. But when it came to issues concerning life together, such as whether or not it was acceptable to eat meat that had been sacrificed to idols (1 Cor 8–10), Paul recommended an attitude of tolerance. The "strong" Christians knew those idols did not exist anyway (1 Cor 8:4); hence they should tolerate the Christians who avoided the meat sacrificed to the gods out of a conscience that was not yet informed by this knowl-edge (1 Cor 8:7). What Paul found problematic was not a given position in the debate (although he favored the view of the "strong"), so much as the way those on each side of the debate could see their own position as *the* marker of identity for the church. Interestingly, Paul especially targeted those with whom he most agreed, the "strong," who knew the truth that food is irrelevant in our relation to God (1 Cor 8:8): "But take care that this liberty of yours does not somehow become a stumbling block to the weak" (1 Cor 8:9). The unity of the church was not conditioned upon being right or wrong about proper food consumption. More important was reaching out to one another from within the body of Christ to emphasize the gospel

---

[15]   See, for example, Alex Murashko, "'Progressive Christianity' a Form of Her-esy Says Author [Lucas Miles] of 'the Christian Left,'" *Media on Mission*, March 16, 2021, https://mediaonmission.org/progressive-christianity/.

as it connected with persons where they were at. To do otherwise is to "sin against Christ" (1 Cor 8:12). Thus Paul was willing to avoid meat for the sake of the weak, if doing so would prevent their "falling" (1 Cor 8:13) from their confidence in Christ and the church. Paul directed his comments to the "strong" Christians, letting them know that their strength resided in greater knowledge. But greater knowledge would have to be used not to insist on being right, but in a way that navigated the conscience of others by discerning contextually where and when not to eat meat sacrificed to idols (1 Cor 10:23-33): "'All things are permitted,' but not all things build up. Do not seek your own advantage, but that of the other" (1 Cor 10:23b-24).

It is in this Pauline spirit that we invite reflection on how we justify beliefs about the shape of justice. Alongside refusing to call a Christian with a different view of justice a "heretic," attention to polarization in the process of belief-justification is central to what we have in mind. Beliefs do not come ready-made into minds and hearts. Rather, we try to make sense of them, usually when we query them in our own minds, or when we are asked to explain them to others. This practice is always a practice in the presence of others, whether they are present to us as conversation partners or in our imaginations. The important point here is that we engage in this practice in relation to others, real or imagined. And these practices shift in the way we take into consideration those real or imagined others. The presence of the imagined other in our practices is significant in our contemporary polarized context. As we make sense of our beliefs in this context, we often imagine the other in oppositional terms. Polarization thus insinuates itself into the very practice of making sense of belief. This polarization increases the temperature, so that making sense takes on intensities of affect, defensiveness, and caricatures of the imagined other. Here the practice of justifying our own beliefs morphs quickly into defensive posturing and aggressive demonization of the other who holds an opposing belief. This occurs more often than not in the face of the imagined other. In our polarized context of high conflict, we rarely meet those on the other side. And the hearsay of their beliefs is translated into our intensified accounting of our beliefs. The process very quickly hardens into positioning that then detracts from the very process of inquiry, of attempts to make sense of and understand.

Whether or not we are self-aware about it, such a polarized way of defending our own beliefs about what is right and wrong often selectively attends to a truth around which we defend our position as if it were *the* mark of moral purity, losing sight of other truths and—as Paul worried—of our larger belonging to one another in the body of Christ. A habit of polemical self-justification might be hazy and inchoate, percolating up into our consciousness with emotional verve as we note our judgments of this or that in the world around us. Or it might be on full display with the sophistic sharpness of a trained lawyer, as when some Republican congresspersons rationalized why they voted against certifying the 2020 US presidential elections on trumped-up procedural grounds, like the expanded options for voting that counties developed in response to the coronavirus pandemic. In both cases, we are drawn to stand our ground on a particular pure truth of fact or feeling, where we are certain we are in the right. *This* truth is either the most salient one, leaving all other related matters in the shadows, or it is the one truth sufficient to ward off criticism of one's position.

Such rigidness invokes the language of orthodoxy and heresy. To be sure, language of orthodoxy and heresy can sound like it is meant to decide who belongs and who does not to the body of Christ. Orthodoxy, in other words, means who is right, and heresy, who is wrong. But these terms of inclusion and exclusion do not take into consideration the actual practices of justifying beliefs in the way and toward the end that has happened in some of the key formations of orthodox doctrine. Once we discern that we arrive at justifications for our beliefs about the shape of justice through practices of affectively and contextually shaped reasoning in view of others, we can begin to notice connections between our modes of debating about justice-seeking and the *way* orthodoxy is itself discerned and upheld.

Three Elements in Orthodoxy Formation

There are three dimensions of the distinction between orthodoxy and heresy in doctrinal debates that can inform a process of justice-seeking as an act of ordinary faith—one ruled or ordered by mutual listening in shared community—rather than a polemical faith that conditions belonging upon bold denunciations that demonize one's opponents. The processes of identifying creedal, ecumenical orthodoxy provide an apt theological resource for practicing metacognition about our own and one another's ways of justifying our beliefs in a polarized political and cultural climate.

First, by starting with Paul's own development of the doctrine of justification by faith as an orthodox statement about Christian identity itself, we recall that for Christians, the heart of orthodoxy as a criterion of belonging is *this* doctrine. While Paul may have encouraged expelling some members for egregious moral behavior where there was genuine disagreement in the community as a whole, he reminded the church again and again that the condition of belonging was not the side one took in that disagreement but their baptism into Christ's body.

Second, we invite reflection on the "orthodoxy/heresy" pairing not as the *de facto* judgments of what we consider to be orthodox and heretical, but as two ways of navigating *how* we justify beliefs in the presence of others, real or imagined, who also belong to the body of Christ. As such this pair is not invoked to find ways to attack others of heresy—to go heresy-hunting—but to remember that creedal orthodoxy itself involved a process of listening and coming to understand the way others justify their beliefs as well as vice versa (i.e., how others might come to understand our own positions). Heresy, by contrast, is ultimately identified as a point of view that *does not listen deeply and widely enough* to the spectrum of truths that need to be brought into the chorus of an orthodox stammering of what is so about God and God's relation to the world. By analogy, in relation to a process of justice-seeking within the body of Christ, a heresy is the spirit of claiming the moral purity of one's position in a way that becomes defensive and accusatory in the face of one's imagined or real interlocutors. As a *process* of entering into a debate about justice in the Beloved Community, heresy involves a rationalization manifesting as a refusal to listen at all to those with whom we disagree, except to point out where they are in error.

Have not many of us been heretics in this respect from time to time? Rationalizations involve selective attention to the truths most relevant for our cause. Rationalizing heretics are adept at motivated reasoning; they can be persuasive public communicators, speaking and penning opinion pieces that line up the evidence toward an inevitable conclusion. Others may be unsure of exactly how to begin to think in another way, unless they really listen to a commentator from the "other side." Social media has created bubbles of rationalizing commentary on all manner of ethical or policy positions. We do not lack for loud voices with meme-worthy defenses in virtual and physical spaces. Many of us contribute to them when we have a revealing story or verbal zinger to add to the chorus. Indeed, there is emotional satisfaction in naming well a supporting point for a position we have come to hold deeply. The moral and theological danger may arise not so much in what is present as in what can be absent from our argumentation.

Selective attention to the truths relevant to a matter of common concern may be the prime generator of a polemical atmosphere. This is not to say that we ought not offer robust justifications for our beliefs, or that

our beliefs on a controversial subject always fail to take account of the perspectives and observations of those who arrive at a different sort of moral
or policy point of view.

Indeed, and third, at some key moments, the actual crystallization of
orthodox doctrine has depended precisely on listening to *and incorporating* what is at stake for participants in a debate. But it can take more
than one generation to discern a perspective that all can agree is the
"right teaching" on a matter that integrates insights from all disputing
parties. Here, in thinking about debates regarding justice, we draw from
the history of creedal development in a heuristic or analogical way. For
where there is earnest rather than specious debate, agreement on the
shape of justice in the Beloved Community is not a condition of ecclesial belonging. Perhaps agreement on the shape of justice on some matters will remain eschatological. In the meantime, though, the *process* of
listening for what is at stake for both ourselves and others in the body
of Christ is what faithfully corresponds to the journey in and toward
orthodoxy.

A Story from History: The Arian Controversy and the Nicene Creed

Let us look more closely at an example from the history of the early
Christian Church in order to illustrate how an orthodox doctrinal claim
emerged from deep listening over time to competing positions. The
orthodox position of the Trinity as three persons in one divine essence
did not fall down from heaven, but emerged through a century of hard
philosophical work and navigating difficult personalities in a political
context of high conflict, along with a generous dose of the Holy Spirit.
Throughout this process, accusations of heresy were bandied about with
abandon. At the risk of oversimplifying, the kind of single-minded focus
on a particular position or intuition is often what came to define a heretic. The Greek root, *hairesis*, means "choice"—one who chooses to identify with a particular point of view or a particular school of thought.
The negative connotation of such "choice" arises only when that school
of thought is deemed erroneous by those who hold a different point of
view. But is orthodoxy just a process of picking among competing "heresies" in the sense of competing choices, competing schools of thought?
At important junctures in the development of orthodox Christianity,
such as those voiced in the Nicene Creed, the process of deciding what
counted as a *rejected* point of view involved not just denying it, but

finally getting what was meant by one's theological opponents through the process. The resulting orthodoxy, rather than excluding so-called heresies, actually found a new synthesis that took account of insights from competing perspectives.

In the Arian controversy of the fourth century, the 381 CE Council of Constantinople continued—like the 325 CE Council of Nicaea—to reject the Arian view that the Son was subordinate to the Father in the Trinity.[16] (To remind our readers: the orthodox position asserts that the Son is of the same essence as the Father and hence of equal divine status as the Father.) But between 325 and 381, many Arian-leaning theologians moved toward affirming the Nicene Creed which stipulated co-equality between Father and Son. The reason for this shift was because the Greek Cappadocian theologians developed a Trinitarian understanding that the Father was distinct from Son, in spite of co-equality. This emerging understanding of distinctness was prompted by Arius' intuition that the Son's subordination to the Father presupposed a kind of distinctness from the Son. The Nicene formulation that the "Son is consubstantial with the Father," yet distinct in personhood, expressed a synthesis of the anti-Arian insistence that the Son was fully divine (*homoousios* with the Father, or of the same divine essence) *and* the Arian concern to avoid collapsing the Son into the Father without distinction. Between the 325 and 381 versions of the Nicene Creed lay a newly minted doctrine of the Trinity that expressed this synthesis with the proposition that God is one being in three *hypostases*, or what in English we call "persons."[17]

As the Nicene example suggests, even within intense debates, orthodoxy entails a capacity to be stimulated by listening to different accounts. In this sense, orthodoxy is generous, capacious, and yes, catholic with a small *c*. Orthodoxy does not mean the resolution of all disagreement. Christians have been discussing and debating the meaning of the Nicene Creed ever since 381. Yet orthodoxy signals that the center of Christian faith holds quite different intuitions about God and Jesus together, while

[16]   For an excellent survey of this controversy, see Lewis Ayres, *Nicaea and Its Legacy: An Approach to Fourth-Century Trinitarian Theology* (Oxford: Oxford University Press, 2004).

[17]   For one account of how the Cappadocians' Trinitarian ideas reconciled many Arians to a newly clarified understanding of the Nicene Creed that took to heart Arian concerns about the Son lacking any distinction from the Father, see Richard E. Rubenstein, *When Jesus Became God: The Epic Fight over Christ's Divinity in the Last Days of Rome* (New York: Harcourt Brace, 1999), 204–10.

smoothing them into a particular unifying orientation. What the Trinitarian controversy of the fourth century CE demonstrates is that theologians who came together to discuss the problem of how the Son could be divine were engaged in the process of justifying their beliefs from different perspectives. As they tried to formulate the meaning of the God-human's two natures, they learned from a position they had dismissed as "heretical" and included at some level consideration of the legitimacy of the alleged heretic's concern.

Differences persist between Eastern Orthodox and Catholic/Protestant versions of the Nicene Creed itself (with the Orthodox giving a certain primacy to the First Person of the Trinity, from whom both the Second and Third Persons proceed, while Western Christians perceive the Spirit proceeding from both Father *and* Son). We will not rehearse here these debates or their partial resolution in additional ecumenical councils, nor the way that political context shaped what syntheses stood (such that loyalty to the Council of Chalcedon in Persia looked like loyalty to the Roman Empire, fostering different doctrinal syntheses among Nestorian and so-called Monophysite churches). And while most non-creedal Protestants accept the doctrines that emerge from the creedal debates, we recognize that a minority of Christians reject the doctrine of the Trinity and have adopted some form of Arian subordinationism (such that God the Father alone is fully divine; a view held by Oneness Pentecostals and Jehovah's Witnesses, among others). What we want to note here, however, is that even when some persons and views were declared heretical in patristic era debates, the emerging orthodox doctrines that stood the test of time were those that had absorbed the most compelling ideas from opposing sides of a question. In this respect, orthodoxy formation involves empathy and breadth of vision, however much it emerged through contention.

Orthodoxy emerged in the process of discussion, coming to express one's position by providing reasons for it, and doing this in the presence of the real and imagined other. A development that foreclosed the concerns of "heretical" others too quickly would have led to quite a different orthodoxy than the one we regard today as such. In other words, orthodoxy took shape by shifting away from polarization between alleged orthodox and heretical positions and toward practices of discussion between different perspectives that led to a more commodious orthodox position. Let us take up this spirit of the Cappadocians today!

Applying Orthodoxy/Heresy to Ordinary Faith
amid Justice-Seeking

Theologically construed, our various justifications of our political and cultural affiliations and our policy positions can all be perceived and evaluated through what might initially sound like a provocative application of the lens of debates about orthodoxy and heresy. To be sure, in ways we have noted as problematic, something like this move has already been made wherever Christians have conditioned belonging on the basis of holding certain ethical views or political identities. If fourth-century Christians were tussling over the Son's exact relationship to the Father, today many Christians casually and routinely out one another as heretics on the basis of whether or not they support same-sex marriage, a legal right to abortion, or women's ordination—each view intertwined with debates about what in effect constitutes orthodox or heretical views of scriptural authority and interpretation.

We suggest that a more faithful approach to Christian disagreements about justice is to call one another back to the kind of debate about orthodoxy that generates potentially synthetic perspectives that can be more widely shared. We can pursue this, as we suggest, by reframing the discourse of orthodoxy and heresy to be—in this case—about the process of deliberating together in the body of Christ. How do we form and justify our particular positions and allegiances in ways that continue to listen to the voices, stories, and emotional truths held by our neighbors who may disagree with us? We propose that positions formed in ways that shut down awareness of a wider spectrum of truths and experiences are positions that tend toward heresy, defined heuristically here as standing on a particular point of truth, as if it alone suffices to make sense of and direct our shared lives.

Likewise, with regard to ecclesial practices of justice-seeking, we define—again, heuristically—orthodoxy as a position or allegiance that is justified on the basis of an ongoing process of listening to as wide as possible a spectrum of empirical truths, narrated experiences of persons affected by a policy or position, and structural analyses of unjust or inequitable (or just and equitable) social patterns. In the process, we inevitably reform our own positions in a way that acknowledges the intuitions and concerns in other construals of truth and justice. In the context of moral and political reflection, this means: orthodoxy is not about a specific judgment so much as it is about the *process* of coming to form, act upon, and revisit our commitments and convictions in the public sphere. In this circumscribed sense, orthodoxy refers to a certain way of practicing the art of justification of beliefs in the spheres of social ethics and political theology: a way of rightly aligning our values and perspectives on particular civic and public issues with a metacognitive awareness that emphasizes due process for our neighbors and ourselves.

This is not at all to suggest that the *content* of doctrinal orthodoxy does not matter. Rather, we are inviting a way of drawing connections between a well-established orthodox Christian doctrine—like justification by faith—to a process of self-reflection and of discerning together what justice looks like in our common life in Christ. An orthodox posture is one that attends to the other's concerns and attempts to articulate those concerns in one's own process of self-reflection and discerning. Heresy is whatever circumvents or narrows that process of reflection and discernment, such as quickly dismissing someone's else's question. Heresy might also take the form of declaring that another Christian is heretical *because* they hold a different understanding of the shape of justice.

Orthodoxy, we are suggesting, is an ordinary, ongoing spiritual-ethical practice of advocating for a position while continually trying to notice and incorporate what is at stake for those who disagree. We may not come to a consensus in our own generation. Yet orthodoxy even then remains a practice of collective vision-seeking that is grounded in faith-borne baptismal identities and oriented to justice as a collaborative work of making sense of why we hold truths dear and how we can listen to the truths that others propose. Orthodoxy, in this respect, is orthopraxy: a way to practice truth-seeking together.

Yet orthodoxy also has to do with content, and specifically the insistence on its truth. Here we draw attention to the orthodoxy/heresy divide that has all too often been weaponized to excommunicate and even do violence against those deemed heretics on account of the content of their ideas. The killing of abortion providers, such as Lutheran parishioner Dr. George Tiller, is a case in point.[18] Further back in history, among the medieval inquisitors, heresy-hunting involved plenty of gaslighting—clever efforts to foster self-doubt in the accused, or to verbally trap them into confessing to their heretical beliefs and naming

---

[18] Jeff Gardner, "The Shooting of George Tiller," *National Catholic Register*, June 5, 2009, https://www.ncregister.com/news/the-shooting-of-george-tiller.

other accomplices.[19] Martin Luther's excommunication from Rome had to do with his being judged a heretic by Catholic theologians of his time. Luther's position on justification by faith rankled his colleagues because he refused to allow any compromise on the issue of works contributing to the divine act of forgiveness. Yet Luther turned around and condemned many Anabaptists because he deemed them heretical for advocating baptism for mature persons. In Luther's case, heresy-hunting is connected to orthodoxy on matters of theological significance. Ironically, however, heresy-hunting can look precisely like the kinds of behavior we are ourselves deeming heretical here: sniffing out any possible way that someone might hold the wrong view of justice and calling them out on it.

Orthodoxy and heresy discourse *is* potent. It signals that what is at stake matters, and matters ultimately. The sharpness and energy around language of orthodoxy and heresy fits with the particular zeal that animates this collaborative project: to think together as Christians not only about *which* ethical and policy positions we hold, but about how we are mutually and widely attentive to all the relevant truths, stories, affectivities, and perspectives that matter to us. How widely and well we listen to the insights of those with different visions of justice matters mightily for the sake of the common good and for our ability to avoid blaspheming God's name. That is why we do not want to keep language of orthodoxy and heresy in the closet. That said, we appeal to orthodoxy and heresy in the context of justice-seeking on diverse Christian grounds. Thus we invite appreciation for an introspective humility with regard to ourselves and our allies who share a particular view of justice, a receptivity to listening deeply to those with whom we most disagree, and a remembrance that the condition of ecclesial belonging is centered in justification by faith in Christ.

Guided by the spirit of orthodoxy so understood—as much perceptively integrating as discriminating among competing ideas—we can run with the Spirit toward a vision of justice without running aground in a constricted notion of what justice looks like. We can repent and remake our world in light of a vision of the Beloved Community without diminishing our ability to see the faces and hear the words, needs, and insights of our neighbors.

---

[19]   For an example of an interrogation by fourteenth-century inquisitor Bernard Gui, see Paul Halsall, "Medieval Sourcebook: Bernard Gui: Inquisitorial Technique (c.1307–1323)," *Internet History Sourcebooks Project*, Fordham University, January 1996, https://sourcebooks.fordham.edu/source/heresy2.asp.

Conclusion: Justifying Justice-Seeking in the Community of Ordinary Faithful

In this chapter we have described how we think about the processes by which Christians reflect on why we hold on to particular visions of justice-seeking. We have hoped to remind our readers that recognizing that Christian belonging is rooted in our justification by faith in Christ—not our positions on contested moral debates—can orient us amid conflict within the Beloved Community *about* the Beloved Community. Justification by faith is a beginning point to which we return again and again when we feel wronged, misunderstood, or aghast by one another's understanding of the shape of justice or morality.

Within this framework of Christian belonging (one indebted to the Pauline epistles), a few things stand out regarding the processes of justifying our beliefs about what justice looks like. One is that we have been depicting a routine process of coming to hold a Christian belief. When Christians cite Scripture as evidence, when we appeal to an authority who holds the same point of view—these are justificatory practices that we almost instinctively apply. Yet they are also *practices we can reflect on*: Why do we hold this value? What or whom does it serve? How do we make connections among all the truths and consequences at play?

A second observation is that we are at our best when we analyze reasons for our justice-related beliefs in the presence of others. Sometimes we do not bother to furnish reasons because we are proverbially speaking to the choir. We assume that others hold the same visions—as if there is "a" Christian perspective on a contested matter—and hence assume that we all have the same justificatory pathways. But those pathways can be probed when others ask us questions like "why" or "how"—and we might certainly ask such questions ourselves, in an inner dialogue. Thus reflection takes on an intersubjective dimension. We think in the presence of others, and we feel things too in the presence of others, so that our justifications take place while a community is taking shape around us. Our justifications for a particular belief are to a certain extent dependent on how this community of shared conversation takes shape, as the posing of specific questions prompts us to consider particular aspects of justice-related narratives and their affective dimensions.

Indeed, we have suggested that the justification of justice-related beliefs is most effective when it emerges in the face of a real or imagined-as-present interlocutor whose resistance to our point of view can invite a more nuanced perspective—one that takes into account more of the morally relevant concerns at hand. Rather than wielding accusations of heresy to distinguish "us" from "them," heresy may be more aptly described as that which diminishes one's own vision because it forecloses important concerns of others, and so it sets up the polarities that rupture the body of Christ. Mechanisms of delegitimating another's grounding in the body of Christ in the name of justice-seeking is a terrible problem, and one that needs attention and correction.

So rather than associate a defense of proper or "orthodox" Christian views of justice with the single-minded zeal of a truth-telling prophet, we offer a more modest proposal that we believe is more in sync with the way that orthodox views finally came into view, at least with regard to the creedal formulations behind the Nicene Creed. Our proposal for Christian justice-seeking is modest insofar as it does not spotlight dramatic showdowns between good and evil as the usual way of doing business in the field of justice work. Rather, sorting out the face of justice in the Beloved Community involves something more like routine attention to a neighbor over time, gabbing over coffee, and exchanging and interrogating stories of our own and stories from afar. We may need to expand our circle of interlocutors; we may need to move the location in which we gather, or invite others in. Sometimes we argue, yes, and fiercely too—but as Christian siblings, not as Christians in battle with a "secular" world—a posture that too readily presupposes an easily spotted, monolithic Christian position even on contested ethical issues.

As the history of Christian witness at its best shows, the practice of mutual listening that is part of ordinary faith does not prevent Christians from speaking truth to power or marching in protests. Justice-seeking is not all chitchat, talking while doing nothing. Ordinary time always yields moments of *kairos*—seasons when it is opportune or timely to make a dramatic change (like the end of apartheid in South Africa, and of slavery and segregation in the United States). But the hard work of finding and of justifying our beliefs about the shape of justice involves formation in conversation, in taking in the weight of one another's stories. And the truth of the memed question, "Who is included at the table?" is imperative if our efforts to discern what justice among us looks like are not simply going to reflect stories from narrowly drawn eco-chambers, where rationalizing displaces openhearted listening to what is at stake for those who seem most at odds with us.

We have set the stage for our next chapter, which is a test case for all the items we have discussed until now: the topic of abortion. On this particularly virulent topic—one at the fulcrum of polarization in the United States—we hope to pull out practices of justification as they emerge in the Beloved Community in ways that attend to orthodoxy as we have described it, and restrict heresy-naming as a way to delegitimize someone else's efforts to think through justifications for their belief. Where the divide is the worst, there we hope to move toward theological wisdom in order to work together in a way that is oriented by orthodoxy, which is basically trust in the Holy Spirit to guide the church.

4

Abortion

Is This the Issue on which the Church Stands or Falls?

A Most Divisive Issue

So often, complex theological ideas are summarized as concise propositions. The assertion, as Luther wrote in his famous 1525 text against Erasmus, *On the Enslaved Will*, is how the Holy Spirit speaks. "Take away assertions and you take away Christianity. . . . Moreover, the Spirit goes to such lengths in asserting that she takes the initiative and accuses the world of its sin [John 16:8], as if she would provoke a fight."[1] The Holy Spirit, according to Luther, speaks in succinct formulas that identify in clear terms where one must put one's loyalty. The simple assertions of faith are easily taught and easy to memorize. They can also summarize the opinion of an opponent. In this case, assertions usually focus exclusively on the opponent's error.

Abortion divides contemporary US Americans, including Christians. Each side has its own slogans, posters, and demonstrators. On the one side people wear the red and white habits from the women in Margaret Atwood's feminist dystopia, *The Handmaid's Tale*. On the other side people carry posters bearing images of violent fetal death. Volunteers endure verbal attacks by pro-life demonstrators as they escort women from their cars to the Planned Parenthood clinic; those defending the life of the fetus insist on their right to discourage women from carrying

---

[1]   Martin Luther, *The Bondage of the Will, 1525*, trans. Philip S. Watson in collaboration with Benjamin Drury, rev. trans. Volker Leppin, The Annotated Luther Study Edition, ed. Kirsi I. Stjerna (Minneapolis: Fortress, 2016), 164. We use the title "On the Enslaved Will" as in Graham White's translation of the Latin *De servo arbitrio* in his essay, "Modal Logic in Luther's *Enslaved Will*," in *The Medieval Luther*, ed. Christine Helmer, Spätmittelalter, Humanismus, Reformation / Studies in the Late Middle Ages, Humanism, and the Reformation 117 (Tübingen: Mohr Siebeck, 2020), 91–103.

out abortions. The American story of abortion includes the murder of Dr. George Tiller, the Lutheran ob-gyn in Wichita, Kansas, who took on the most tragic of third-trimester abortions.[2] The loudness of the extremes, the binary polarization, and the rejection of the other's position characterize all too painfully the way in which the issue of abortion divides the Beloved Community.

It was not always this way. Until the 1970s, Protestants, also evangelicals,[3] held on to a variety of opinions about the different issues of abortion: fetal viability, the time of "quickening"—meaning the first fetal movement detected around sixteen weeks of pregnancy—the status of fetal "personhood," birth control, the circulation among women of knowledge about self-inducing an abortion. Likewise, Roman Catholics have not always condemned abortion. The key issue for Roman Catholics was disagreement about when personal life begins for the fetus in the womb. Thomas Aquinas, to cite a famous example, considers six weeks the time at which the fetus should be considered a potential person.[4] But in the late twentieth century, the idea of when life begins in the womb was pushed back earlier and earlier. New technologies allowed medical practitioners to hear electrical impulses at six weeks of pregnancy and to project uterine contents on a screen. Sounds and images of the fetus were related to the question of the origins of personal life. The proposal, now common among some Christians, emerged that "life begins at conception." How life relates to personhood, how possibility relates to reality, how maternal health relates to race and socioeconomic status—these are some of the many topics that inform an increasingly polarized landscape.

The division in US American Christianity today is both religious and political. The idea of a single-issue vote—and this means abortion—was the key to the 2016 election. Donald Trump garnered the support of 80 percent

---

[2]   "Kansas Reacts to Tiller Killing," *NPR*, June 1, 2009, https://www.npr.org/templates/story/story.php?storyId=104791132.

[3]   See, for example, Joe Early Jr., "From Permissible to Intolerable: Southern Baptists and the Abortion Debate in the 1970s," *Baptist History & Heritage* (Summer 2020): 73–91; for legal questions, see Leslie J. Reagan, *When Abortion Was a Crime: Women, Medicine, and Law in the United States, 1867–1973* (Berkeley: University of California Press, 1997).

[4]   Christine E. Gudorf, "Contraception and Abortion in Roman Catholicism," in *Sacred Rights: The Case for Contraception and Abortion in World Religions*, ed. Daniel C. Maguire (New York: Oxford University Press, 2003), 68–69.

of the white evangelical community on this issue alone.[5] For many, abortion trumped all other aspects of his personal moral failings. Meanwhile, more progressive mainline Protestant denominations have crafted social statements supportive of legalized abortion (although usually discouraging it except under certain conditions). More rarely have pastors and leaders of those same denominations supported abortion rights in the pulpit or in public political advocacy[6]—perhaps in part because for decades, the decision of *Roe v. Wade* had not necessitated it.

The disagreements among US Christians about abortion are set within a larger context of historical and cultural changes in the United States, as women gained greater legal rights and access to public spaces once occupied primarily by men. Abortion became legal for American women in all states when *Roe v. Wade* was passed in 1973, as the 1960s and early 1970s brought women's rights to the forefront. Women's rights, as Justice Ruth Bader Ginsburg advocated, are reproductive rights.[7] The manual *Our Bodies, Ourselves* became the central text studied by many women to gain knowledge about body parts, birth control, sexual pleasure, and reproduction.[8] The gain in women learning about their personal body was mirrored by their entrance into the body politic and into colleges. Women were ordained as pastors and became NASA engineers. In the last decades of the twentieth century, US women increasingly became visible as agents permitted to realize their ambitions, as persons who can have credit cards in their own name, as women whose uteruses belong to their personal bodies; these are some of the details in the history of women's becoming recognized as equal to men.

For many Christians—who may be broadly supportive of at least some of the changes in women's rights—abortion remains more than ever the

[5] Tom Gjelten, "2020 Faith Vote Reflects 2016 Patterns," *NPR*, November 8, 2020, https://www.npr.org/2020/11/08/932263516/2020-faith-vote-reflects-2016-patterns.

[6] For a summary and analysis of various denominational statements, see ch. 5 of Kira Schlesinger's *Pro-Choice and Christian: Reconciling Faith, Politics, and Justice* (Louisville: Westminster John Knox, 2017). For more on perspectives about abortion across the world's religions, see Daniel C. Maguire, *Sacred Rights: The Case for Contraception and Abortion in World Religions* (Oxford: Oxford University Press, 2003).

[7] See Cianna Garrison, "RGB's Quotes about Reproductive Rights Will Inspire You to Keep Up the Fight," September 26, 2020, https://www.elitedaily.com/p/ruth-bader-ginsburgs-quotes-on-abortion-care-reproductive-rights-focus-on-protecting-women-34394176.

[8] Boston Women's Health Collective, *Our Bodies, Ourselves: A Book by and for Women* (New York: Simon and Schuster, 1973).

non-negotiable litmus test for Christian and political affiliation. Yet what does this way of denoting Christian identity say about one's membership in the Beloved Community? Abortion, indeed, is an issue of social and political justice for those on either side of the divide. It identifies the ways in which justice-seeking can manifest diverging religious commitments that inform social and political understanding. Yet precisely *as* a matter of justice-seeking, one's own conscience-informed approach to abortion does not in and of itself determine one's belonging (or not) to the Beloved Community. Justification by faith in Christ is the basis for participation in the Beloved Community; it is the origin and touchstone of belonging, as well as of repentance and grace. Here identification with Christ draws Christians into heartfelt dispute to work together, to discuss with one another how they imagine justice-seeking in the area of abortion. When Christians pull back from the temptation to equate their primary Christian identity with a position on justice and move "back" toward a primary belonging through justification by faith, something shifts: justice-seeking incorporates a process of listening and articulating in the presence of others.

We address abortion as a test case to see if there *is* such a possibility of working out justice-seeking strategies on the basis of justification by faith. We write this chapter, even after the Supreme Court took up *Dobbs v. Jackson Women's Health Organization* and on June 24, 2022 reversed the "decisions that originally asserted the fundamental right to an abortion prior to the viability of the fetus . . . and, the authority to regulate abortion is 'returned to the people and their elected representatives.'"[9] Given that *Dobbs*, as this ruling has come to be called, assigns the regulation of abortion to the states, abortion will continue to be an issue of live debate, perhaps more so. Hence this chapter takes up this deeply divisive topic in order to model how a theology based on justification by faith can proceed to inspire building bridges across the divide between those who assert that abortion must be regulated and those who assert that abortion must be a constitutional right for women. Can an understanding of the Beloved Community as a common Christian identity marker be used productively to imagine shared justice-seeking on a topic as divisive as abortion? We decided to try, and we invite our readers into this thought experiment.

9   "*Dobbs vs. Jackson Women's Health Organization* (2022)," Legal Information Institute, Cornell Law School, https://www.law.cornell.edu/wex/dobbs_v._jackson _women%27s_health_organization_%282022%29; for the full text of the *Dobbs* decision, see https://www.law.cornell.edu/supremecourt/text/19-1392.

Our discussion invokes the third article of the Creed. Can this article on the unity of the church created by the Holy Spirit orient Christians to see unity as a mandate for mutual justice-seeking? We appeal also to a shared humanity. As humans living and cohabiting in this world, we cannot be so far apart that no conversation is possible. As Christians within the Beloved Community, we cannot be so divided from each other that we have lost the humility to talk with each other about a topic that resonates so deeply and personally with many of us.

In what follows, we begin by describing what we are calling incommensurable ontologies: competing value-laden worldviews that define good and evil in seemingly opposing ways, and in the process interrupt remembrance that for Christians, our baptism into Christ is the basis of ecclesial belonging—*not* on which side of the abortion debate we stand. We lay out what we call a "collage" of stories that variously uphold and complicate those seemingly incompatible worldviews: journalistic and data-informed narratives about abortions and silence and shame surrounding them, as well as the real-world consequences when women are denied access to abortion; stories of conversion from one worldview about abortion to the other; macrostories that function as moral-theological framings (justificatory vs. reproductive justice paradigms); and finally, archetypal or iconic stories that gender the sacred in ways that bear on women's reproductive choices. We explore what the various theological imaginaries around pregnant women imply for women's spiritual and moral lives. In doing so, as part of the practice of justice-seeking *together* within the Beloved Community, we invite taking ownership of the consequences—material, emotional, and spiritual—of supporting or withholding access to abortion.

We anticipate that some of our readers will find this chapter problematic or limited, in several ways. While we have been inviting fellow Christians to listen and think together through the medium of stories, the stories we tell here are often representative ones, not thickly described personal stories. We invite readers to move through this chapter with the ears of their heart mindful of stories they have already heard, as well as stories they may become more open to hearing. Christians who believe abortion is a grave sin might feel as though we used this chapter primarily to make a case for a pro-choice Christian theological position. If we have done so, it is because this perspective is rarely sought, heard, or pondered by the many Christians who have been politically active in opposing access to abortion. We feel Christians ought to be more literate and fluent about theological positions in favor of reproductive justice, even if they disagree with them. At the same time, some progressive Christians who have been at the forefront of the reproductive justice movement might wish that this chapter be much more concerned with tangible policy suggestions. Indeed, what are we to make of the longtime relative silence about abortion among so many Christian leaders—including clergy and theologians—who are comfortably outspoken on other progressive issues, from racism to climate crisis? The challenge is that no one *aspires* to be a person who had an abortion—certainly not the way that birthing and raising a child with hope and intention is aspirational. Affirming legal access to abortion as part of the common good of the Beloved Community requires us to look with care at concrete, existing women and their good—the conditions of their well-being. Who gets to define those conditions? There is nothing like the subject of abortion to push us to confront the ways that patriarchal (or matriarchal) control of women's bodies and lives can seem inevitable whenever we center the image of a newborn child, abstracting out all other moral complexity and considerations. By contrast, the contextless image of a woman who is aborting a fetus can look selfish or criminal; thinking from this image swiftly sparks misogyny (of a sort that some see as satisfyingly justified). It takes more moral energy to perceive and think together the goodness of women's reproductive autonomy and the goodness of childbearing. With such challenges in mind, we hope we are framing here a Christian conversation about abortion in a way that invites readers to form their own positions, thinking with and beyond us.

One additional note: because the debate around abortion overlaps with a debate about gender essentialism—about whether there are specific identities and roles assigned to males and females in the order of creation—we will usually speak of pregnant *women*, rather than pregnant *persons*. We hope that transgender or non-binary persons who are capable of experiencing pregnancy will listen to what we share here as part of an ongoing conversation and contribute their own stories and perspectives that further enrich understanding of the empirical, ethical, and spiritual dimensions at play in debates about reproductive justice.

Incommensurable Ontologies?

Just how polarizing *is* abortion? This question is an important one because it gets at the possibility of a conversation between Christians on different sides of the issue. When we perceive a shared world, a shared common ground, we will be more likely to engage in conversation with one another. Even if there is only a glimpse of something shared, conversation is more likely. But if one perceives that there is no shared value or experience, then there is no conversation.

The debate about abortion often admits no shared terminology. The terms "pro-choice" and "pro-life" are drawn up as mutually exclusive positions. "Pro-choice" refers to a legal, rather than religious, position associated with the "left." It identifies the legality of abortion in the United States since *Roe v. Wade*. A pregnant woman has the right to choose whether to permit the fetus to develop to the point at which it can be viable outside the womb. This position has been re-termed by its opponents as "pro-abortion." Polemics cast "pro-choice" as "pro-abortion" to identify choice—which by definition is open to different outcomes—with only one outcome. When this term is mapped onto the dichotomy between life and death, it is employed in dramatic terms as the position that ultimately chooses death. Pro-choice advocates reject the "pro-abortion" label because they insist that the right to choose different outcomes resides with the pregnant woman. "Pro-life" is a positioning on the right that insists on life for the unborn. Its protagonists advocate for the "unborn" that is deemed to have no voice by which it can defend itself. *Roe v. Wade* exacerbates the way that the "unborn" is seen to have no advocates—legal, moral, or theological. The term "pro-life" assigns life to the unborn, including the idea that the rights of personhood begin at conception. Its polemic is directed against the willed disintegration of that life, termed "murder."

The opposition between both sides of the abortion divide makes shared terms undetectable, because the morally weighted facts are not agreed upon. A pro-life protagonist might use the term "murder of an unborn child" in order to express that their position advocates for the unborn. The terms "murder" and "child" point out that the opposing "pro-choice" position must be identified in relationship to these terms of action. Yet a pro-choice protagonist would insist that the terms "murder of an unborn child" do not accurately identify the action of abortion. The accurate term "terminate a pregnancy" refers to abortion; the term "murder" is not accurate because murder refers to a person whose life is viable outside the womb. And the term "unborn child" is more accurately identified in the biological terms of stages of development, like zygote, embryo, fetus, or prenate. The term "murder of an unborn child" only make sense within a semantics that sees its position in defense of the life and personhood of a fetus. In a pro-choice semantics, the term "murder of an unborn child" is unrecognizable. This semantics is concerned with distinguishing between fetal life and life of an infant outside the womb. Terms such as fetus, fetal termination, and death are recognizable because they draw a distinction between fetal dependence and a pregnant woman's capacity for decision-making with respect to the prenate.

What makes the semantic differences so intense is that each position implies a qualitatively different legislative outcome. The political stakes are high: abortion is either legal or not. Only one side will hold the legislative gavel. The terms of debate highlight the semantic divide. One side speaks of an "unborn child" while the other one uses "fetus": murder versus termination; person versus prenate. The semantic differences expose the political fact that there is no middle ground in legislative terms. There is nothing shared; not even the meanings of terms are shared. The same terms mean different things in these two semantic worlds. And the respective semantic contexts of these words legitimate each speaker's own worldview and prevent speakers from finding and using common terms.

A second opposition highlights the ways in which empirical facts are interpreted. Each side interprets the empirical fact of the developing fetus in different ways and with different terms. The pro-choice side uses the biological term "fetus" or "prenate" to connote its difference from a baby that can breathe on its own outside the womb; the pro-life side uses the term "baby" to imply that development coincides with the goal—the fetus's development in the womb is oriented toward the goal of birth, and thus life outside the womb as a baby. Of course there are developmental demarcations between the term neonate, infant, and toddler, which are different developmental demarcations of "baby" where preference is given to the envelope term, baby. Different terms denote different moral values. A baby is assigned personhood. When the term "baby" is used to denote prenatal life, then it is by implication a person assigned with the right to life ("inviolability"). When, on the other hand, the term "fetus" is used to denote the developing prenate, then the ascription of personhood is diminished with respect to its developmental status. The fetus is not yet biologically capable of living outside the womb and thus its rights to live are weighed together with the rights assigned to a person, who is pregnant.

The abortion debate thus underlines a situation in which terms are taken to mean different things by different sides. The terms invoke a polemic that the other side identifies as misrepresenting its position. The terms imply opposing legal and moral outcomes.

This situation identifies, as we call it, "incommensurable ontologies." The space inhabited by each "side" of the division is hermetically sealed off from the other side. Each side inhabits a discursive framework in which words function and are used differently within the "other" side. The terms used stir different affects: love, horror, care, or shame. What counts as an argument is different: is it moral or legal, theological or political? One side believes *it* occupies a logical space, while deeming the other side's logical space as "crazy." The two sides of the abortion debate are so far apart that they inform two different worldviews that are incommensurable with each other. No conversation between them is possible. Positions have become entrenched in their own deployed vocabularies, phrases, assertions, and polemics.

The language of "conversion" reinforces this incommensurability. Rev. Robert L. Schenck, evangelical pastor and founding director of the Dietrich Bonhoeffer Institute in Washington, D.C., caused ripples in his evangelical Christian community when he wrote about his regret at long-time activism to overturn *Roe v. Wade*.[10] In an op-ed in the *New York Times* from May 30, 2019, Schenck wrote about his "conversion" to a pro-choice position. He describes his change of heart from one of callousness toward a pregnant women's fear and desperation to one of respect for a pregnant woman's capacity for moral deliberation as well as an antipathy to the harm and pain inflicted on women (and their supporters) by people willing to profit from political cruelty, as his most recent blog on the Texas Senate Bill 8 articulates.[11] Schenck's story of his "conversion" from one side of the abortion debate to the other side is compelling because it presupposes the incommensurability between the two sides. Conversion is a Christian term that connotes the dramatic shift of belief in false gods to faith in the true God, a shift from sin to grace. When one "converts" from one position to another, one dramatically shifts the terms in which one lives—the move is from one position to an incommensurable other. If words cannot convey some basis of agreement regarding definition, then they lose their ability to communicate content to another. Only those playing the

---

[10]   Rob Schenck, "I Was an Anti-Abortion Crusader. Now I Support *Roe v. Wade*: Overturning the Supreme Court's 1973 Decision Would Not Be 'Pro-Life.' It Would Be Destructive of Life," *New York Times*, May 30, 2019, https://www.nytimes.com/2019/05/30/opinion/abortion-schenck.html.

[11]   Robert Schenck, "Texas Abortion Law Is Anything but 'Pro-Life,'" *Reverend Rob Schenck Blog: Inspiring Messages of Faith, Hope and Love*, September 3, 2021, https://www.revrobschenck.com/blog/2021/9/3/texas-law-is-anything-but-pro-life.

same "language game" can talk to each other in ways that the other understands. Conversation is not possible across the incommensurable divide.

The incommensurability is persistent, daunting, even as it so readily simplifies complex moral reasoning into easy formulas. Yet the very fact that there is an incommensurability implies the presence of uncertainty. Certainly there is a lack of consensus about abortion. Incommensurability between positions dramatically points to that lack. Still, the lack is open to a sensing, even a wavering, when one pays attention. Incommensurability is the easy answer—but uncertainty pries open the lack of consensus. What one has assumed to be the case is sensed as something to be questioned. This lack of consensus is peculiarly connected to the unease that is sensed regarding the status—scientific and moral—of the prenate. What *is* the moral status of a prenate? The right has a moral high ground insofar as its pro-life position is simpler to grasp: despite the lack of consensus about when personhood begins (from as early as conception to as late as the first breath outside the womb), a fetus is undeniably human, or at least on the way to becoming recognizably human. Abortion prevents the birth of a human life that, until then, existed in formation. But the left has an abiding moral grounding too, insofar as it assumes a difference between the abortion of a prenate and the killing of a born human being. At least the nomenclature distinguishes between abortion and infanticide. When asking questions about the prenate, or in other terms the unborn child, one can sense an opening that makes the other position possible.

The incommensurable ontologies seem nigh impossible to bridge, even as contemporary reproductive justice theorists have been developing a discourse that depicts "the prenate as a 'human becoming' rather than a human being"[12] and so resists pinpointing some exact moment when the prenate's inviolability begins, tying the moral status of the prenate to the moral imagination of the pregnant woman herself. For a pregnant woman, a prenate's inviolability emerges when and as she becomes emotionally attached to her prenate, which may happen as soon as she finds out she is pregnant; she may be pro-choice and still call her own prenate a "baby." As Rebecca Todd Peters notes, pregnancy is a liminal season in which the prenate is not yet a born person, but also something with a real but fluid moral significance. Pregnancy's liminality is such that even when a woman miscarries a prenate she was planning to carry to term, she may be devastated or

---

[12]   Rebecca Todd Peters, *Trust Women: A Progressive Christian Argument for Reproductive Justice* (Boston: Beacon, 2018), 159.

peacefully accepting ("It was just God's will," as one woman put it to Amy; the woman already had several children). Viewing pregnancy as a liminal season in which the prenate's moral status is fluid to the person gestating the prenate implies that the moral status of the prenate is bound up with a pregnant woman's own moral reasoning and sense of life circumstances and direction. This ontology is one in which the prenate's and a pregnant woman's moral status are interdependent and in motion throughout a pregnancy.

Even though ontologies of becoming, like that of Todd Peters, reflect the phenomenological accounts of pregnant women in their variety and breadth, pro-life Christians are likely to view the language of a prenate's human "becoming" as something that makes the worth of an unborn human dependent upon the subjective feelings of a pregnant woman herself. This looks capricious, arbitrary; it is no surprise that some Christians argue that the slippery slope to all moral relativity begins with the denial of full human moral status to an unborn child from its conception. In turn, viewing their own lives through the lens of those who absolutize the value of a prenate, pregnant women may feel that their moral perceptions and capacities matter not a whit—that they are not seen as moral agents, only carriers of a vulnerable human life that depends utterly on its gestating mother's continual support of its existence.

The discussion of the fetus in relation to the semantics of personhood shows that the terms used to characterize an issue enter into a value-laden worldview. A worldview relates to other dimensions of shared existence as well, as we find when looking at how each "side" of the abortion debate opens into a picture of the world that is permeated by specific sorts of gender norms.[13] A patriarchal worldview that assumes gender essentialism and gender complementarity assigns to women the role of birthing and childrearing. A feminist worldview, defined against patriarchal

[13] Interesting in this regard is Fritz Oehlschlaeger, *Procreative Ethics: Philosophical and Christian Approaches to Questions at the Beginning of Life* (Eugene, Ore.: Cascade, 2010). Oehlschlaeger recognizes that work against gender inequality is a vital factor in the debate about abortion, and is one of a number of Christian opponents of abortion who believes that abortion should remain *legal* (at least in cases of rape or incest, 59), and that Christians should instead focus their political advocacy energies more on creating social policies that enable pregnant woman to find it materially, socially, and economically viable to choose to carry a pregnancy to term. Similar views are voiced by Timothy R. Sherratt, *Power Made Perfect? Is There a Christian Politics for the Twenty-First Century?* (Eugene, Ore.: Cascade, 2016), 83–84; and Frederica Mathewes-Green, *Real Choices: Listening to Women; Looking for Alternatives to Abortion* (Ben Lomond, Calif.: Conciliar Press, 1994), 173–78.

assumptions about gender roles, implies that navigating reproductive rights as a woman is, as Ruth Bader Ginsburg stated, integral to women's social and political rights. Certainly much is at stake for species reproduction with regard to persons with uteruses bearing children. Unless technology enables artificial wombs (itself a morally fraught path), both a patriarchal and a feminist or egalitarian worldview depend on persons with uteruses for the propagation of the species; hence there is a vested interest in survival that is crystallized in the background of the abortion debate. Reproductive processes have a deep bearing on women's autonomy in a patriarchal worldview that dictates those processes.

The abortion debate thus always concerns how society views women, including their moral agency. A pregnant woman's moral agency is called into question when she is prescribed educational steps (like watching an ultrasound image or waiting twenty-four hours) to allegedly inform her prior to her final decision about continuing or ending a pregnancy. Alternatively, from a perspective in which abortion is murder, if a woman *is* ascribed moral agency when choosing to abort, she ought to be delivered to the criminal justice system. The reality *and* ideologies about women's rationality, moral agency, will, and autonomy are all at play in proximity to reproduction.

The difference between patriarchal and feminist worldviews is interwoven with disagreement about what constitutes the structural or systemic sin in the abortion debate. Which is the sin one worries over: a society that permits abortion, or patriarchal control of women's bodies and lives?

By opening this conversation for justice-seeking, we reflect on our own assumptions and commitments, particularly in relation to the abstract discussion of the fetus's ontological and moral status and the conceptual questions surrounding the abortion debate's relation to patriarchal or feminist worldviews. We assume that it is important to insist on a space in which a commitment to hearing women's reproductive stories is important. In telling their own stories, women take seriously their moral commitment to reflect on their own lives. Our commitment is to invite listening to persons who make decisions—or are coerced into making decisions—regarding their reproductive capacities, whether they choose to terminate pregnancies or abort fetuses, whether they are assigned roles of childbearing by religion or politics or family pressure, and how they navigate these choices and roles. We understand that there are voices who insist on speaking for the fetus, and these are important to consider insofar as fetuses have no literal voices because of their dependence on maternal gestation. But we now listen to persons who have something to say, some shamed into silence, some coming out decades later, some advocating on the basis of their experience. It is a place to start, and an exercise in faith that invites stepping out of one's entrenched comfort zone and exploring a space of stories. This in turn invites inhabiting an ethical and aesthetic space characterized by receptivity—a feeling of one's way into the affective landscape conjured by stories told and conversations experienced.[14]

Below, then, we look at ways to explore a creative space of story-listening that adjusts incommensurability by shaping the conversation from a different perspective—that of working out a trust in belonging to an already present Beloved Community, one redeemed in Christ who bears all our wounds and wounding of one another. How can we listen to stories in the framework of the Beloved Community? We assume that the basis for listening is indeed the constant return to one's core faith-based identity, along with others in the Beloved Community, as rooted in justification by faith. Justice-seeking presupposes a perennial reminder that Christian identity is situated in the Beloved Community.

The sections below propose a way to embark on justice-seeking as Christians who disagree at times profoundly with one another. We present this exercise as one of listening to different stories, each from their own experiential perspective, each with their distinct affective and reflective resonances. The stories form a collage with overlaps, gaps, and differences. The exercise here is to listen to the stories along with their gaps, silences, and emotional registers. Listening through the lens of the Beloved Community is an exercise that cultivates a widening of perspective, an acknowledgment of affective responses in the work of preparing a particular justice-seeking proposal.

Because such a conversation among Christians presupposes at least one shared assumption—our belonging to one another on the basis of our faith in Christ, not on the basis of which incommensurable side of the abortion debate we each may stand—we can dare to sojourn into a variety of aesthetic, ethical, and affective landscapes regarding abortion and associated sensibilities about the sacred. We use spatial metaphors because in telling and interrogating stories about abortion—including archetypal stories—we draw attention to the way those stories presuppose and evoke

[14]　For a theological and literary reflection on the ethics involved in reading and pondering stories, see Cynthia Wallace, *Of Women Borne: A Literary Ethics of Suffering*, Gender, Theory, and Religion (New York: Columbia University Press, 2016).

inhabited worldviews that are never only about God, or the moral status of a prenate, but also about normed expectations regarding those who identify as women in relation to both.

Any existing person might migrate among different affective land-scapes or worlds or might feel as if she is living by one while feeling the draw of another, unable fully to connect with it because it does not do justice to the fullness of her own life and circumstances. That sort of ambivalence is an important affective dimension of the mix of empathy and critique we are attempting here, as theologians inviting a similar practice by our readers. As we try to enter and imagine inhabiting the landscape of different pieties and stories, we pay attention to what each one feels like. What sounds and feels right? What does not? Why? Where does a sense of the sacred lie in each landscape? Our attention moves from here into critique and argument, sometimes suggestively or experimentally, sometimes with conviction. In the generous spirit of orthodoxy and of contributing to a synthesis that avoids the heretical temptation to fixate narrowly on selective truth claims, we seek here less to practice an apologetics using abortion-related narratives and their affective landscapes, and more to explore what such narratives reveal, what they might eclipse, and where in them one might perceive the presence of God.

Listening to Women: A Collage of Stories

> The unborn child is easy to privilege; after all, she is innocent and uncomplicated, perfect fodder for all of our projections. A woman, however, is complicated and ripe for judgment for what she did or did not do.[15]

We have all heard stories about abortion. In fact, some stories are so well-known that they are represented by symbols: the coat hanger; dismembered fetal body parts; red and white habits from Margaret Atwood's *The Handmaid's Tale*. These images assert positions with their affective power. They are graphic and evoke strong reactions of identification, loathing, and aversion—shock stories that are intended to highlight the only morally relevant facts or attitudes. The images help us to rally around the truths we want to protect. They help us to simplify complexity: the rules are made clear so that we can navigate the world. Simplicity and shock characterize a fraught landscape; graphic images shape positions in the

15 Schlesinger, *Pro-Choice and Christian*, 50.

absence of stories because they represent the legitimating positions of stories regarded as normative.

But what if we took seriously the enfleshed nature of the Beloved Community—that there are real people and first-person accounts behind the symbols? What if we take those persons seriously as authors of their own stories? What if we back down from already established ideas and symbols and get into stories that might have possibilities for generating moral, theological, and political reflection? What if we sought to attend to the silences and listen, attentive to what a different ontology might draw our attention to, to how stories are connected to certain vocabularies and to what is valued and represented by focusing on some but not others?

Stories play both normative and morally reflective roles here, for they point to persons behind the statistics and show that justice-seeking regarding pregnancy has to do with pregnant persons who have their personal stories. Stories are also told about ideals that inform positions and the way first-person stories are themselves told. As we shall see, the power of those idealizing stories frames abortion within broader archetypal roles having to do with gender, sin, and redemption. Justice-seeking involves an exercise in listening to this range of stories, including how first-person narratives interact with norm-bearing idealized stories about pregnant women.

The initial stories we present introduce complexity regarding abortion through first-person narratives. The question here is how to render more plastic the pro/con paradigm that so rigidly negates complexity by hardening incommensurables. While we can use formulaic stories to justify positions, lived stories open up affective and reflective registers that either legitimate or add depth to one's position. Stories told by family members and people one knows are most effective because listening is based on a shared commitment. We are affected by persons who tell stories, as we begin to take their real lives into consideration. To be sure, abortion unfolds in as many individual stories as women and childbearing persons who have experienced it—diverse stories, each with their own affective register and meaning making embedded in them. Our aim is to introduce stories into the justice-seeking endeavor in order to add depth, affectivity, and complexity. To ease the dichotomy of the incommensurable worldviews in the binary public debate about abortion, we look at stories that reveal how affectivity plays a significant role in decision-making and living out the consequences of abortion. We invite readers to add their own stories and ponderings while listening.

Silence

In her op-ed in the *Washington Post* on September 22, 2021, Uma Thurman joins a chorus of prominent women speaking out about the abortions they had.[16] She writes that in the wake of the Texas Senate Bill passed in summer 2021 she is sharing her story "in the hope of drawing the flames of controversy away from the vulnerable women on whom this law will have an immediate effect." Thurman expresses the shame she has experienced over the years regarding an abortion she had in her late teens after an accidental impregnation by an older man. She writes that the abortion itself was a painful procedure. She felt she "deserved the pain." While the feelings of shame and regret endured, she knew that her choice was the right one. As a teen, she knew she was unprepared to be a mother. "I have no regrets for the path I have traveled. I applaud and support women who make a different choice," she writes. "The abortion I had as a teenager was the hardest decision of my life, one that caused me anguish then and that saddens me even now, but it was the path to the life full of joy and love that I have experienced. Choosing not to keep that early pregnancy allowed me to grow up and become the mother I wanted and needed to be."

Statistics estimate that one in three women to one in four women will have an abortion at some point over the course of a lifetime; half of pregnancies in the United States are unplanned.[17] The single teen who is still

---

[16]   Uma Thurman, "The Texas Abortion Law Is a Human Rights Crisis for American Women," *Washington Post*, September 21, 2021, https://www.washingtonpost .com/opinions/2021/09/21/uma-thurman-abortion-law-texas/. See also, e.g., Diane J. Cho, "Celebrities Who Have Shared Their Abortion Stories to Help Women Feel Less Alone," *People*, last modified July 15, 2022, https://people.com/health/celebrity -abortion-stories-busy-philipps-jameela-jamil/?slide=96fff4ac-3b9a-4756-ab5d -7440aa139a68#96fff4ac-3b9a-4756-ab5d-7440aa139a68.

[17]   See Todd Peters, *Trust Women*, 2, who cites Rachel K. Jones and Megan L. Kavanaugh, "Changes in Abortion Rates between 2000 and 2008 and Lifetime Incidence of Abortion," *Obstetrics and Gynecology* 177, no. 6 (June 2011): 1358–66. Since this study, the rates seem to have dropped to about one in four women, according to a Guttmacher Institute analysis. See also "Abortion Is a Common Experience for U.S. Women, despite Dramatic Declines in Rates," *Guttmacher Institute*, October 19, 2017, news release, https://www.guttmacher.org/news-release/ 2017/abortion-common-experience-us-women-despite-dramatic-declines-rates; Planned Parenthood of the Pacific Southwest, "1 in 4 American Women Will Have an Abortion by Age 45," *Care Matters* (blog), https://www.plannedparenthood .org/planned-parenthood-pacific-southwest/blog/1-in-4-american-women

trying to finish her GED; the forty-three-year-old married woman who has already raised four children; the twenty-year-old whose birth control failed—an occurrence that happens with surprising regularity; the ten-year-old victim of incest; the twenty-nine-year-old who has just begun the career that she worked very hard, against many odds, to achieve; the forty-year-old whose fetus's prognosis is death seconds after birth.

There are as many stories as there are women who have experienced abortions. Stories tell of circumstances and relationships, reasons and feelings, fears and desires. Stories frame decisions complicated by regret and resolve, feelings between shame and resignation, relationships that support or reject. Many are introduced with the preface, "I have never told anyone."[18] Yet as Rebecca Todd Peters notes, both pregnancies *and* abortions are a normal part of women's lives, despite the punitive, often classist and racist shaming of women for unwanted pregnancies voiced by critics who seem unaware that contraception is not always reliable: "50 to 60 percent of the women who have abortions were using birth control during the month that they got pregnant."[19]

The multitude of stories are all too often whispered in secret. The stories can be buried within women's biographies for decades, told only years later in confidence. The thirty actors who told their stories in the media since 2019 intended to break the culture of silence surrounding abortion. Some, like Thurman, expressed the recognition that the telling of their stories would precipitate hate. She writes in her op-ed that she personally has nothing to gain and "perhaps much to lose," but that her goal is to provide hope to "women and girls who might feel a shame that they can't protect themselves from and have no agency over."

One sort of abortion story is that of silence and silencing itself, for sharing abortion stories is *discouraged*. Here what is crucial is the way in which women bear the cross of the abortion (or not, with distinctive consequences). The burden of sin and shame becomes a lifelong regret,

---

-will-have-an-abortion-by-age-45; and Jeff Diamant and Besheer Mohamed, "What the Data Says about Abortion in the U.S.," Pew Research Center, January 11, 2023, https://www.pewresearch.org/fact-tank/2022/06/24/what-the-data -says-about-abortion-in-the-u-s-2/.

[18]   According to one survey, 95 percent of women who abort do not regret the decision, but two-thirds think others would look down on them if they knew they had an abortion. Todd Peters, *Trust Women*, 139.

[19]   Todd Peters, *Trust Women*, 2.

or lifelong "sin" and condemnation that so easily blames women in this catch-22, lose-lose-situation. Such dynamics help to explain the relative dearth of widely shared abortion stories, the secrecy shrouding the decisions, and the reasons why women only relay their stories decades afterward and in the hushed whispers of a close confidante. Their stories are rarely public or easily told but shrouded because of all sorts of condemnations—internal and external—that place moral culpability on women for their supposedly tragic choice.

To tell one's own story about abortion is thus to have one's very life read with or against the grain of a norming narrative that condemns women for unwanted pregnancies as well as for ending them. In *Down Girl: The Logic of Misogyny*,[20] philosopher Kate Manne analyzes the many ways in which a patriarchal culture exercises misogyny in order to enforce women's silence about areas of their lives that deviate from patriarchal norms. Sexism persists in the valuation of men as superior to women insofar as men's stories, freedoms, and career paths are valued as intrinsically important, with women most accepted when they are supporting and centering men. Patriarchy is the dynamic in which women's stories, freedoms, and decisions are subservient to those of the men in their lives. Moreover, women themselves often enforce upon one another the patriarchal norms that pressure and shadow their lives, emotionally and financially rewarding the women who comply with them. The particularly virulent issue at stake in the patriarchy, Manne claims, is that a woman's identity is intrinsically bound to her capacity for caretaking. In fact, this capacity is so essentialized that womanhood in our society is synonymous with caretaking, and specifically, mothering. The patriarchy exists to guarantee that this identity remains unchallenged. As long as women are mothers, their existence is perceived as unthreatening. But once they disrupt this enforced conformity, they are singled out for punishment. Manne describes the many ways in which misogyny is enforced through a punitive regimen against women who choose careers over children, and in so doing "allegedly diminish" their caretaking role in order to pursue public leadership.

Manne directs her analysis to women whose career paths take them into public leadership roles that diminish their essential identities as caretakers. She acknowledges that her study is devised on the model of

---

[20] Kate Manne, *Down Girl: The Logic of Misogyny* (New York: Oxford University Press, 2018).

middle-to-upper-class white women, yet her study is also relevant for most women who end their pregnancies, taking an active role in rejecting the culturally imposed identity of caretaking without limits. These women, like Uma Thurman or a neighbor who lives close by, tell their stories with the preface, "I haven't told anyone." The fear of hostility and shaming that they rejected the childbearing function assigned to them by a patriarchal society frames these stories.

Reproduction and Risks

There are other stories that are part of the reproductive dimension that are not about abortion *per se* but about the ways in which women's reproductive capacities are controlled. These stories play a role in abortion, as they shape the ways in which women perceive abortion against the backdrop of reproduction as a gendered expectation (albeit one permitted more to some women than to others) and a danger.

While not an illness, pregnancy is not without risks. Maternal mortality in the United States has staggering statistics compared to other developed nations, and mortalities are on the rise again, although they declined when abortion was widely available in the United States after *Roe*.[21] Risks to pregnant women run the gamut from illnesses triggered by pregnancy, such as preeclampsia, which can be fatal, to risks of birth—ranging from C-sections to all sorts of surgical "repair" (not to speak of the "husband's stitch") that damage female genitalia, to incidents of postpartum episodes, including postpartum depression, obsessional disorders, and psychic/mental health trauma. The trauma around and health risks of birth are especially exacerbated when race and class are taken into consideration. According to the Centers for Disease Control and Prevention (CDC), "Black women are three times more likely to die from a pregnancy-related cause than White women."[22] The CDC acknowledges that "social determinants of health," such as access to adequate medical care before and after pregnancy, diminish maternal opportunities for "economic, physical, and emotional health." Furthermore, the incidence of maternity care deserts, places where there are "no

---

21   Lauren Carroll, "Hillary Clinton: Pregnancy-Related Deaths Dropped after *Roe vs. Wade* Legalized Abortion," *PolitiFact*, June 24, 2016, https://www.politifact.com/factchecks/2016/jun/24/hillary-clinton/hillary-clinton-pregnancy-related-deaths-dropped-a/.

22   "Working Together to Reduce Black Maternal Mortality," *CDC*, April 6, 2022, https://www.cdc.gov/healthequity/features/maternal-mortality/index.html.

obstetric hospitals or birth centers and no obstetric providers," extends to 36 percent of counties in the United States, many in the Midwest and South, "affecting nearly 7 million women of childbearing age and some 500,000 babies."[23] All too often, the traumatic dimensions that can accompany pregnancy and childbirth are couched in silence; childbearing is seen as "normal," and this normative narrative tends to silence the complications of maternal health. Pregnancy entails a vulnerability to risk and is fatal for some women.

The history of forced reproduction is also part of the storytelling shrouded in silence. *Philomena*, the film starring Judy Dench, tells of Irish Catholic women who became pregnant and, because of shaming around premarital sex along with religious prohibitions and then illegal abortions, had to carry their pregnancies to term in religious and government-run institutions dedicated to this particular group of women stigmatized as unwed mothers.[24] Manual labor was to be their compensation for sin, and they were forced to give up their children to adoption. The report issued on November 16, 2021 by the Commission of Investigation into Mother and Baby Homes and Certain Related Matters reviewed these eighteen homes from 1922 and 1985 and attributed the 9,000 deaths or 15 percent of the 57,000 children (in 1945 to 1946), more than twice the national average, to appalling living conditions that precipitated early deaths due to disease, cold, hunger, and emotional neglect.[25]

"Stealthing" is another kind of forced reproduction, now recently made illegal in California. Stealthing involves poking holes in condoms or pulling off a condom before penetration. Katha Pollitt noted in *Pro: Reclaiming Abortion Rights* that 16 percent of women have experienced "reproductive coercion" in which a male partner uses threats or violence to override their reproductive choice and 9 percent have experienced

[23] Rachel Treisman, "Millions of Americans Are Losing Access to Maternal Care. Here's What Can Be Done," *NPR*, October 12, 2022, https://www.npr.org/2022/10/12/1128335563/maternity-care-deserts-march-of-dimes-report.

[24] *Philomena*, directed by Stephen Frears (London: BBC Films, 2013).

[25] Government of Ireland, Commission of Investigation into Mother and Baby Homes and Certain Related Matters, *Final Report*, November 16, 2021, https://www.gov.ie/en/publication/316d8-commission-of-investigation/#. See also the documentary by the *New York Times* on the home in Tuam, County Galway: https://www.nytimes.com/video/world/europe/100000005168975/tuam-ireland-babies.html?action=click&gtype=vhs&version=vhs-heading&module=vhs&region=title-area&cview=true&t=12.

"'birth control sabotage,' a male partner who disposed of her pills, poked holes in condoms, or prevented her from getting contraception."[26]

Maternal risks and stealthing contribute to one argument for why abortion should be an unrestricted right: violations resulting in conception must be counterbalanced by choices regarding consequences.

Shaming in the United States involves a history of forced sterilization against Native American, Black, and other women of color. Developmentally disabled or mentally ill women experience collective shaming because, within the rubrics of implicit white supremacy and ableism, they are regarded as unworthy of being mothers. Furthermore, over 40 percent of Native American women were sterilized between 1968 and 1982,[27] and some Black female inmates in Californian prisons could be sterilized without their consent until recently.[28] Here the logic of misogyny is twinned with race and ableism to deny the possibility of motherhood. In all of these cases, misogynistic, racist, ableist notions of ideal white womanhood diminish actual women, whose stories include forced sterilization and shaming as well as denial of their personhood and reproductive decision-making.

Women Who Speak Out

Silencing women is a misogynistic practice that guarantees an implicitly (if not explicitly) patriarchal right to make decisions about women's reproductive capacities. The relative invisibility of women's stories about sexual assault, sterilization, and abortion reflects a patriarchal regime in which women are not permitted agency over their bodies or their stories, and their stories are not allowed to enter into public consciousness so that public awareness—and the cultural and legal systems associated with it—can change. The punitive regime is swift, uncompromising, and complete. The title of Kate Manne's book, *Down Girl*, points precisely to the fact that every woman who speaks out will encounter the wrath of the patriarchy. The immediacy of hostile reactions, diminishing an experience with verbal arrogance, invoking fear of financial and career ruin, or freeing a convicted sex predator based on a prior prosecutorial agreement,

---

[26]   Katha Pollitt, *Pro: Reclaiming Abortion Rights* (New York: Picador, 2014), 17.

[27]   Todd Peters, *Trust Women*, 114; citing Barbara Gurr, *Reproductive Justice: The Politics of Health Care for Native American Women* (New Brunswick, N.J.: Rutgers University Press, 2014), 125.

[28]   *Belly of the Beast*, documentary, directed by Erika Cohn (New York: Black Public Media, 2020).

even as many women told their stories—all these practices preserve the culture of women's silence.

Storytelling has to do with power. Those who tell stories that people listen to exercise the power of their persons. Those who are valued as "less" have "less" power than the default standard. Women with non-normative stories fear retribution because they have less power than others who impose the regime of fear. This power difference is represented in theology by those who inhabit the institutional power of the church and the academic power of the university in which a learned clergy is trained (at least in the traditional churches of the West). These theologians have listened to some stories, and as representatives of the Christian tradition, have sought to make sense of the various stories involved—stories about the image of God, the Bible, Jesus, and historically influential theologians like Aquinas and Calvin.

Yet the stories are going to be limited if those selected only highlight representations that feel comfortably familiar in a context so long shaped by patriarchal assumptions. Conversations are only as good as the interlocutors, and the Holy Spirit is poured out upon all flesh (cf. Acts 2:16–18, citing Joel 2:28). Hence in the twentieth century people traditionally excluded from theological conversations have begun to join in new iterations of them. Women began to gain medical knowledge over their own bodies and to become ob-gyn doctors and scientists interested in women's bodies. Women began to promote changes in legislation regarding the right to vote, reproductive laws, ending rape in marriage, the capacity for financial independence, and the right to own property and to have a credit card in one's name. Women became pastors and theologians, adding newly told stories and new ways of reading the tradition into a shared ecclesial conversation. In this way, Christian discourse about abortion also became more complex and multifaceted as different constituencies contributed their heartfelt stories to inflect the issue.

Such cultural changes around gender, however, do not automatically translate into an invitation to speak. When women speak theologically, there are still ways in which their speech is disciplined and their voices silenced by those who hold the power in church and academy. Especially on controvertible issues, the power difference in theology is often staged between male pastors who are "pro-life" and women theologians who are "pro-choice." This difference has to do with the power to speak; male pastors have that power in their own churches, while women theologians have some degree of authority with respect to their own institutions as ordained clergy or academic faculty. Yet possessing professional competence does not always translate into being part of conversations characterized by a real reciprocity of speaking and listening. In her own experience as a woman theologian, Christine has encountered the silencing regimes of the patriarchy—usually within her own Christian circles, not to mention attempted conversation with male theologians who represent different values than she does. The smackdown can be immediate and aggressive. For example, a recent article that both of us wrote for the *Lutheran Forum*[29] on abortion led to an immediate "down girl" by David Scaer, an older white male theologian in a Lutheran denomination that refuses to ordain women, and because of hiring practices at its colleges and seminaries, has no women theologians on its faculties either. Scaer's review was extensive, detailed, and equivocated between addressing our argument on abortion and addressing women's ordination, as well as mistakenly assigning a particular Lutheran denomination to one of us without checking the record. This is one example among an entire professional lifetime full of experiences for Christine in which the speaking of her voice in a public professional setting, as a theologian embodied in her particular chromosomal makeup, has been met with hostile questions, obvious gestures of anger, prompt and outright rejections (without attempts to understand), and verbal diminishments of rather outrageous kinds.[30]

Even our writing of this chapter that invites conversation presupposes our position that conversation is required, that the Holy Spirit has not summarized the whole issue in an assertion, and that in spite of the backlash that we as women theologians anticipate when we write about an issue as controversial and power played as this one—abortion—we have decided that conversation is better than the either/or, that the body of Christ that is broken by abusive uses of positionality must be mended, and that attempts to understand by listening is a strategy that is oriented to this mending. While we have no hopes that the positionality will

[29] Amy Carr and Christine Helmer, "Claiming Christian Freedom to Discuss Abortion *Together,*" *Lutheran Forum* 53, no. 2 (Summer 2019): 48–51; David Scaer, Theological Observer review of "Claiming Christian Freedom to Discuss Abortion *Together,*" *Concordia Theological Quarterly* 84, no. 1–2 (2020): 175–76.

[30] Christine Helmer, "Luther Scholarship under the Conditions of Patriarchy," *Journal of Lutheran Ethics* 22, no. 4 (August/September 2022: Gender Identity, Gender Expression, and Sexuality), https://learn.elca.org/jle/luther-scholarship-under-the-conditions-of-patriarchy/.

cease—women theologians are so rarely listened to and the political issue so fraught with walls that preclude listening—it is our hope that at the very least we can bear witness that justification by faith does play a role in the justifications of one's positions on justice concerning abortion. That is why we have been inviting our readers to pause, even just for a moment, to discover where attempts to understand those with whom we might disagree are worthwhile, theologically, ethically, and politically.

Stories about Those Who Died—and Other Tales from a World without Legal Abortion

If women telling their own stories about abortion are silenced, then who else can tell them? Medical doctors have recently been writing them in public forums. One ob-gyn wrote in the *Washington Post* about his decision to medically induce an abortion in Texas since the passing of Senate Bill 8, knowing full well that he would be sued by some persons now empowered to take the law literally into their own hands.[31] He gave the reason for his civil disobedience: his daughters, nieces, and granddaughters, and his experience as a medical doctor in the time preceding *Roe v. Wade*. He tells of the women who had been transported to the hospital after they had tried to self-induce abortions. One, he writes, arrived with her body cavity stuffed with rags. She died of sepsis a few days later. Another doctor, an immigrant ob-gyn in Texas, writes in the *New York Times* op-ed pages of her ethical responsibility to provide abortions as one dimension of reproductive health care for women. She knows, as do the statistics, that low-income women and (especially undocumented) immigrants are less likely to have the means to find abortion providers if their own state denies them access.[32]

Women now in their sixties and seventies tell stories of women and abortions prior to 1973. A high school classmate studied for a test one day and did not come to class the next. Speculation fills in the absences. Women have always had abortions, whether it is legal, medically safe, or not. When the law prohibits safe abortions, women retreat into the silence of rooms in which they—or a trusted confidante—might administer

[31]   Alan Braid, "Why I Violated Texas's Extreme Abortion Ban," *Washington Post*, September 18, 2021, https://www.washingtonpost.com/opinions/2021/09/18/texas-abortion-provider-alan-braid/.

[32]   Ghazaleh Moayedi, "How Texas Has Made My Job of Helping Women More Dangerous," *New York Times*, September 20, 2021, https://www.nytimes.com/2021/09/20/opinion/texas-abortion-provider.html.

Lysol. The coat hanger has become the symbol of women's voices silenced by their deaths—an instrument of abortion, among others, including just the right quantity of toxic herbs like the hellebore or mugwort that women since the ancient world have used and told each other about.

We can also find troubling stories in other parts of the world where abortion is illegal. Women in El Salvador disappear into prison when a miscarriage is used by a vindictive partner as an accusation of abortion. When abortion is illegal, men get rid of women by precipitating a miscarriage and then having her jailed. There are many other stories. An eleven-year-old Argentinian victim of incest-rape was forced to carry her pregnancy to term and had to have a C-section to deliver because her reproductive organs were not adequately developed. In Ireland, where there was a Roman Catholic aversion to C-sections, women's pelvises were broken to deliver vaginally, a procedure known as symphysiotomy.[33]

The more privileged find ways to access abortion elsewhere. This is so even without the shame of illegitimacy in patrilineal structures, where a woman's virginity must be guarded until marriage. *Downton Abbey* portrayed such a context, when Lady Edith entrusts her news of pregnancy to her aunt Rosemary, who then announces that the two will go to Switzerland for a few months to learn French.[34] There, the shame of pregnancy—physically apparent on women—is diminished by hiding this episode in her life and secretly giving the child away for adoption. Edith returns with her aunt, and no one asks any questions, until much later.

Stories of the Terminated

There is another silence, one described vicariously by spokespersons telling the story of the only entity who is completely silent: that of the embryo, the fetus, the prenate, the unborn child. The entity within

---

[33] Michael Brice-Saddler, "An 11-Year-Old Pleaded for an Abortion after She Was Raped. She Was Forced to Give Birth," *Washington Post*, February 28, 2019, https://www.washingtonpost.com/world/2019/03/01/an-year-old-pleaded-an-abortion-after-she-was-raped-she-was-forced-give-birth/; "Twelve Facts about the Abortion Ban in El Salvador," *Amnesty International*, September 25, 2014, https://www.amnesty.org/en/latest/news/2014/09/twelve-facts-about-abortion-ban-el-salvador/; Homa Khaleeli, "Symphysiotomy—Ireland's Brutal Alternative to Caesareans," *The Guardian*, December 12, 2014, https://www.theguardian.com/lifeandstyle/2014/dec/12/symphysiotomy-irelands-brutal-alternative-to-caesareans.

[34] *Downton Abbey*, season 3, episodes 7 and 8, directed by David Evans, written by Julian Fellowes (London: Carnival Film & Television, 2013).

the uterus is silent—it will not have the linguistic tools until much later, when memory, brain development, and language skills kick in. At this stage it is silent. But there are others who would speak in the name of the voiceless unborn. These spokespersons point out that the fetus is completely dependent on the pregnant woman and thus by giving voice to the fetus they insist on its right to exist.

As we have noted, proponents of both pro-choice or pro-life positions often point to an affective moment in the conversion of someone to their own viewpoint. Images of the fetus through an ultrasound, combined with the knowledge that it lacks a voice of its own, move many to sympathy with a pro-life position—or to choosing against abortion personally. *Christianity Today* emailed its subscribers an ad by James Dobson's *Focus on the Family* that describes a pregnant woman who had intended to abort then changing her mind when she saw an ultrasound of the fetus, which looked to her to be in the shape of a baby in prayer. She felt that the baby was praying for her to carry it to term. On the other hand, Willie Parker describes how listening to women facing unwanted pregnancies led him to convert away from his Black fundamentalist Christian upbringing and into his life's work as an abortion-providing doctor.[35]

How do we think together as Christians amid such a collage of morally weighted stories—to which we trust you have added some of your own?

Framing Women's Pregnancy Stories within Justice-Seeking Visions

There are many stories that continue to be told by women, their partners and family members, by those who speak on behalf of women and give voice to the silent unborn. Stories elicit reactions because abortion is never neutral and ethical debates play on a highly reactive and emotionally fraught landscape. Our effort to listen to stories is one disciplined by questions. We are curious, we ask, we need and want to hear. If we shut hearts and ears to each other then we prematurely cut ourselves off from the experience of others from whom we can learn. This is the disposition that we advocate—one that attends to others in spite of and through the complex and challenging conversations we need to have about abortion today.

---

[35] Willie Parker, *Life's Work: A Moral Argument for Choice* (New York: First 37 Ink / Atria, 2017).

If we do not prematurely shut ourselves off from others, and open hearts and ears, then we discover that we can be moved intellectually and emotionally by others. New stories are added into old stories, and our minds knit them together in distinctive ways. This process of knitting and stitching together new and old is one expression of "meaning making." These stories are not "one-offs," told as jokes in a bar and promptly forgotten. As we listen, we relate them to other principles and commitments. We try to make sense of them by applying to them a set of meaning-making tools that we have accrued through our life experience and reflective resources.

More abstract principled arguments express some of those cross-story meanings connected to biblical and doctrinal themes. As Hans-Georg Gadamer depicts through the idea of a hermeneutical circle, we move back and forth between a current perspective (shaped by a synthesis of all the information we have gathered up to this point) and a revisioning of our perspective when we encounter new information that does not fit into a current conceptual framework.[36] In the seemingly abstract discursive world of apologetics or doctrinal argument, that revisioning takes place through the give and take of theological conversation with voices we respect, or voices with which we feel we must reckon. Thus Arminians and Calvinists seek to know and accommodate (or have a rebuttal for) one another's theological intuitions. (How can Arminians acknowledge divine sovereignty? How can Calvinists articulate the realness of individual agency?) Likewise, theologians who make feminist arguments bring into conversational play the voices of inherited doctrinal traditions and appeals to overlooked women's experiences that expose and reframe patriarchal spins on Christian doctrine.

Some stories become more important as they deploy particular meanings that then impose on other stories. As such, these stories become anchored as what might be called "interpretive frameworks," or "meaning-making macrostories"—frameworks in and through which we justify the particular moral beliefs we hold. These terms get at the process of how some stories are stretched and shaped in relation to other stories so that particular nodes become meaningful and then anchor other stories. These paradigms inform the arguments we formulate as we try to make sense of a complex issue. They help give us the reasons for justifying our points

---

[36] Hans-Georg Gadamer, *Truth and Method*, trans. Marvin Brown (New York: Crossroad, 1982 [1960]).

of view. Sometimes these moral interpretive paradigms are rigid; they are templated onto experience so that they insist on one meaning. Attention must be paid to them so that they can retain flexibility, so that they can be tweaked and edited when new stories come across our bow. As we look below at some of the moral interpretive frameworks around abortion, we envision the formation of an interpretive framework that can be both stable and flexible, that moves beyond reactivity to the kind of listening that is informed by reflection on deep listening. This is the tool that can help us make meaning of life's complexity and not reduce it to an affective reaction goaded by slogans and images.

Bible stories for many Christians have this paradigmatic function. Christian communities rally around the Bible, and sometimes texts are seen as paradigmatic for meaning making and for interpreting other stories. Bible and ethics is an immediate connection that many Christians make—one that is sometimes lacking in theological reflection and analysis. In the context of the abortion discussion, the Bible emerges on both sides of its divisive ontologies. Yet a close look at biblical passages shows that there is ambiguity about the precise moral status of the prenate, at least in the terms stipulated by the contemporary debate. Note, for example, texts about God calling prophets from the womb (Jer 1:5), or each of us being knitted by God in our mother's womb (Ps 139:13)—they do not pinpoint when personhood begins in the gestational process. Moreover, as Kira Schlesinger notes, these verses "say more about the all-being and all-knowing characteristics of God than they say about the personhood of an embryo or fetus in the womb."[37] Humans may be made in God's image (Gen 1:26–27), but generations of theologians have debated what constitutes this *imago dei*, or the way in which divinity is reflected in humanity and in what way divinity sanctions humanity as worthy of bearing this divine imprint. Is it the possibility for knowing God, as Calvin queried in the opening lines of his *Institutes*; a divine sense and taste for the infinite, or a restlessness for the divine that can only be quenched when divinity and humanity meet, as respectively Schleiermacher and Augustine thought? And is the divine image imprinted on humans even while they are developing in the gestational state? Many others have explored how the

[37] Schlesinger, *Pro-Choice and Christian*, 58. She adds that if we were to take Psalm 139 in a literal sense regarding when human personhood begins, we would also have to take literally Psalm 137:9: "Happy shall they be who take your little ones and dash them against the rock!" (57). And as Schlesinger notes (64), what of God's own striking down of the firstborn of Egypt in Exodus 12:12?

imago dei relates to philosophical and theological notions of personhood and when it might begin. Meanwhile, Genesis 2:7 suggests that human life proper begins with the first breath: "then the Lord God formed man from the dust of the ground, and breathed into his nostrils the breath of life; and the man became a living being." Likewise, Exodus 21:22–24 conveys that the life of a pregnant woman is valued more than the life of her prenate. The text describes two men fighting who accidentally cause a nearby woman to miscarry. The judgment issued is that the "one responsible shall be fined"; if she herself is harmed, "you shall give life for life, eye for eye, tooth for tooth, hand for hand, foot for foot." As biblical scholar Cheryl Anderson notes, "The penalty [for the violence causing a woman to miscarry] is just the payment of a fine which would not have been possible if a human life had been taken (Genesis 9:6 and Exodus 21:12)."[38] Moreover, Numbers 5:11–31 goes so far as to describe the process by which a husband may ask a priest to prescribe a forced abortion on his wife if he suspects her of adultery. As on so many ethically fraught issues, biblical texts speak to diverse moral intuitions.[39]

To be sure, whatever our view of scriptural authority, Christian appeal to the Bible is already infused with preexisting conditions of interpretive stances. Part of listening to stories is to interrogate our own assumptions about the meaning-making apparatus we impose on the experience of others. In the spirit of Gadamer, then, as we move from stories (biblical or experiential) to visions of justice with which to frame and interpret them, we invite you to think about what stories you yourselves think from with regard to abortion, and how—if—your own mind has changed along the way. What were the first conversations you recall having about abortion? How do they shape your sentiments today? After describing one of our own responses to this question, we consider some justice-seeking framings of the in/justice involved in legal access to abortion.

[38] Cheryl B. Anderson, "Christians and Reproductive Justice: Hearing New Voices," *Ecclesio.com*, September 25, 2012, http://www.ecclesio.com/2012/09/christians-and-reproductive-justice-hearing-new-voices-by-cheryl-anderson/.

[39] For a deeper look at "pro-life" and "pro-choice" biblical arguments about personhood, see Schlesinger, "What the Bible Does (and Doesn't) Say," ch. 4 in *Pro-Choice and Christian*; and Margaret D. Kamitsuka, "Biblical Arguments for Personhood," ch. 2 in *Abortion and the Christian Tradition: A Pro-Choice Theological Ethic* (Louisville: Westminster John Knox, 2019), 49–71. For a broader engagement on questions of abortion and fetal personhood with regard to church history, Christology, and Christian philosophy, see Kamitsuka, *Abortion and the Christian Tradition*, chs. 1 and 3–4.

Amy's First-Heard Stories of Meaning Making about Abortion

Amy recalls that her first conversation about abortion was with a fellow member of the high school debate team, a friend who is Lakota on her mother's side and a member of the largely Ojibwe Keweenaw Bay Indian Community located in their county in Upper Michigan on the shores of Lake Superior. (Amy is white—or as some in her town would say then, rattling off our immigrant connections while "Old World" languages were still spoken around us, "half Finnish American and a quarter each Slovenian American and German American"). Her friend was active then in Native Catholic efforts to canonize Kateri Tekakwitha. She said that the reason she did not support abortion was for faith reasons *and* because of the history of forced sterilization of so many Native women ("as high as 80 percent on some reservations"; as Rebecca Todd Peters notes, "42 percent of Native women were sterilized between 1968 and 1982, compared with a 15 percent rate among white women during the same period"[40]). Another member of Amy's debate team also had Lakota and white ancestry; the daughter of Protestant pastors, she became Catholic when marrying her husband of Lebanese-Italian descent. This mutual friend admired the consistent life-ethic (from womb to death) of Catholicism, but was as matter-of-fact about supporting a woman's right to an abortion as she was in describing—with the same methodical detail she brought to her lectures in college chemistry courses—the birth of her first daughter, which she compared to pushing a watermelon through a pinhole.

The contrasting attitudes to abortion Amy picked up in these two formative friendships reflect themes we find in broader narratives that we might call norm-bearing analytic frameworks: ways of framing and interpreting the ethical, medical, and affective dimensions of abortion. For example, among those who support a legal right to abortion, we can find two normative frameworks that each grant pregnant women moral agency but do so with different assumptions about what is morally permissible: a justificatory framework and a reproductive justice framework. These two frameworks differ in the macrostory they tell about the moral trustworthiness of women and about the ethical norms around shame. After pausing to consider the theological anthropologies (views of human nature, gendered) at play in justificatory and reproductive justice frameworks, we will move into exploring, more poetically, some of the spiritual and theological views of the divine and gender at play in the pieties of

---

[40] Todd Peters, *Trust Women*, 114.

those who view abortion variously as a tragic choice, a practical choice, and a morally reprehensible choice. Part of our listening will attend to the ways competing senses of the sacred lie in the background of the debate about abortion's legality.

Two Contemporary Meaning-Making Proposals about Abortion to Consider

In her book *Trust Women*, Rebecca Todd Peters contrasts a justificatory framework for abortion with a reproductive justice framework. A justificatory framework affirms that abortion before viability is justifiable only on certain grounds capturable with the acronym PRIM (Prenatal defects, Rape, Incest, Maternal health): when the life of the prenate is not viable or birth defects would be too grave; or in cases of rape, incest, or when the mother's own life is threatened. Todd Peters unpacks the history of legal and cultural arguments in support of PRIM, unfolding how they are informed by the same paternalism toward women that informs arguments against abortion under any circumstance. Paternalistic practices include asking a woman to wait a certain number of days after requesting and before having an abortion, or requiring her to view an ultrasound image to be sure she understands what she would be doing by terminating her pregnancy. By contrast, a reproductive justice framework associates justice with the means and permission for women to discern when and when not to bear children—trusting women to that discernment is *itself* a moral good, without asking a pregnant woman to justify her abortion.

To some extent, the reproductive justice perspective can account for both kinds of justifications of belief Amy heard in her early conversations about abortion. Reproductive justice is about more than access to abortion and contraception; it involves women's moral agency in choosing the sizes of their families, as well as finding the economic, medical, and social resources they need to support a decision to bear and raise children. Reproductive justice includes awareness of once politically acceptable policies of forced sterilization that perpetuated genocide or eugenics against Native American, Black, and disabled women. A reproductive justice framework accommodates women who have no moral qualms about aborting a prenate, as well as those who believe it would be wrong for them personally to have an abortion and who may seek support in deciding whether to give up the child for adoption. A reproductive justice framework does not, however, accommodate those who would prevent *all* women from having abortions, either conditionally or absolutely.

The title *Trust Women* distills Todd Peters' critical commentary on both justificatory and reproductive justice frameworks into a lucid commandment that bucks the idealized, essentializing views of women's obligations within a theological and cultural worldview that portrays them primarily as mothers. (In this respect, taken out of context of a fuller argument, "trust women" can also function as an assertion or meme in the public abortion debate.) While recognizing the choice and practice of motherhood as morally significant, Todd Peters is laser-focused on portraying and advocating for women-identifying persons as capable of navigating the moral complexities of their lives regarding reproduction. Construing abortion as immoral "has disordered our ability to think and talk thoughtfully and ethically about abortion's important role in helping women achieve some measure of order and control in their lives."[41] Before the mirror of a theological and legal prohibition on abortion, women can only see themselves as morally obligated, under all circumstances, to continue an unplanned pregnancy as part of their fulfillment of the divine command to "'be fruitful and multiply'" (Gen 1:28) and not to murder.[42]

Yet the moral intuitions of pregnant persons vary with regard to the status of what Todd Peters calls a prenate, with many people—of all genders—experiencing the moral intuition that there is something distinctly different between a prenate and a birthed infant, such that natality involves what Todd Peters calls a continuum. During that period of prenatal status, a prenate may be invested early on with the hopes and dreams of its mother or parents; or it may be a collection of cells toward whom a pregnant woman may feel no emotional connection, or feel only emotions of fear and anxiety because she had not intended at this time to become pregnant.

A reproductive justice framework centers the lives of pregnant women and trusts them to discern whether they seek to bring a prenate through to full natality. Not only are they trusted to make the best morally significant decisions for themselves and their families, but they themselves are centered in moral imagination; their lives and well-being matter—on terms that come into focus for them amid the complexity of their circumstances and their respective vocational pulls, not by measuring themselves against a normative portrait of females as childbearers, perhaps even as competitors (as Leah and Rachel were) in seeing who can bear the most children. The awe, wonder, decentering, and recentering unique to pregnancy and giving

41 Todd Peters, *Trust Women*, 122.
42 Todd Peters, *Trust Women*, 124.

birth can be a calling for those who enter willingly and with sufficient material means into a parental covenant. Rebecca Todd Peters describes this as a process of a pregnant woman's developing moral obligations—including whether and when she develops an attachment to the prenate—rather than a question of competing rights (a question less pointed when the prenate is understood as a potential person).[43] But it violates a pregnant person's bodily and spiritual integrity, and often her or her family's material well-being, to make motherhood (or forced birthing of a child to be adopted) a norm for every woman or the telos of every unexpected pregnancy.

Those who oppose all or most abortions take their bearings from the idea that a fetus has the same moral status as a born person, so that abortion can only be seen as murder. From this lens, a pregnant woman's moral intuitions are profoundly misguided, reducible to emotions that have no more significance in determining the moral status of a prenate than her emotions would have in determining the moral standing of a born child. For those Christians who do see women as most fulfilled in motherhood, when a pregnant woman's moral sensibilities are properly ordered and redeemed from any sinful distortions, she would recognize that it is her duty, if not always her joy, to risk her life—and perhaps her well-being in other respects—for the sake of carrying a prenate to term. Here the prenate is given more moral significance than the woman carrying it in her womb; its life matters more than the fullness of the life of the woman carrying it, except insofar as one rationalizes that if a woman knew her true worth, she would see, perhaps even feel, that her own moral mattering was precisely bound up with her willingness to say "yes" to her continuing her pregnancy.

To be sure, a Christian does not need to have an all-out notion of gender complementarity to perceive the prenate as the most vulnerable being in a pregnancy; all one needs is the conviction that the moral standing of a prenate at any stage of development is identical to the moral standing of a born infant. Moreover, even when the fetus's viability outside the womb is the standard of full personhood, abortion opponents point out that medical technology is making the time of viability earlier and earlier. Will there come a time when any fetus can be extracted from the womb and brought to full term outside it? Apart from questions of who would be responsible for raising children brought forth in this manner, developments in medical technology may one day enable gestation and birth to

[43] Todd Peters, *Trust Women*, 162–66.

bypass the need for a woman's body entirely, which could put the moral pressure not on a pregnant woman but on society as a whole. In the meantime, though, moral discernment—and whatever moral pressure others place upon her—belongs primarily to a pregnant person herself.

Affectivity of Shaming in Moral Meaning Making

A society practicing reproductive justice would ideally lift all moral and shaming pressure on a pregnant woman to carry a prenate to term. Qualifications still apply, for others involved in a pregnancy would have some degree of moral authority or voice; a pregnant woman's partner might really want another child, while she herself does not, or she is ambivalent about the possibility. This sort of moral pressure could be present even if a woman were not yet pregnant, and need not be tied to coercion or domestic violence. But reproductive justice advocates do insist that pregnant women should never be shamed into believing their abortions are morally wrong or sinful. The Religious Coalition for Reproductive Choice (RCRC) states as its advocacy position:

> We reject the shame and stigma that religious conservatives have long attached to sex, sexuality and reproduction. Publicly, we challenge these views which have polarized the debate on reproductive issues. In the secular reproductive issues movement, we present moderate and progressive faith perspectives to counter religious extremists. In our congregations and communities, we offer women spiritual support and solace as they make their reproductive choices.[44]

Indeed, the wider context of reproductive justice addresses the shame women may face not only with regard to abortion, but also with regard to pregnancy or breastfeeding.[45] Amy has a young friend, committedly opposed to abortion, who noticed that her priest seemed visibly uncomfortable when she breastfed her son while they had coffee together at a restaurant. Why would a priest, who puts up displays of fetuses at various stages of development to educate the children at the Catholic elementary school, be anything other than enthusiastically supportive of a mother breastfeeding in front of him? One can imagine reasons why he

---

[44] "The Moral Case," *Religious Coalition for Reproductive Choice*, https://rcrc.org/the-moral-case/.

[45] See the Religious Coalition for Reproductive Choice webinar, "Pregnancy Shaming in Religion and Culture," RCRC Learning Center Webinar Series, December 15, 2020, https://youtu.be/-dlRDa-FjE0.

might *feel* uncomfortable—from an unmet longing for erotic intimacy to an internalized shame about female bodies—whether or not he finds his own feelings morally justifiable. But whether feeling shame or shaming others is intended or unintended, their occurrence signals something of significance in the wider debate about abortion access.

Shame in the sense of not measuring up to normative expectations can arise no matter one's position on abortion. Should a feminist Christian commandment to trust women's reproductive decision-making translate into the idea that feeling shame or regret about having had an abortion is itself something to be ashamed about? Ought the origin of such shame be explained as due simply to bad patriarchal theology or endemic misogyny? Even if many feminists might be tempted to say "yes," faith-based reproductive justice advocates recognize that these feelings do exist, or that some women face others who tell them they *ought* to feel shame. Amy recalls at a Benedictine oblate retreat a Catholic woman standing up to testify about how ashamed she felt about having had an abortion years ago. With tears in her eyes, she embodied a repentant spirit and was grateful for the support of Benedictine sisters and oblates in walking with her amid her sense of shame. While reproductive justice advocates might encourage her to understand her abortion as a morally sound, if agonized choice rather than as sin, the Religious Coalition for Reproductive Justice provides interfaith liturgical resources for journeying in a sacred way with the range of feelings a woman might feel about having chosen an abortion. Likewise, even if the majority of surveyed women who have had abortions do *not* experience regret, Margaret Kamitsuka points out that many do refer to those they aborted as "babies" and may speak to them as possibilities they had to let go of, for now.[46] For instance, in Japan, there is a tradition of ritually mourning a miscarried or aborted pregnancy.[47]

The senses of loss or shame for some (not all) pregnant women who choose abortion, even when they identify with a reproductive justice framework, are the sort of affective experiences that can be weaponized or approached pastorally but are also a window into forms of spirituality or piety and their interface with images of God and of gendered views of being human. Those who oppose abortion's legality might see a woman's mourning or shame about an unchosen possibility as a sign she *does* have a

46   Kamitsuka, *Abortion and the Christian Tradition*, 6.
47   See Bardwell L. Smith's study of *mizuko kuyō* in *Narratives of Sorrow and Dignity: Japanese Women, Pregnancy Loss, and Modern Rituals of Grieving* (Oxford: Oxford University Press, 2013).

conscience: it is evidence that even a woman who says she does not regret having had an abortion is still aware it was *wrong* to have one. Some feminists might be tempted to weaponize those feelings as well, finding their very presence morally problematic. This is part of a larger pattern among feminist perspectives that tend to interpret various self-incriminating emotions as a product of false patriarchal consciousness, from shame about abortion to feeling polluted after being sexually abused or raped. Without addressing all that such feelings might indicate about being vulnerably human and affected by what others do with or to our bodies, here we might note minimally that a Christian feminist gospel against shaming is necessary but insufficient unless it is located within an account of maternal decision-making that makes space for what some pregnant women will experience as a tragic sense of options, with regard to a potential human life (even if that human life is not construed as a full-fledged person who has been murdered). At the same time, if we take our bearings from Christian perspectives that cannot take their eyes off the moral fact that an emerging human life has been snuffed out, we might perceive not a feminist ideal of trusting women to navigate the moral complexities of their lives in ways that best honor themselves, but a certain kind of saintly ideal: staying attuned to the absolute sanctity of a prenate's life as an end in itself. Here the world is perceived as morally callous to the extent it does not maintain this saintly maternal ideal for all expecting mothers.

We have suggested that as a heuristic amid polarized debate, heresy involves holding to a particular truth or insight in a way that eclipses a fuller spectrum of truths. With regard to abortion, heresy might involve regarding only some affective responses of women as relevant and normative—morally guiding—for all pregnant women. Shame, for example, can be weaponized in the context of a diminishing of women's moral authority and capacity to know and decide what the best course of action is in a situation intimately concerning themselves. When we treat shame as if it were itself sufficient evidence that one is morally (or ontologically) mistaken, then we complicate our ability to articulate and debate diverse Christian understandings of what justice-seeking looks like for pregnant women in the Beloved Community. Indeed, women themselves can shame one another by holding pregnant women responsible for having been sexually active,[48] even though statistics bear out

---

[48]   Reading her US Representative Darin LaHood's September 24, 2021 Facebook post opposing a new federal abortion-related law, Amy was struck by the number of anti-abortion comments by women engaged in this kind

that in the United States, at least, many unintended pregnancies involve contraceptive failure.[49]

We turn now to entering the spiritual spaces conjured by various theological imaginaries about what a woman-identifying person is supposed to do and to be, especially with regard to her womb as the most morally contested space of her body.

The Theological Imaginary: Ideals, Icons, and Archetypes

It is inevitably painful to listen for God amid the debate about abortion's legality and morality. What parable might we tell to get at the moral intuitions regarding legal access to an abortion? *Let those who have ears to hear, hear*: Can one parable get at all the moral intuitions at play in this debate? Do we need at least two parables? In trying to listen to those who agree or disagree with our own take (if it is settled) about the moral status of a prenate in relation to the moral status of a pregnant woman, it is as if we are walking barefoot across a room with broken glass. We have only shards of a shared moral vision.

Here are some unsystematic, exploratory forays into that landscape, picking up some of the shards and looking through them for what they might suggest about our views of God and moral (and gendered) norms in relation to each.

Those who condemn and refuse to listen to persons—especially women—who support abortion *sound* (to those they silence) as if they are outing misogyny as their core value. From the perspective of those who feel viscerally that abortion is equivalent to murder of a person outside the womb, those who make a case that abortion is morally acceptable in any sense whatsoever *sound* like a coldhearted clanging gong trying

---

of shaming of women for having unintended pregnancies in the first place. LaHood's own original post: "I voted NO on Democrats' extreme abortion bill today that would strip nearly every pro-life protection for the unborn, green-lighting abortion on demand until birth in every state. This radical bill devalues the sanctity of life and goes far beyond Roe v Wade. I am proud to be pro-life and I will always lend a voice to the voiceless in Congress." https://www.facebook.com/replahood/posts/pfbid0de1S84AjM99oxATSPqoVF4tcW6b2dn5r2b84pQSjX7G1LUW971vnrZGFKQ2qRSa9l.

[49] "Studies demonstrate that between 50 and 60 percent of women who have abortions were using some form of contraceptive the month they got pregnant. This statistic is not surprising, given contraceptive failure rates" (Todd Peters, *Trust Women*, 32). The study she cites is Rachel K. Jones, Lori Frohwirth, and Ann M. Moore, "More than Poverty: Disruptive Events among Women Having Abortions in the USA," *Journal of Family Planning and Reproductive Health Care* 39, no. 1 (2013): 36–43.

to defend the indefensible, daring to call evil good. Taken together, the silencing and the clanging generate a composition that plays a song about patriarchy. Unless there is agreement that women must be trusted to discern for themselves whether to consent or not consent to continuing a pregnancy, the life and value of a pregnant woman cannot be framed in anything other than a patriarchal way: she is evil if she aborts; she is good only if she orients her own value around the birthing of and caring for children—immediately dropping any other life projects as a priority, even the emotional and financial well-being of herself and her current family. Women's capacity to bear children leaves them always vulnerable to being shadowed by patriarchal expectations.

It is no wonder that early and medieval Christian women gained spiritual authority through lifelong celibacy, within or without a monastic community. Only then would their lives not be determined and interpreted so overwhelmingly in light of their reproductive capacities.

Perhaps the impulse these women had toward celibacy is the same one that led Amy to find herself emotionally unable to imagine having a child *and* a career. She had internalized the values and expectations of the women in her rural community, where she knew no women who defined themselves around a professional career. The only professional women (with college degrees) she knew were teachers; and they were also cast maternally as caregivers. Shaped by these initial role models, Amy could not easily imagine motherhood as a possibility for herself, unless it were the primary choice around which she organized her entire life (and then she was drawn to becoming a foster mother of many children at the same time). Yet she felt more strongly other callings—to an intellectually intense life—that seemed threatened by motherhood. She remembers marveling that this sense of having-to-pick did not seem in the atmosphere at all for her female classmates in college and graduate school who grew up in urban places, whose own mothers and even grandmothers had attended college and had careers. These classmates blithely seemed to take for granted a capacity to imagine becoming both mothers and professional women. With different role models in their childhood, they had not internalized an either-or sensibility regarding mothering and a career.

But at stake is not only the time and energy it takes to be defined by motherhood *and* by a demanding career that draws one's focus for many hours a day away from family caregiving. Also at stake is a sense of what constitutes a life rightly lived before God—the shape of the moral law, be it construed in a patriarchal or feminist key. And the irresolvable difference between these sensibilities regarding the moral law (even if one might not identify with the labeling of "patriarchal" or "feminist") flares into expression at the level of archetypes of women in relation to the sacred.

The Iconic and the Demonic

Entering into that space of the iconic, of a sacred imaginary, is one way that some Christians contend with a cognitive dissonance in society and among Christians about abortion. How can some Christians justify, even as a moral good, what other Christians call murder? Is this not the height and depth of blasphemy? Christians who view abortion as murder, plain and simple, might ask, "What is really going on here? Why don't all Christians agree?"

One answer is: "The demonic has distorted the secular world's perception, and it is infecting our churches too." So Matt Walsh views acceptance of abortion as the foundation of all moral decline,[50] the first of an "unholy trinity" that includes nontraditional marriage (feminist and same-sex) and gender fluidity that has its roots in Lucifer whom Walsh calls "the first liberal."[51] Likewise, Carrie Gress blames "toxic femininity" on the demonic spirit of the "Anti-Mary,"[52] which channels women's desires to nurture something into a feminist sisterhood that is always discontented because in it women are not, like Mary (who reversed Eve's sin by consenting to God's command), saying yes to the centrality of fertility and fruitfulness as the core of their identity and happiness.

When a Christian who supports abortion access reads Walsh and Gress, she might feel she has been taken into a horror house that is presented as the mirror of society's actual spiritual condition before God, beneath the veneer of professional women's public egalitarian successes. It would be hard for a great many contemporary Christians to take Walsh and Gress' caricatures of feminism seriously (even when they are grounded in anecdotal examples), or to find plausible their Catholic neo-traditionalist depiction of and rationale for rightly ordered gender relations. That may be because both Walsh and Gress follow in that strand of the apocalyptic tradition in which the only weapon against a hegemonic dominant worldview is the rhetorical one of attributing it to demonic deception. Both

---

[50]   Matt Walsh, *The Unholy Trinity: Blocking the Left's Assault on Life, Marriage, and Gender* (New York: Image, 2017), 15–18.

[51]   Walsh, *Unholy Trinity*, 1.

[52]   Carrie Gress, *The Anti-Mary Exposed: Rescuing the Culture from Toxic Femininity* (Charlotte: TAN Books, 2019).

associate their own views with the minority tradition of the persecuted pure—with saints, martyrs, and Mary (if also with a natural law view of gender essentialism that—as if it were itself the long arc of justice cited by their opponents, the social justice warriors—will have the last word of truth in the end, and which always pokes through even now despite the best efforts of feminists).

That voices such as those of Walsh and Gress tread in the waters of conspiracy theories does not mean they are outside the Christian tradition. To be sure, other Christians might judge them as heretical because they fail to attend to the complexity of lived experience, to the nuances of evolutionary biology, and to the richness and diversity of Christian thought itself. But perhaps those most drawn to demonizing discourse turn to it when something profoundly at stake for them is itself felt to be silenced or delegitimized. For Christians like Walsh and Gress, a rationalization of abortion is the fountainhead of a moral depravity that calls good what is evil.

Peter Kreeft extends the blasphemy accusation to the sacramental dimension itself: "Abortion is the Antichrist's demonic parody of the eucharist. That's why it uses the same holy words, 'This is my body,' with the blasphemously opposite meaning."[53] The analogy is fuzzy; how is destroying a fetus to protect the body and well-being of a woman parallel to consuming/eating the body of Christ? The comparison would seem to be between the fetus and Christ's body, since both are "destroyed." The pro-choice woman saying, "This is my body" is not asking anyone to eat her; if anything, it is forcing a woman to continue an unwanted pregnancy that feels to her more like the parody of the Eucharist (she is being consumed by all the pressures upon her—and in sacrificial service of another's well-being).

Kreeft's demonization of abortion rights acutely expresses the cognitive dissonance between the valorizing of prenatal existence and the legal acceptance of abortion. By our heuristic definition of heresy, Kreeft's statement is also heretical, for it spotlights what he believes to be the only truth that matters—abortion is murder—and renders opposition to that claim in theologically macabre ways (emboldened by the macabre of the cross itself, and the Eucharist; an abortion is construed as a re-crucifixion of Christ). His meme eclipses the fuller spectrum of moral concerns and

---

[53] A meme found on Facebook and Twitter, and https://quotefancy.com/peter -kreeft-quotes.

human truths precisely *by* depicting a pregnant woman as inherently dangerous: she is dutiful and responsible if she carries a prenate to term; or she is the devil herself, self-centered and murderous. And claiming the value of her own life ("this is my body") is the heart of what's demonized, in the name of a genuine loss of a potentially born human life. To be pregnant is to be capable of being the antichrist in a way no person without a womb could ever be.

It is as if the fact that abortion interrupts a potential human life justifies spiritual sadism toward women, creating a safe space for voicing misogyny full throttle. There is a kind of satisfying glee in someone making a statement like Kreeft's, without any sympathy even for a justificatory paradigm in which a woman may only have an abortion for acceptable reasons. How can a raped woman, a woman pregnant through incest—however small their number—hear a sentence like Kreeft's and not feel damned, whichever decision she makes?

Calling abortion a feminist anti-sacrament is the ultimate in gaslighting for a pregnant Christian. Reading her own life in light of it, she can do no other than doubt her own ability to wrestle with a morally weighted decision, when such a sign—*this way lies hell*—is placed before any option other than carrying her pregnancy to term. *This way lies your own act of desecrating Christ himself.* Before such signage, a pregnant Christian feels damned even for asking herself what responsible uses of her own resources she might want or need to honor. And what—in hell—is going on with that male pastor or theologian who must invest so deeply in a refusal to open his "ears to hear" the cry of a woman with an unwanted pregnancy that he does not simply sorrow and plead, but zealously antichrist-ens her? It is as if her very presence and circumstance challenge him to become something he is viscerally uncomfortable about being or becoming. So he scapegoats a woman who chooses an abortion for everything he wants to ward off, perhaps including "fragile masculinity," the sense that he can only be someone if she is not in the spotlight ahead of him—and how comforting that *she can be Very Bad in a way he can never be*—unless he is an abortion-providing doctor. A demonic cult of abortion is a misogynist's conspiracy theory: every abortion proves a woman is the gateway to hell, vulnerable to impurity and pulling the rug out from under the whole human race.

The Feminine Sacred?

What, then, if those of us who identify as women—pregnant or not—step into the space defined by voices that equate abortion with murder, or that regard abortion as a feminist anti-sacrament? Some women do comfortably feel that their own life choices and life circumstances are at odds with the normative expectations that women carry every pregnancy to term, even when it is unplanned. Such women know a particular kind of blessing of belonging. And where conservative male theologians and pastors might focus more on demonizing "feminism" and proclaiming abortion its sacrament, conservative women may tend more often to uphold patriarchy—protecting themselves within and from it—by condemning and policing other women's behavior, especially with regard to their sexuality. Both male and female conservative Christians fear that not-right women will upend the world. Other Christian women, however, do not find themselves at home within the theological imaginary in which abortion is murder. They bring to bear different moral intuitions about prenatal life, and factor a pregnant woman's larger life circumstances into any reproductive decision (including abortion). Insofar as Christian women themselves disagree about whether or not abortion is murder, then, their wombs become a site of contestation between competing moral and sacred orderings.

In this respect, debates about the legality of abortion function in many countries rather like religious Jewish debates about what counts as proper or improper behavior for women at the Western Wall. As part of the ruins of the Second Temple in Jerusalem destroyed in 70 CE, the Western Wall is a shared sacred space for Jewish groups who each have a different notion of religiously appropriate behavior for women. At their respective Orthodox and Reform or Masorti/Conservative synagogues, Jews may create distinctive spaces where they pray with (Orthodox) or without (non-Orthodox) gender segregation, with or without women donning tallit and tefillin and carrying a Torah scroll. But at the Western Wall, the choice is either/or: either there are some egalitarian prayer spaces where Jewish women may pray as they wish (even as the men do), or there are not. Likewise, while individual pregnant women may choose or not choose to seek an abortion (though able safely to choose an abortion only where it is legal), the contested site in public political debate is about whether the state sanctions *any* space for women to elect to have access to safe, legal abortions.

Note that at both sites—the Western Wall, the law of the state—only one side in the debate refuses to share space with women who live by different values regarding what they wear, touch, sing, or choose to do about their reproductive possibilities. At the Western Wall, those who advocate carving out an egalitarian prayer space at the Wall recognize that there will continue to be a prominent space at the Wall for those who prefer gender-segregated prayer, with women invisible to the men, praying quietly. Likewise, those who support legal abortion make space for women to hold and to practice different values about whether they believe it is ever acceptable to end a pregnancy.

The men and women who loudly and violently interrupt egalitarian prayer services at the Western Wall feel deeply that women who don a prayer shawl, who carry and chant the Torah, are desecrating a sacred space. They perceive such women as committing sacrilege in the very place that carries the sacred name of God. Likewise, the men and women who loudly, sometimes violently, interrupt the passage of pregnant women into abortion clinics feel viscerally that every woman who aborts a fetus is committing murder and, moreover, that any law that permits such sacrilege is polluting the land they share. It is as if every womb is a kind of Western Wall: a border around where the most holy place for the name (or image) of God dwells.

Within the same psychic space, what some call misogyny is what others call a sacralized image of femininity. Patriarchy (or gender complementarity) of this sort carries a veneration of the birth mother, on whom every man depends for his very existence, through whom each person passes into our shared world. So fierce is this existential dependence on the birth mother that any woman who controls her own fertility is felt to be a profound threat, for she has the power to negate the possibility of the one thing a man himself alone cannot do: bring into this world another male, another human being. At the heart of patriarchy is not only a desire to control women's permitted ways of being in the world, but also a profound fear of the power of women—like God—to bestow or withhold life itself. Patriarchy in this sense is always ironically associating God with an idealized woman: a stylized yet potent image of the sacred feminine that is rooted in the real vulnerability of men to women's ability to give birth.

To be sure, patriarchal control of women's lives can be more an unintended consequence than a conscious agenda of those who oppose abortion all or most of the time, especially when they are motivated by what

Christian ethicist Matthew Lee Anderson calls a "dual awe" about embryonic new life and a woman's ability to gestate it. In an autobiographical testimony for his pro-life position, Anderson appeals to a sacralizing, rather than demonizing, image of women capable of saying "yes" or "no" to the gestation of prenates. Listening to those facing unfulfilled wishes for conception, or facing "the fears and anxieties of an unwanted pregnancy," has "deepened [his] sense that human life is a wonderful, tragic mystery."[54] It is this sensibility—not ethical arguments, not a desire for patriarchal power-over—that he believes most animates the pro-life movement:

> The pro-life outlook is more enchanted, more infused with a secular sense of the sacred, than most of our philosophical arguments allow. Identifying that ethos, and attempting to name it, is crucial for understanding how pro-lifers think—and why they are so earnestly devoted to their cause.[55]

Regarded with "wonder," a "clump of cells" "*is*—a living human being":

> For the pro-lifer, that "clump of cells" is as wondrous, as potent, as mysterious as, well, the cosmos. The recognition of the "baby" induces a hushed reverence. The universe once appeared out of nothing, a fact that reasonably seems to induce the strange vertigo of awe, but the formation of a new human being is not so different from this. The embryo contains a whole world of possibilities and adventures. . . . Human beings are capable of the most heinous evils and exploring the vast reaches of the cosmos—and so the pro-lifer meets the early embryo as a sign of the possibilities before us.[56]

But this "natural awe at the emergence and power of new human life"—and at the risks and sacrifices pregnant persons may undergo to bring forth a child—"is inseparable from a reverence toward the mothers who bear it." The embryo's "radical dependence upon its mother" offers moral insight into the interdependency of all life: "The autonomy of our lives is an illusion that our origins within the womb dispels [*sic*]."[57] It is not hate,

54   Matthew Lee Anderson, "People Criticize Pro-Lifers for Focusing so Much on Abortion. But There's a Reason We Do," *Vox*, February 3, 2017, https://www.vox.com/first-person/2017/2/3/14487208/pro-life-abortion-movement.
55   Anderson, "People Criticize Pro-lifers."
56   Anderson, "People Criticize Pro-lifers."
57   Anderson, "People Criticize Pro-lifers."

but love, awe, admiration, and recognition of our interrelationality that motivate participation in the pro-life movement.

Anderson names abiding, deeply felt human truths that are at home within Todd Peters' reproductive justice framework. Both presuppose a reverence for women's reproductive capacities, but Todd Peters centers wonder about new life in a way that makes room for those capable of giving birth to decide whether or not to continue a particular pregnancy. Anderson insists it is "egalitarian" to value embryonic life because it is not conditioned upon knowing whether that embryo will become the next Beethoven. According to Anderson, there is an urgent sense that the prenate's inherent value shines more brightly than the value of an existing gestating woman, *except* insofar as she remains in the glory of a sacrificial pregnancy, which other Christians should be moved to support in emotional and material ways (however insufficiently in practice):

> For the pro-lifer, there is no clearer instance of the marginalized, the voiceless, and the vulnerable than in the womb—and no more profound source of wonder at the limitless possibilities that human life is capable of achieving. The early embryo looks nothing like us, has none of our capabilities, drains the mother's resources, and often requires the mother to sacrifice many of her interests. If in these conditions one can see something worthwhile, something that can be a benefit or a blessing to the world even when unwanted, then one can start to glimpse why pro-lifers are so animated and so patient in their efforts.[58]

Maternal self-sacrifice reflects and inspires the most profound human ideals. But the adoration of the prenate and of its mother motivates political action that would enforce this ideal upon non-consenting women in a way that other ideals of self-sacrifice are not mandated. The justification for this selective idealism would seem to turn us from arguments informed by pregnancy's moral beauty back to arguments about the criminalization of abortion—both of which would render normative the expectation that any pregnant woman serve as an icon of Mary. Before the dual awe in Anderson's defense of the pro-life movement, a woman, once pregnant, may be revered and valued only if she consents to continue that pregnancy.

---

[58] Anderson, "People Criticize Pro-lifers."

The flip side of Anderson's adoration of mothers is Kreeft's demonization of women (who abort, who do not conform to mothering
norms). Although Anderson and Kreeft have different attitudes towards
pregnant women, the political implications of their positions are similar. Their condemnation of women for a crime (abortion) that men can
never commit in their own bodies is arguably tied to an awareness of the
capacity to do something the men themselves can never do: bring forth
more human beings into the world.

Is such a maternal-worshiping patriarchy a kind of idolatry? Perhaps the
answer to this question is "no" insofar as there is something profoundly true
about the particular life-giving power women possess as birth mothers, but
"yes" insofar as three-dimensional, living, breathing women are eclipsed
whenever in a potent polemical debate they are reduced to their wombs and
their decisions regarding life or potential life within them.

Those who feel deeply that a woman's ability to control her own fertility is both vital and ordinary are attuned to another, yet not wholly other
sensibility of the sacred: one in which there is both awe at the capacity to
bring forth life and an awareness of the fuller textures, dimensions, con-
tingencies, and complications of giving birth and supporting an infant's
life. This is the sensibility at play among those who support a legal right
to abortion, and among those who recognize there are times when they
are certain that, given their circumstances at hand, an abortion is the right
choice for a particular pregnancy of their own. What is sacred here is not
only the ability to birth and nurture a child; the well-being and varied
vocational dimensions of an existing woman's own life are also of spiritual
significance. In addition to her child, she too is in the image of God. A
legal right to abortion allows a woman to discern how to approach the
prospect of bearing a child in a way that also honors her own particular
life and its circumstances.

Some will justify taking away a woman's right to choose to end a particular pregnancy by stressing that the most vulnerable neighbor is never
the pregnant woman, but the one she bears in the womb.[59] Here the parable of the Good Samaritan (Luke 10:25–37) might be recast into the parable of the Good Mother who, weighing the possibility of an abortion,
opts to go out of her way to invest in caring for the fetus, the prenate, the
unborn. Framed as a matter of a prenate's life or death, all other factors

<hr/>

[59] Dan Fienen, "Can We Talk? Another View of the Abortion Discussion,"
Lutheran Forum 54, no 1 (2020): 58–61.

about a pregnant woman's life fade from view and significance—or are cast as practical neighbor-need matters that the rest of the body of Christ should attend to as well, so long as a pregnant woman chooses not to put an end to the particular potential life currently in formation. Those who oppose abortion and call it murder see all of society's moral callousness flowing from legal acceptance of abortion. Those who support the right to an abortion will regard it as something along a spectrum from a tragic to a realistic, long-practiced, ordinary choice of a woman to control her fertility for the sake of her own and her family's flourishing, with a deep and also widely shared intuition that abortion is markedly different from murdering a person already born. As Margaret Kamitsuka notes, citing Jeanne Stevenson-Moessner: the Good Samaritan did not give everything away when he helped the wounded traveler, but retained enough resources to finish his own journey.[60]

Owning the Iconic Consequences

One thing is certain: it matters a lot how we carry or inhabit these competing yet overlapping senses of the sacred with regard to women's capacity to give birth. A refusal to acknowledge the truths and valuations shining in both can impel us to demonize and caricature those who identify deeply with a very different icon of female power and authority—be it an icon of a woman who fiercely protects every unborn child within her and every born child in her care; or an icon of a woman who, with or without children, fiercely guards her sense of what it means to be responsible to her life's circumstances and vocational callings, including deciding whether or not she will continue a particular pregnancy.

Here are two ways of perceiving a wise woman, both with valences of the sacred about them. Some Christians might visualize the first icon in terms of Mary as mother of Jesus; some might depict the second icon as the more properly feminist one. The two icons are compatible wherever a woman fully chooses *of her own accord* to identify with the first icon, even at the risk of her own life when a pregnancy is dangerous to carry to term (and any pregnancy potentially is death-dealing). But the two icons are in tension when a woman is *forced* to identify with the first icon, against her will and her own acute sense of vocation and of the viability of gestating and/or raising yet another child. The second icon never forces a woman to choose against carrying a prenate to term. The second icon stretches to

---

[60]   Kamitsuka, *Abortion and the Christian Tradition*, 172–75.

make room for the development of many Spirit-moved ways of carrying out life as a woman or female-identifying person.

Can we also make space for the dreams and visions of those who surround the life of a pregnant woman? Or is there a space for bearing witness to what one hopes a pregnant woman will do? May we trust that pregnant women are not so fragile that they cannot handle facing diverse moral perspectives about abortion with regard to their own decisions—at least when those perspectives are invitational rather than cruelly on display to a woman walking past taunters to an abortion clinic? Is some level of familial and ecclesial support and respect for her own choice key here? Do we have ideally an obligation to foster the moral freedom to lift up our favorite icons of women with one another, while also acknowledging the others in circulation?

If abortion's legality cannot preclude women from having abortions in the callous way that abortion opponents fear/assume, likewise its legality cannot prohibit moral pressure on women to conform to a maternal icon of virtue that implies shame—even an existential denial of her expected role in creation—for choosing an abortion. The absence of coercion does not mean the absence of competing moral voices—within oneself, one's family, and one's formative faith community. It would be another form of paternalism—as well as nigh impossible—to seek to prevent women from *ever* hearing the voices of those who yearn for every prenate to have the opportunity to be born (and who may even offer resources along the way). Among Christians, it would also be a way of conditioning belonging to the body of Christ on holding identical views about the shape of justice with regard to women's reproductive capacities. Ideally, trusting pregnant women as moral agents means trusting they can sift through the many moral claims brought to bear amid their own vocational, ethical, and practical considerations when they find themselves pregnant—although their ability to do so presupposes both the legal availability of abortion and access to voices that support their own moral discernment as a framing moral good. Only in such a context of support can we risk facing the voices that urge women with unwanted pregnancies to resist abortion. Some of those voices invite reflection as a matter of shared Christian discipleship, as in Catholic ethicist Lisa Sowle Cahill's claim that we sometimes have mutual obligations "to which we have not explicitly consented."[61] Other voices pressure women to

---

[61] Lisa Sowle Cahill, "Abortion, Autonomy, and Community," in *Abortion: Understanding Differences*, ed. Sidney and Daniel Callahan (New York: Plenum Press, 1984), 265; cited in Todd Peters, *Trust Women*, 126.

identify with essentialized gender notions, as in Missouri Synod Lutheran Rose Adle's declaration in a handbook for Christian women that a "lady's place in God's creation was set for her. We didn't get to choose our own space, but this is no injustice. It's simply what it means to be *created*."[62] Such a voice would not exist if a "lady's place" were so obvious, even if some women do welcome the expectations Adle describes. Others find a perspective like Adle's humorous because it is so out of sync with how they and those they know express gendered and familial relationships, though they might find it dangerous to their well-being if their social circle were dominated by a perspective like hers. Is it easier for pregnant women to navigate such dissonance in the moral audiosphere when the legal context (and preferably their communal context) assures that pregnant women themselves have the moral authority to decide how to weigh all ethical considerations involved during a pregnancy—and in fact have access to safe, affordable reproductive care? Surveys reveal that most women do not choose abortions casually.[63] These women recognize abortion itself can be a moral good, even as some women do regard it as a tragic choice.[64] The crucial legal framing that allows women when pregnant to sort out the inner and outer voices they will heed is expressed in a speech Representative Maurice West made on the floor of the Illinois legislature after facing threats to his life for filing a Reproductive Health Act that expanded abortion access: "I'm a black man. My ancestors had physical chains and laws that governed their bodies. We fought a civil war because we [many in the country] wanted to keep black bodies chained and enslaved and now you're asking me, a black man, to put policy chains on a woman's body, on reproductive health. . . . I've decided to trust women to do what's best for themselves. Women, I trust you."[65]

Stories and Macrostories That Hold the Affective Landscapes

Exploring affective landscapes by describing and inhabiting narratives may not take us to a middle ground that satisfies both proponents and opponents of legal abortion. But we hope by this exploration to begin embodying empathetic, non-heretical practices of shared moral deliberation—shared

[62] From the description of Rose Adle, *Christian Life for Christian Women*, Lutherans for Life (St. Louis: Concordia, 2020), 1, https://y4life.org/wp-content/uploads/2020/11/LFL305B_Christian_Life_for_Christian_Women.pdf.

[63] Todd Peters, *Trust Women*, 40–41, 166.

[64] Todd Peters, *Trust Women*, 10, 203–4.

[65] Cf. Rebecca Anzel (@RebeccaAnzel), "Rep. Maurice West (D-Rockford) made a speech on the floor that received applause from his colleagues. Here's a transcription," Twitter, May 29, 2019, 3:57 a.m., https://t.co/cZZt4LoSIB.

efforts to discern and justify our ethical beliefs—that are rooted in mutual listening within the Beloved Community. As with the various ways of imagining how the person and the human and divine natures of Christ relate to one another, we may find that there are some affective landscapes in which more strands around reproductive justice can hold together; or we may find that more than one sort of landscape is sensible, with each tending to foreground or background different sets of goods and harms, different ways of valuing ourselves and one another.

It is precisely this dynamic of making-sense and of not-making-sense that animates and sustains both the hardened convictions and the ambivalences of those who support *or* oppose legal access to abortion. There are worldviews that perceive beauty and goodness in consistently valuing life from the womb to the grave, evoking pieties in which aspiration to a sort of sainthood shines like a sun over all of a person's moral choices. That particular vision of beauty is interrupted by a person whose aspirations, or even sheer survival, are at odds with the choices held out to her as the only good and moral ones. There is likewise an inhabitable landscape that radiates what we might today call a fierce feminist Christian beauty that takes its bearings from Galatians 3:28: "There . . . is no longer male and female; for all of you are one in Christ Jesus." This biblical indicative of equality is a call to abandon essentializing notions of gendered norms and ideals, a world in which all persons are challenged and supported in discerning their individual callings and gifts within the corporate body of Christ. But vocational pulls are messy and a pregnant woman who is not ready to bring a child into the world may wonder how to balance them. Or she may feel the tug and beauty of both worldviews. In short, those who are morally queasy about abortion may also be uneasy about banning it, and those who believe firmly in the right of women to choose to abort may not feel comfortable having an abortion themselves.

How often does theological argument for those opposing legal abortion proceed by way of principles of moral purity rather than by stories of moral complexity? How often is the reverse true in theological arguments that support legal abortion?

Conclusion

We have outlined a process of storytelling that invites attention to ways in which justice-seeking can take place within the Beloved Community. Our commitments to the process are based on the Beloved Community as a space capacious enough for listening and storytelling. Our primary motivation was to imagine a construal of justification and justice-seeking that would facilitate reflecting about—as well as resisting—the one-sided positioning and polemics characterizing this divisive issue of abortion. In our terminology, heresy situates two sides of the abortion divide. The symbol of the coat hanger compresses the many stories of women who have died under illegal abortions; the images of fetal body parts compress the many stories of the unborn and validate their personhood. Silence and shame envelop the divide, while stock stories are circulated for religious identification and political gain.

We wanted to show that even an issue as divisive as abortion can be the subject of a search for something akin to a capacious orthodoxy, one that calls out as heretical a position that refuses to hear what is at stake for those with a different but deeply held vision of justice-seeking about abortion. Justification by faith recognizes that each person is renewed to live within Christian freedom by virtue of our baptism into Christ; justice-seeking acknowledges that diverse persons are needed to engage in articulating any shared vision of justice-seeking—even on issues on which agreement is not yet possible. In the meantime, we wanted to nudge reflection on stories, particularly those mustered to support one's own position, including their intended or unimagined consequences. Those consequences include reckoning with profound moral and theo-logical questions about what is lost through a terminated pregnancy, as well as the concrete economic, material, physical, and spiritual implica-tions of forcing pregnant persons to continue a pregnancy. We have also suggested that behind the abortion debate lies a wrestling with compet-ing visions not only of gender norms, but also of the range of ways that women do and may image the sacred itself.

Acknowledging our baptismal belonging to one another in Christ means recognizing one another as fellow Christians across both our dis-agreements about abortion and the gender norms that circulate within any ethical appraisal of it. Should our moral framework be such that all pregnant women are obligated to give the greatest moral weight to the potential life of the unborn? Should pregnant women be morally expected to conform to the ideal of the maternal? Or ought a society grant primary moral weight to valuing women as persons, respecting their agency to discern how to realize their vocations, and how to navi-gate their network of obligations amid an unplanned pregnancy? When we ponder all these things in our hearts, the greatest challenge might be to perceive that we offer our answers to such questions in the presence of fellow Christians. As two particular women within the body of Christ, we hope that whatever our Christian siblings' respective convictions about the legality and morality of abortion, we can all grow in our capacity to listen to the range and register of pregnant women's lives—affectively, materially, spiritually, and in all ways relevant to a pregnant woman's own inner sense of direction. "Let anyone who has an ear listen to what the Spirit is saying to the churches" (Rev 3:22). To listen to the voice of the Spirit in the church surely involves no less than listening to the breadth and depth of pregnant women's own insights and moral reasoning before the Holy One.

5

Ordinary Faith in Political Justice-Seeking

A Practice of Christian Freedom

Introduction

Justice-seeking inevitably involves politics. As we demonstrated in the previous chapter on abortion, moral deliberation is carried out in the Beloved Community. Christians belong to the Beloved Community because we are justified by faith. Yet our thinking and acting extends beyond the Beloved Community into the political space. Christians offer diverse visions of justice to public spaces of political decision-making. Debate can become intense when different Christian visions clash with each other and with visions offered by other religious and civic communities. Some forget that their Christian neighbors are also part of the Beloved Community and denounce them as "secular" and "demonic." Others cancel their Christian neighbors as "crazy" and "anti-Christian." Christian identities rally political positions; Christian moral deliberation all too easily becomes overt political posturing.

How Christians navigate the political sphere is the serious question all of us who are Christians should be asking today. What does it mean for a Christian to convey Christian faith in politics in a diverse nation? Today, the political discussion is permeated with references to "faith commitments," how various Christian groups vote, and what Christian freedom means in the public square. Voters are interested in the faith commitments of religious leaders, with the implication that affinity of belief implies affinity in voting on some issues. Sometimes Christians vote politicians into office who align political positions with faith-based commitments. Some even insist on a direct link from faith to politics. This public discussion of faith in politics is one that demands reflection, particularly on the part of those who are shy about working out faith in public ways or those who depict their distinctive brand of faith as the only kind that has political purchase. How Christian belonging to the Beloved Community relates to political justice-seeking is the theme we reflect on in this chapter.

While justice-seeking often involves the tussling introduced by opposing positions, what becomes concerning is when Christian identity *itself* is invoked to support a justice issue. In the previous chapter, we discussed a specific issue—abortion. Our solution to the problem of invoking Christian identity as allied with a particular political "pro-life" or "pro-choice" position began with the turn toward a more primary notion of Christian identity—that of belonging to the Beloved Community. By orienting Christian belonging to Christ, and not to a political affiliation, we made the theological claim that a space of belonging to Christ welcomes all Christians, especially those with whom one disagrees. Unity in Christ, given by grace, provides the Christian identity from which the navigation of political positions emerges, but with which it is not conflated. We drew on this theological picture to imagine welcoming others into a space of belonging in which reflective discussion, paying attention to affective tenacities, and thinking "otherwise" could take place. Admittedly justice-seeking is messy and always risks the temptation to self-delusion and demonizing others. But when we are theologically mindful that Christian identity is grounded in Christ, a space of freedom is created from which we are able to regard even our political opponents as coworkers in the same vineyard of justice-seeking.

The current political context is especially challenging because the notion of a shared political space is contested. Especially concerning today is the idea that Christians are free to dismantle a shared political space in the name of advancing a particular justice-seeking vision. When Christians co-opt a pluralistic public space by their particular political interests, they try to restrict that space to one defined by only their own take on faith-rooted commitments. When Christians cancel another perspective—including other Christian perspectives—and refuse to interrogate its merits and demerits, they restrict the public space to the like-minded.

This politicization of Christian identity may seem relatively recent. Like other Western nations, the United States was based on values developed since the eighteenth century that included the expectation that citizens check their religious commitments at the door (or at least bring them into play implicitly rather than in the name of religious authority), in order to engage in coercive-free debate. Of course, this notion does not get at the way that the very idea of the United States is rooted in providential readings of the biblical narrative of Israel as a promised land—a narrative appropriated by many European Christian colonizers and extended to the lands they claimed and settled, displacing Native inhabitants. But the premise of US democracy, with its refusal of an official state religion, includes the notion that religion tended to create unnecessary conflict and that if people just relied on rational processes to articulate their justice-seeking, then just laws and policies would transpire. Yet what this idea did not take into account was the degree to which religion actually plays a huge role in the formation of beliefs about political justice. And it is this recognition that has come into play in a new key in the contemporary US political arena, as well as globally. So the question before us is about the role that religion (in this case, Christianity) plays in justice-seeking, and how religious commitments can be open to debate and discussion, even as they are earnestly expressed and votes rallied to support them.

Here we are particularly disquieted—as we have been throughout the book—that when holding a specific Christian moral position is equated or associated with Christian identity itself, then that particular position will be taken into the public arena as *the* Christian position. In reality, however, Christians often advocate for different sides of any given issue. There are, in fact, diverse and often competing Christian visions for justice-seeking, just as there are different visions proposed by practitioners of other religions or by those who do not adhere to any religion. Hence justice-seeking also involves discussing and navigating among proposals that themselves are based on distinctive ways of understanding how religion is (or is not) relevant to justice-seeking. A theology of justice-seeking includes an assessment of how different perspectives can be theologically framed as integral to justice-seeking. This assessment does not remove struggle from justice-seeking: what is significant is *how* that struggle takes place, and how it might be oriented by a spirit of delightful capaciousness.

We aim here, then, to work out a theology of belonging to the Beloved Community that is open to justice-seeking in the political realm. There are rich and varied ways of relating religious belonging to national belonging—or, classically put, to distinguish yet relate church and state. While we touch on some of those ways, our primary theological premise here stands in the tradition of not conflating the religious with the political, for the Beloved Community is evoked and sustained by God's grace in Christ, not by humans bringing forth a more just world, however they conceive it. The Beloved Community inspires us to compete in sharing, debating, and enacting visions of justice for all the communities in which we dwell and to which we are responsible—including our local, state, national, and global ones. Hence, we presuppose that political justice-seeking is inevitably contested and must remain so if the mutual belonging of Christians—amid their differences—is to be honored. If we are right, then a theology of how faith is navigated in politics must take into account how the political space can be sustained as a place of robust discussion. Indeed, the theological perspective we are advancing here honors Christian differences *and* recognizes that the political process of justice-seeking involves the participation of those who do not consider themselves Christian.

It may be worthy of note that our primary aim here is not to sketch a political or even public theology *per se*. That is, we are not proposing a normative Christian account of forms of government, or of particular justice-seeking public policy approaches (although we do show our hands in finding democratic forms of government the most able to honor religious diversity,[1] and we own the directions our own reasoning tends with regard to various ethical or policy values). In many respects, we assume more than urge Christian engagement in the public sphere; it is Christian dissension about that pursuit which catches our attention. The interface between church and world is always at first (or as well) an interface among Christians with competing ideas about matters of justice or ethics. In that respect, our work contributes to efforts to foster thinking together across differences.[2]

Certainly others have also contributed their careful, focused work on making a case for how Christian theological reasoning can support particular sorts of advocacy directions and forms of justice-seeking. For example, Kathryn Tanner offers a sustained argument about how Christian doctrines (like divine transcendence and creation) can be engaged in a way that supports liberatory movements. She considers a specific pattern of theological reasoning that arrives at justice-related beliefs, as

---

[1]   For two examples of Christian arguments for democracy, see Luke Bretherton, *Christ and the Common Life: Political Theology and the Case for Democracy* (Grand Rapids: Eerdmans, 2019); and Aristotle Papanikolaou's Orthodox Christian defense of democracy in *The Mystical as Political: Democracy and Non-Radical Orthodoxy* (Notre Dame: University of Notre Dame Press, 2012).

[2]   See, for instance, Katie Day, *Difficult Conversations: Taking Risks, Acting with Integrity* (Herndon, Va.: Alban Institute, 2001); Leah D. Schade, *Preaching in the Purple Zone: Ministry in the Red-Blue Divide* (Lanham, Md.: Rowman & Littlefield, 2019).

we did in chapter 3.[3] James K. A. Smith shares our conviction that having an ecclesial center moves one to attend to the common good in ways that critically and self-critically participate in the political sphere. Smith develops the theme of a publicly engaged "resident alien" (attentive to a heavenly city and its king) in ways we do not ourselves hold, although we draw upon other facets of Christian (and Augustinian) theological imagery and history to spur self-aware Christian engagement in public justice-seeking.[4] Smith articulates a liturgical public theology in which a stable church is on edge about its relation to the world. Yet in our work, we invoke the centrality of justification by faith as the defining heart of the Beloved Community whose members are disputing and growing (if eschatologically) toward a shared vision of just relations. Anna Madsen's *I Can Do No Other: The Church's New Here We Stand Moment* may sound closest to our own endeavor in its Lutheran emphasis on justification by faith stretching toward justice. But where Madsen makes "a case that justice, anchored in justification, is our new Reformation moment,"[5] we call for a return to more deeply recollecting justification by faith as the basis for faith *amid* justice-seeking, lest justice *itself* become our creed in ways that define Christian identity around particular views of what justice ought to look like.

None of this is to say that we advocate neutrality about justice-seeking in the world. But if we are right that justice-seeking in ordinary faith resists equating Christian identity itself *with* an "us versus them" position amid ethical, political, and justice-seeking debates, then we are called in Christ to participate in the often painful process of collaborating through and across our genuinely held differences.

Our theological task in this chapter is to offer an account of the participation in politics of both Christians and those who do not identify

---

[3]   Kathryn Tanner, *The Politics of God: Christian Theologies and Social Justice*, 30th anniversary ed. (Minneapolis: Fortress, 2022). Other authors (among many more) who make a case for progressive Christian political advocacy include Ilsup Ahn, *The Church in the Public: A Politics of Engagement for a Cruel and Indifferent Age* (Minneapolis: Fortress, 2022); Guthrie Graves-Fitzsimmons, *Just Faith: Reclaiming Progressive Christianity* (Minneapolis: Broadleaf Books, 2020); E. J. Dionne Jr., *Souled Out: Reclaiming Faith and Politics after the Religious Right* (Princeton: Princeton University Press, 2008).

[4]   James K. A. Smith, *Awaiting the King: Reforming Public Theology*, Cultural Liturgies 3 (Grand Rapids: Baker Academic, 2017).

[5]   Anna M. Madsen, *I Can Do No Other: The Church's New Here We Stand Moment* (Minneapolis: Fortress, 2019), 8.

as Christian, while maintaining that the particularity of Christians has to do with their fundamental belonging to the Beloved Community as the basis for their own participation in justice-seeking. Our interest in keeping politics open to meaningful discussion is particularly pressing in regard to heated issues, such as those discussed in the previous chapter on abortion. It is too easy to resort to power-seeking in the face of incommensurable positions, and thus to foreclose the possibility of coming to terms with stories that might challenge one's position. Yet even as the heresy-like behavior of simplifying a picture of reality is always a danger—we are after all interested beings, keen to make sure that our opinion is heard and followed—we offer a theology of how the voices of people of faith can be robust even amid politically volatile disagreements. Our work, in other words, leaves no room for a Christian position that inserts its power and perspective alone into a space that ought to be kept open for the precise reason that the freedom wrought by justification by faith demands it, for Christians and non-Christians alike.

We applied in the previous chapter a close-angle lens to study the specific contested topic of abortion. Now we use a wide-angle lens to survey the broader questions of how Christian belonging can be navigated in the politics of justice-seeking. How do we make sense of faith in politics, particularly when faith-based commitments can inspire such different proposals on how faith can be active in politics? How do we understand theologically the relationship between belonging to the Beloved Community and belonging to a nation-state as the context in which justice-seeking is pursued?

Christian Freedom in Politics

Talk of freedom in the context of belonging to community can seem odd, especially in these times: does not belonging to a community constrain one to think and act according to what the community dictates? Is not freedom narrowed by community? One is bound to other members of the community who place limits on one's freedom. Yet a particular notion of freedom is central to community, in both a political and theological sense! The term "freedom" is central to US American public discourse: recall the freedoms in the US Constitution, the popular discussions of the freedom to choose, to self-actualize; to wear (or not) masks; and the incessant talk in the public sphere about choice. The imagined "community" of the United States as a nation is informed by freedom as its constitutive concept. But the term "freedom" also plays a major role in theological thinking and is especially relevant in the Protestant tradition that associates the sixteenth-century Reformation with freedom from religious and state tyranny.

In the chapter on justification by faith (ch. 2), we discussed freedom in the soteriological (salvation-minded) sense: freedom is Christ's gift to Christians that releases us from the bondage arising from our sinning and being sinned against. Freedom in this sense *is* justification, and thus the significant marker of Christian existence in the Beloved Community. But this same freedom in justification also frees one *for* attentive service to one's neighbors. The political sphere is one domain in which we express service to our neighbors through laws and public policies—ideally, at least, for laws can do a disservice to our neighbors as well.

The topic of Christian freedom has its classic treatment in Martin Luther's 1520 treatise of the same name, *The Freedom of a Christian.*[6] This treatise is one of three that posterity acknowledges shaped the objectives of the Protestant Reformation. In this treatise Luther focuses on the relation between Christ and the individual; *The Babylonian Captivity of the Church* addresses reform of the church's sacramental practices while *To the Christian Nobility of the German Nation* advocates for reform in the political sphere.[7] This last text is significant because it assigns to the temporal sword the authority to interpret Scripture—a papal prerogative until then—on the basis of the priesthood of all believers. The text on Christian freedom is significant for our purposes because in it Luther advocates a notion of freedom that is determinative of Christian existence *per se*, but that is created solely by Christ's work of justification. Freedom in this sense is constitutive of the "new creation" in Christ (2 Cor 5:17). Luther explains that Christ sets a Christian free from the consequences of disobeying the divine law. The freedom Christ offers undoes the bondage

---

6   Martin Luther, *The Freedom of a Christian, 1520*, trans. W. A. Lambert and Harold J. Grimm, rev. trans. Mark Tranvik, newly rev. Timothy J. Wengert, The Annotated Luther Study Edition, ed. Timothy J. Wengert (Minneapolis: Fortress, 2016).

7   Martin Luther, *The Babylonian Captivity of the Church, 1520*, trans. A. T. W Steinhäuser, rev. trans. Frederick C. Ahrens and Abdel Ross Wentz Newly, new rev. trans. Erik W. Herrmann, The Annotated Luther Study Edition, ed. Paul W. Robinson (Minneapolis: Fortress, 2016); Martin Luther, "To the Christian Nobility of the German Nation concerning the Improvement of the Christian Estate, 1520," trans. Charles M. Jacobs, rev. trans. James Atkinson, newly rev. trans. James M. Estes, in *The Annotated Luther*, vol. 1, *The Roots of Reform*, ed. Timothy J. Wengert (Minneapolis: Fortress, 2015), 376–465.

created by sins committed, including presumptuous attempts to prove ourselves worthy of divine acceptance. It also offers deliverance from bondage to sins of omission, which today we know to include complicity with structures that diffuse power in ways exacerbating injustice. Moreover, although Luther himself mentions this idea more implicitly, Christ offers freedom from our determination by the sins of others, both interpersonal sins and those that entangle us in unjust structures that damage the lives of some to the benefit of others.

Hence freedom in Christ offers forgiveness and soul healing, and with this, the liberty of being a self that, by virtue of being grounded not in itself but in Christ, is free to consider the needs of the neighbor. As Paul put it: "For you were called to freedom . . . only do not use your freedom as an opportunity for self-indulgence, but through love become slaves to one another. For the whole law is summed up in a single commandment, 'You shall love your neighbor as yourself'" (Gal 5:13–14). Consequently, Christian freedom, in Luther's sense, is a space-making operation! Christ sets a Christian free for spacious existence, rather than an existence that feels condemned or restricted. In forgiveness our lives are carried by and in Christ Jesus, whose own earthly journey contended with the legacy of all human sin in a way that opens us to breathe and begin again. Grounded not in ourselves but in Christ, we are able to attend to the needs of our neighbors for their own sake, rather than to earn favor with God. Forgiveness in Christ does not obstruct our accountability to one another, but instead provides a context for mutual accountability that liberates us from trying to do good to others *in order* to prove ourselves worthy before God. To be sure, we might *feel* Christian freedom to varying degrees throughout our lives; the "old Adam" remains with those baptized into Christ. Luther urged daily recalling one's baptism to repeatedly reorient one's life in light of it as a fact to remember—receiving the gift of a more open space in which to listen well to God, others, and ourselves. The political, then, is part of the shared human realm in which Christian freedom fosters spacious vision-seeking, collaboration, and negotiating what it means for needs to be met justly. Christian freedom is thus crucial for grounding the whole of ourselves in Christ while simultaneously making room for others.

What does it look like when we take Luther's idea of Christian freedom into twenty-first-century politics? How can Christian freedom be the way that Christians belong to the Beloved Community while also foraying into the political realm in order to realize visions of justice? In part, as we have been suggesting, freedom means the ability to imagine forms of justice that are commodious of our neighbor's voices—indeed, regarding one another *as* neighbors instead of parceling them out into allies and enemies. This being-set-free-for-spaciousness is a radical idea in a political context that usually polarizes Christians. We tend to exist in groups restricted by ideology, living on one side of a polarity, seeking affirmation of the sanity of our respective worldviews—an affirmation exploited and manipulated by algorithms and informational ecosystems. Such polarization contrasts with the open-spirited attentiveness of Christian freedom.

Yet freedom in the abstract can be a dangerous norm of Christian life. Indeed, the phrase "religious freedom" has many connotations. In the United States historically it has meant freedom *from* the imposition by law of a state religion and freedom *to* practice a life of faith free from government control. The latter has been developed by some Christians to mean an exemption from state and federal laws with which one disagrees on the basis of religious conviction. More broadly, the idea that religion plays significant roles in political justice-seeking situates talk of Christian freedom squarely within the conflicts we experience today around contested moral and political issues. Freedom as a space for shared deliberation can narrow to freedom to dissent, or to impose on all one's own sense of the right position to take on a contested topic.

The Christian freedom we have been describing is not the same as religious freedom in the political sense, but Christian freedom has a bearing on how we in turn practice religious freedom. Indeed, tyranny can arise when Christians assume there is a simple straight line from belonging in the Beloved Community to a particular vision of justice implied by it, without a mediating space of Christian freedom to discern the meanings of neighbor-love in concrete policy ways. This move bypasses justification by faith as the condition of belonging in order to make one's own take on the moral law *itself* become the primary condition of Christian belonging. Some Christians appeal to a notion of religious freedom to further legitimate this conviction that "true" Christians are those who share their own perspective on a politically contested issue. We have seen this recently in the sustained movement of conservative Christians who, in the name of religious freedom from "liberal secular" values, impose their particular take on Christian justice-seeking into the political realm. A civil servant refusing to perform a gay marriage because they can accept only heterosexual marriage on account of their religious beliefs—this is a familiar example of claiming that the freedom to express one's own religious commitment should trump any legal argument that civil servants should carry out their duties to the state. Is such a refusal of civic duty like, or unlike, the crossing of the color line in the civil rights movement against legal segregation? Or a church making a sanctuary for "illegal" immigrants? In practice, when claiming religious freedom exemptions from the law, there is a fine line between acting with the attitude that "we alone are Christian" and with the conviction that "this is the truly Christian thing to do."

It is especially the former sort of appeal to religious freedom that we query and analyze. By looking from a theological perspective of ordinary faith, we situate Christian freedom not around extraordinary oppositions between a praiseworthy "Christian" and a demonized "secular" perspective, but around a daily recalled justification by faith in Christ. Thus we endeavor, with the biblical prophets and the gospels, to hear and respond to our neighbors' needs in all their complexity. Christian freedom creates a space for listening, debating, and advocating on behalf of the justice-needs we perceive—a space compatible with democracy itself as a practice of shared public deliberation. This means that Christian commitments can be negotiated in political justice-seeking in ways that acknowledge that justice-seeking cannot—on theological grounds of Christian freedom—be reduced to sheer power-grabbing. Christian freedom is understood and honored when it draws us into engaging in genuine debate about the norms of justice-seeking. What is important is identifying how our own beliefs might foreclose the relevant moral insights of others, and seeking to mitigate that.

We have been presupposing that democracy fosters a political space that assists Christians in navigating Christian freedom by working within a public sphere to practice justice-seeking for the common good. While the term "democracy" has several meanings, here we refer simply to a political system that allows for some means (often electoral) of citizen participation in choosing state decision makers, as well as for articulating different visions of a just society without recriminatory violence, censorship, or persecution. While electoral politics technically allows for majority rule (with a complex relationship in the United States to the judiciary branch, which can override some laws in the name of the Constitution), minority positions may be expressed without censorship. The actual historical expression of these ideals is, of course, tested and contested. And as we are experiencing in our time, although democracy has been the political system in the United States for two centuries, it is fragile. Failures to address the equal humanity of every citizen exert pressure; and the danger of minority rule by sheer power is a pernicious threat. Yet democracy reflects an ideal that inspires its citizens to continue to work to improve it.

What democracy means for Christians is that there is a public or political space for their own contributions to justice-seeking. Christian freedom is not identical to democracy, but like (and with) democracy, Christian freedom makes a space for justifying before others one's beliefs about the nature of justice—whether as an interpretation of the moral law or in the enactment of local, state, and federal laws. And upholding such a space requires a commitment by Christians to learn to disagree and work together toward justice-seeking. Any Machiavellian power move, whether by Christians or any other group insisting on minority rule, is undemocratic—even if it is in the name of justice itself.

In what follows, we sketch some of the patterns in Christian expression of politically engaged justice-seeking in our context of the United States, albeit with some reference to other countries whose Christian political movements are understood by US Christians in various ways. We invite our readers to use the theological lens of Christian freedom to assess the ways that Christians pursue justice-seeking in the political realm, wherever they may themselves dwell. There is a normative *process* implied by our appeal to Christian freedom in the context of justice-seeking. In chapter 6, we will revisit some of the spiritual practices for justifying beliefs that we described in chapter 3, with an eye to reflecting critically on ways that we as Christians engage in justice-seeking in a public realm. Here we highlight one theological tool that can help us discern when we are practicing a capacious sense of Christian freedom in the public square, or when we are instead foreclosing it.

One theological conceptualization of sin that can be utilized in a self-reflective practice of Christian freedom is a right understanding of the term "heresy." Christians who maintain that their moral position is the sole marker of Christian identity and on that basis insert it into the political as the sole normative position not only betray democracy but, theologically speaking, promote heresy. This is not to suggest that there is a moral equivalency among all positions on a contested political or cultural issue. But importantly, in contrast to Christians who equate certain moral or ideological positions with heresy, we have argued that heresy involves attending to one particular truth (if it is indeed a truth rather than a falsehood) and ignoring all other relevant insights or truths. For example, Trump's election in 2016 directly appealed to white evangelical Christians on the basis of opposition to abortion in a way that asked these Christians to become oblivious to various problems, to the point even of the demise of democracy, in order to secure Supreme Court nominees who would overturn *Roe v. Wade*. The abortion issue in particular (with a host of accompanying issues, such as voting rights) has become rife for political maneuvering wherein Christian approaches to it do not allow space for Christian freedom but practice heresy in the name of opposing the "heresy" of abortion. Again, we are using the discourse of heresy here in a heuristic sense, for historically heresy is not about perspectives on justice so much as about doctrinal "choices" regarding how Jesus is to be construed in relationship to God. But heuristically used in a landscape of Christian moral (and political) debate, heresy means placing restrictions on our freedom of listening with nuance and care to others—and doing so in the name of legitimating our own positions. Likewise, just as the process of forming orthodoxy—by finding creedal expressions that synthesize apparently competing insights—is one expression of Christian freedom to converse together about truth and justice, by analogy, in practicing Christian freedom amid justice-seeking, we can slip past the overt marking-out of political positions on genuinely contested moral issues, into a space of listening for where in our opponents' views we can affirm something at stake or of shared concern.

In the political realm, Christian freedom presupposes a living, lively space for sorting out different visions of justice-seeking. If Christian freedom means there is no direct line from Christian identity to political positioning, then there must be a space for navigating and debating different political positions. Christian freedom demands hard work, a lifelong practice of keeping horizons open for justice-seeking together. Reflecting, feeling, and listening clear a space between justification by faith and the justifications for our respective political positionings. Here an orthodox use of Christian freedom is not about holding one's own view of the moral law wherever it is defensibly contested, but about the process of really listening to what's at stake for one another as we journey toward a synthesis that integrates some intuitions and prompts conversion or repentance of others—a journey that may be eschatological, if not simply centuries long.

Recognizing Christian freedom also provides a theological way to acknowledge religious voices in the political sphere while maintaining democracy and curbing on theological grounds illegitimate appropriations of government power. When Christian freedom is misunderstood, Christian identity is co-opted in favor of one political position that is pursued as an end in itself using whatever power one can find at hand—thus corroding democratic justice-seeking. Christian freedom has also been weaponized against non-Christian groups, to marginalize people of other religions or no religion in the public sphere and render them second class.

This is not to suggest that neutrality (or holding all positions as equally worthy) is implied in Christian freedom to love the neighbor in democratic spaces of shared deliberation. A powerful model of advocacy amid democratic pluralism is Martin Luther King Jr., the Christian civil rights leader who articulated a multifaceted vision of the Beloved Community that is at once Christian and pluralistically national. While he may not have explicitly described Christian freedom as creating space for sorting out competing convictions about the shape of justice, he presupposed a shared public space for democratic deliberation and moral exhortation to express his deep belief that Christian and national ideals of justice demanded the end of legalized racial segregation. Indeed, while Christian freedom in theory and in history makes space for a notion like "separate but equal" as one way of envisioning right relations among people (a view once earnestly held by many white Christians and still in circulation), the success of the civil rights movement—to the extent it succeeded—depended in part on Christians who made a persuasive case that all humans are made in the image of God, and thus equal in the eyes of God and (ideally) of US law. While the end of legal segregation had unintended consequences (like the replacement of Black teachers with white ones in integrated schools), it marked a shift in the national narrative about racial justice such that white supremacy became seen as a deviation from a national norm, and theologically as a position calling for white repentance.

Indeed, examining King's theology allows us to jump into one recurring theme in US politics and in anxieties about national identity: contestation about the nature and virtue of the United States as a country built around not only geographical boundaries, but also ideals of democracy, liberty, and justice for all. Engaging King allows us to reflect on what has historically been called church-state relations not abstractly, but in a way that is embedded in the thickness of US political, ideological, and theological debate—and, indeed, *judgment*—about the virtue or vice of the United States itself. Here notions of national belonging drink deeply from Christian images of belonging to the kingdom of God, the promised land, the Beloved Community. Indeed, King taps into legacies of both church and nation that long precede him. We will revisit those complex legacies, for they remain at play in contemporary polarized political discourse. But King's construal of religious and national belonging illuminates one compelling Christian approach to justice-seeking that reckons with the sin and redemption of a nation long stamped by racism—one prominent expression of injustice that contemporary US Christians (and US Americans more broadly) debate about in another way: by asking whether or not racism still exists, and whether or not it defines the nation in an essential or accidental way.

We will return to consider some of these live questions about national identity, considering them through a theological lens of Christian freedom to deliberate about the shape justice takes in a country with a history of racism and colonization. First, though, let us take a closer look at the justice-seeking theology and practice of one of the most paradigm-setting US Christian leaders who thought and acted in concert with a national justice-seeking movement that both preceded and followed him.

Martin Luther King Jr. and the Controversy about National Imaginaries

We have claimed throughout this book that belonging to the Beloved Community is fundamental to Christian identity: Christ frees the sinner for belonging, along with others, to Christ's body. This primary belonging frees Christian identity from ultimate identification with a political position, and it frees a Christian for political engagement with others, even with those with whom one disagrees. The distinction is crucial; belonging to the Beloved Community is based on Christ's action and is distinguished from political action as a practice of human freedom.

We turn now to address Christian engagement in politics, specifically how theology can help us understand the kinds of political belonging that intersect (in some way) with Christian identity, in particular national identity. National belonging is a belonging of a distinctive sort. Any justice-seeking in the political realm presupposes national belonging and a commitment to it and to the local, state, or regional orderings of belonging within it. Furthermore, national belonging holds some of our deepest convictions about belonging and what justice within that belonging entails. For example, human rights and freedoms are guaranteed to those who belong to the United States, at least on paper. And concerns for justice have to do with the concrete awarding of those rights and freedoms to citizens or inhabitants. Any casual observer of a country's political debates and cultural tensions can see that what is at stake are value-laden notions of what belonging to a country is imagined to be. Here we examine how a theological perspective that orients a distinction (yet relation) between the Beloved Community and political justice-seeking facilitates ways of self-critically imagining freedom and belonging in the political realm.

We begin with Dr. Martin Luther King Jr., whose term "Beloved Community" we have been using throughout this book. We think that King's important and influential vision of justice can orient us in making a theological distinction between the Beloved Community and justice-seeking in the first place, as well as in identifying the conditions that are needed to stay committed to justice-seeking, in view of both the inheritances of American history and current criticisms that seek to narrow American democracy as a place for justice-seeking by groups with different interests.

King's God of Love and Justice: Connecting Christian and National Belonging

Dr. Martin Luther King Jr. is recognized as the extraordinary and courageous leader of the civil rights movement from the 1960s, although the movement was blessed with many capable leaders, including women like Pauli Murray, who were at the forefront of major actions. King was pastor of Ebenezer Baptist Church in Atlanta, a theologian with a PhD from Boston University, a Nobel Peace Prize laureate, and an icon of the civil rights movement. His advocacy for peace during the Vietnam War and his increasing concern with wealth inequality were the focus of his work before his assassination on the balcony of the Lorraine Motel in Memphis, Tennessee on April 4, 1968. While his contributions to civil rights are the subject of ongoing appraisal, including in conversation with the Black Power approach of Malcolm X, the significance of his theology of justice-seeking on the basis of the Beloved Community is of interest here.

While King is commonly known as a civil rights leader, he was also a theologian. As such, he was attuned to God—the word "theology" contains the word "God" (in Greek, *theos*). Significant for King is how he understands God from two perspectives: from both a personal theistic lens—as in the personal God of Christian faith—and a "metaphysical" perspective—God as a force transcending history and guiding it toward an ultimate good end. King uses theology to frame these two perspectives on God in distinction from and in mutual relation to each other in order to secure the integrity of faith while also assigning a theological meaning to political justice. In other words, King uses theology to conceptualize God's significance for Christian belonging to the Beloved Community while also orienting this God, albeit in a more metaphysical sense, toward a public that includes many proposals of justice-seeking.

A key text in which King documents this double theological perspective is an essay, "Pilgrimage to Nonviolence."[8] Here King offers a brief intellectual autobiography in which he documents his synthesis of different theological inheritances. King identifies first his training in the liberal Protestant theological tradition. He studied German Lutheran theologian Paul Tillich and American theologian Henry Nelson Wieman, criticizing their nonpersonal ideas of God that King perceived to be prohibiting God's personal relationship with humans. A personal theism is, for King, crucial for orienting a theological framing for Christian identity that grounds political action.

Yet King does not dismiss this liberal tradition entirely. He appropriates it in order to articulate a theological idea about God's providence in history. This view is behind the famous phrase, "The arc of the moral universe is long, but it bends toward justice."[9] The phrase is important because it can be interpreted in light of King's double perspective on God. First, the phrase presupposes a Reformed theological understanding of a transcendent God who guides history toward a final cause, namely, justice. This guiding governance of world history is what the Reformed theologians understand by divine providence. But King insists that the "arc of the moral universe . . . bends towards justice." This phrasing is deliberately non-theological, but in its orientation, invokes a kind of metaphysics of history. History has a purpose, justice; historical moments, however ambiguous, can be meaningful by imagining them as contributing to this arc of justice.

King's twofold theological perspective functions to open a theoretical space—from a theological perspective—for a public realm that is inclusive of different visions of justice-seeking. Those in that sphere are not required to "believe in God." Their participation in justice-seeking has its own integrity based on individual and communal commitments. Yet

---

[8]   Martin Luther King Jr., "Pilgrimage to Nonviolence," in *A Testament of Hope: The Essential Writings and Speeches of Martin Luther King, Jr.*, ed. James Meville Washington (New York: HarperOne, 1991), 12–15.

[9]   Dr. Martin Luther King Jr., "Remaining Awake through a Great Revolution," speech given at the National Cathedral, Washington, D.C., March 31, 1968, https://seemeonline.com/history/mlk-jr-awake.htm; for a history of this quotation (back to Theodore Parker in the nineteenth century), see "The Arc of the Moral Universe Is Long but It Bends toward Justice," *Quote Investigator*, November 15, 2012, http://quoteinvestigator.com/2012/11/15/arc-of-universe/.

King is able to frame their vision of politics from a theological perspective, namely, God's providence. Those who believe in a personal God are invited to consider others working with them on justice-seeking as participating in the same aim of justice. King does not coerce non-Christians to believe in this same God. Rather he offers Christians a way of conceptualizing their belief in a personal God as open to a metaphysical construal of history. As such this view offers to Christians a way of envisioning room for and trust in the public to contribute to justice-seeking without eroding or limiting it. God is "behind the historical scene," so to speak, guiding humans as they establish justice for marginalized populations whose justice is still outstanding. And it is this commitment that gives King the space to acknowledge different visions as working together for this aim.

King deepens his theology for Christians to work out an understanding of God. He first insists on the perniciousness and complexity of human sin to correct an overly optimistic appreciation of human goodness. Human existence is fragmented, alienated, and anxious.[10] On a decidedly Augustinian basis, King then articulates a theology of salvation focused on the personal God's invitation into the Beloved Community. King is adamant about the nature of this invitation: God acts in the Beloved Community to transform its members through the power of divine love. Love is "agape"—the attribute that the New Testament predicates of God (cf. 1 John 4:8). It is also the soul-force that empowers persons to turn the other cheek (cf. Matt 5:39) and to love one's enemies (cf. Luke 6:27).[11] Love is a dynamic power that grounds the Christian community. Yet this love attains its transformative power through a distinctive action. Love is a divine attribute that reveals itself in the suffering on the cross. King's Christologically derived understanding of love resonates with Martin Luther's sixteenth-century insight captured in the 1518 Heidelberg Disputation that divine love is transformative because its power turns hate into love, death into life. Only from Christ's cross can love be understood to achieve transformative power through suffering.

As a Christian theologian, King is keenly attuned to the particularity of Jesus as embodying the transformative power of agape. Jesus is the One who grounds the spiritual transformation needed in the soul as a prerequisite for working justice in politics. Jesus frees the self from determination by racist structures and violence. A new identity, one born of Christ's redemptive suffering, invites transformation and sharing in this

---

[10] King, "Pilgrimage to Nonviolence," 37.
[11] King, "Pilgrimage to Nonviolence," 38.

new identity. As such, a Christian experiences freedom from a cycle of hatred and violence by transcending it, elevating a human self onto the ground of a new being—the being of Christ-centered transformation that is extended to the Beloved Community.

But God is also providential, guiding history to justice. King can take up his Christian theological notion of divine love and expand it—in metaphysical terms—to existential and social transformation. We can see this theological expansion when King writes about his inspiration from Gandhi's commitment to nonviolent resistance spurring on India's political emancipation from Britain: "I came to see for the first time that the Christian doctrine of love operating through the Gandhian method of nonviolence was one of the most potent weapons available to oppressed people in their struggle for freedom."[12] King's theology is wonderfully capacious: given his twofold theological perspective, he can expand a Christology of redemptive suffering to include Gandhi's notion of "satyagraha" (truth-force). For King, non-Christian visions of justice-seeking can demonstrate redemptive and transformative love: "So the nonviolent approach does not immediately change the heart of the oppressor. It first does something to the hearts and souls of those committed to it. It gives them new self-respect; it calls up resources of strength and courage that they did not know they had. Finally, it reaches the opponent and so stirs his conscience that reconciliation becomes a reality."[13]

King's theology of God's love and justice allows Christians to conceptualize political justice-seeking in theological terms that do not explicitly have to be shared by their non-Christian neighbors. King's appeals to justice in view of the US Constitution make this point. American citizenship guarantees rights and freedoms under the law. Yet in the case of oppressed populations, these rights and freedoms are still wanting. The theological claim differs from the political claim in that theology works with the doctrine of God and politics is oriented to the US Constitution. Yet both theological and political claims dovetail in insisting on rectifying deficient justice. King offers a theological vision of justice-seeking that invites agreement from non-Christian persons who prefer to think in political terms about issues of justice. His theology opens up a space for reflection on and work toward justice by those who might disagree on the theological terms for that space, while agreeing on the nature of the vision.

12   King, "Pilgrimage to Nonviolence," 38.
13   King, "Pilgrimage to Nonviolence," 39.

Crucial is King's two-pronged theological argument for why Christians can join together with those who do not have Christ as a primary faith focus and work together for political justice. King theologically frames political action in ways that recognize others along this road to realizing a vision of justice-seeking. The doctrine of God is used to make a space for Christians and non-Christians to identify unjust laws and to promote a democracy that actualizes rights and freedoms for all its citizens. The doctrine of Christ is used to establish the Beloved Community as a space for Christians and non-Christians to ground their freedom from external determination by racism and violence in a spiritually transformative community. While Christians attribute this to Christ, they invite non-Christians into the space that is cultivated for the purpose of freedom to love first themselves and then their oppressors in ways that exchange hate for love, injustice for justice.

King's vision compels precisely because it complicates both a secular account of political justice-seeking and the restrictions imposed by the "culture wars." King's terms are theological: there is a place for religion in politics, and hence it is important to cultivate religious arguments that can be made in the public square in ways that bring others on board. His own theological model demonstrates how different religious and non-religious commitments can contribute to justice-seeking. The public arena must not be co-opted by one religious group, leading thereby to a limited notion of justice. Rather plurality must be sustained in order to facilitate the contributions of different perspectives, religious and secular, and as such, invite a shared working toward a more expansive justice.

Competing Theologies/Ideologies ("Imaginaries") of the Nation in Light of Justice-Seeking

We have highlighted how King's vision of the Beloved Community drew religious and non-religious citizens alike to participate in anti-racist justice-seeking. However, what focusing on the Christian-multifaith-secular dimension of the civil rights movement elided was the resistance to that vision, most often by white Christians of the time who either openly opposed racial integration, or who were simply uncomfortable participating in public nonviolent resistance to segregation. Sympathetic white Christians might rationalize their non-participation by citing the inadequacy of trying to change a law that would not itself erase the racism in the hearts of white people. Moreover, while the civil rights movement succeeded in ending segregation and expanding voting rights (at least for a few decades), often forgotten in the national narrative around MLK Day (the third Monday in January although King's birthday is January 15, 1929) are King's more controversial efforts to speak out about other justice-related issues, like ending poverty and US imperialism in the Vietnam War—not to mention police brutality against Black bodies. If MLK Day's existence attests that a majority of the country now believes that persons should be judged by the content of their character rather than by the color of their skin,[14] it also conceals ongoing ideological disputes about the moral and even metaphysical legitimacy of the United States as a nation, disputes that the Christian right and the Christian/progressive left have often cast as incommensurable.

Tucked into these ideological disputes about national identity are existential cries for belonging in concrete ways to one's community and country—from people of color who continue to live in a climate of systemic discrimination (from redlining to forced sterilization to racial profiling), to those with white working class and rural grievances.[15] Baptismal belonging to the Beloved Community offers us bearings for knowing that we ultimately matter to an intimately attentive God. But we inevitably need to care and be cared for within the texture of many layers of belonging, from the familial and local to the national and beyond. Often identifying with intermediary affinity or shared-interest groups seems to suffice to meet our need for being heard and validated in our person as well as our beliefs, such that we may be inclined at that point to switch off our reflections about any unintended consequences of our beliefs, or we may cease trying to dialogue with members of political groups that might disparage our own.

In addition, Christian freedom to attend to the needs of our neighbors for their own sake is hard to practice without centering some more than others in our respective moral imaginations. Does trying through policy changes to center people of color in metropolitan areas mean that the latter have no obligation to understand or care about the economic or

[14]   Martin Luther King Jr., "Read Martin Luther King Jr.'s 'I Have a Dream' Speech [Washington, D.C., August 28, 1963] in Its Entirety," *NPR*, updated January 16, 2023, https://www.npr.org/2010/01/18/122701268/i-have-a-dream-speech-in-its-entirety.

[15]   Tex Sample, *Working Class Rage: A Field Guide to White Anger and Pain* (Nashville: Abingdon, 2018); Katherine J. Cramer, *The Politics of Resentment: Rural Consciousness in Wisconsin and the Rise of Scott Walker* (Chicago: University of Chicago Press, 2016).

land-based concerns of rural white or indigenous communities (or vice versa)? What has New York City to do with Seney, Michigan, or Butte, Montana? It is not hard to understand how the geographical vastness of the United States alone can leave many to feel left out of national narratives and media portrayals, for one reason or another. Moreover, we all know (and some of us may be) persons whose capacity for empathy overwhelms them if they try to take in more than a fraction of the enormity of human and planetary suffering. We are finite in our capacity to love concretely our neighbors as ourselves not only interpersonally, but also in our time, energy, and emotional fortitude for participating in local, national, or international policy analysis and advocacy on all manner of justice issues.

Nevertheless it matters how, as Christians, we call to mind our primary belonging to Christ—and to one another and the whole of creation in Christ—in relation to the intermediary communities of belonging in which we practice justice-seeking. In liturgy and the sacraments, in praise songs and small group studies, in private and shared prayer and Scripture reading, we are reminded to perceive the whole of our lives in relation to the reality of God, the Beloved Community, and God's larger creation on which the well-being of every one of us depends. If in those devotional spaces we equate the church or Beloved Community with a particular country, social movement, or political group, we risk a destructive idolatry by sacralizing that nation or movement, perceiving sacred energy in it—up to the point of perceiving eschatological fulfillment in a particular election or movement success. Mid-twentieth-century writers like H. Richard Niebuhr, Reinhold Niebuhr, and Paul Tillich wrote perceptively about idolatry of this sort, mindful of Germany's fall into fascism, and mindful also of the liberal Protestant embrace of the US nation in its uncritical support of the war effort of World War I.[16] Yet we know that even if we try to avoid making our national, political, or social identities an idol—or what Tillich also called an inadequate "ultimate concern"—the finite still mediates our relationship to the infinite. Or, as Augustine voiced in his commentaries on 1 John, there is a coinherence

[16]   H. Richard Niebuhr, *Radical Monotheism and Western Culture* (Louisville: Westminster John Knox, 1993 [1972]); Reinhold Niebuhr, *Moral Man and Immoral Society: A Study in Ethics and Politics*, foreword by Cornel West, Reinhold Niebuhr Library (Louisville: Westminster John Knox, 2021); Paul Tillich, *Dynamics of Faith* (New York: Harper & Brothers, 1957).

between our love of God and love of neighbor.[17] When is what we are calling an intermediary kinship belonging (like a nation, political party, social movement) a creaturely gift through which we iconically perceive and are perceived by God, as we seek together to promote justice and flourishing? When is an affinity group instead for us an idol that we confuse with God or with the will of God—the recognition of which can prompt repentance? *How* we recall our primary belonging to one another in Christ shapes how we answer such questions with our lives.

With such profound spiritual concerns in mind about how we invest in political projects, let us turn to look theologically at some of the competing ideas among US Americans about our nation-state and how to live with its often unpalatable legacies. Construed theologically, whether Christians regard our own respective nations as essentially or accidentally sinful influences whether we are more or less inclined to trust the means of political decision-making within them. So too does how we interpret the actors, movements, and systems that seem to thwart justice-seeking: do we see our opponents as lost and misguided, or demonic? Can we perceive what human needs and visions of justice they are taking their bearings by, and why?

King understood himself to belong to a nation that had not lived up to its democratic ideals. National belonging presupposes our collective responsibility for upholding democratic ideals articulated in the Constitution, yet also for revising laws in light of emerging understandings of how deficient justice can be rectified. According to King, we belong to an imperfect nation and our taking responsibility for it presupposes trust in a providential God who guides the nation toward more adequate justice. God's providence provides a frame for picturing belonging and responsibility together. Justice-seeking is rendered a responsibility in an unjust institution that is not *itself* essentialized as evil. Herein lies King's resistance to revolution—a theological vision of justice that invites those who belong to be responsible for lifting up its ideals and making them real, working through their country's institutions and legal frameworks. To cite the Jewish biblical scholar who recognized King's moral leadership, Abraham Heschel notes, "few are guilty, all are responsible."[18]

---

[17]   Augustine, *Homilies on the First Epistle of John*, ed. Daniel E. Doyle and Thomas F. Martin, trans. Boniface Ramsey (Hyde Park, N.Y.: New City Press, 2008).

[18]   Abraham Joshua Heschel, "What Manner of Man Is the Prophet?" in *Abraham Joshua Heschel: Essential Writings*, selected and ed. Susannah Heschel (Maryknoll, N.Y.: Orbis Books, 2011), 62.

By perceiving a compatibility between the gospel and the US Constitution, King understands the United States as a nation that is still becoming more truly a "promised land": "I've been to the mountaintop. . . . I've seen the Promised Land. I may not get there with you. But I want you to know tonight, that we, as a people, will get to the Promised Land."[19] Here King identifies a trope used by European Protestant immigrants. In using it, King trusts that the idea or ideal of the US nation-state is essentially sound, even if—like the human race—it has fallen into bondage to sin—including an original sin of racism.

But not all who are social-justice minded are convinced that the US nation can be redeemed from its colonial and national past. Both secular and theological visionaries and critics today often speak of an "otherwise"—a way of imagining a non-oppressive world that reminds us that the present order of things is not inevitable, natural, or final. Those who appeal to an "otherwise" might or might not feel invested in the institutions of their nation-state, depending on the degree to which they seek to work through or apart from political institutions to pursue that "otherwise." The otherwise is thus one way of conceptualizing a critical imaginary about a nation. Considering such imaginaries with a theological and ideological lens can be helpful in assessing how our political participation as Christians interacts with trends toward either authoritarianism or democracy.

Indeed, what is often called the "culture wars" are in part a debate about how we imagine the essential and unique identity of our nation-state, or about what we might call our national "imaginaries." Is the United States a nation of individuals in pursuit of liberty? Is liberty about the freedom from the tyranny of state mandates? Or is that liberty release from systemic oppression on the basis of race, religion, gender, sexual orientation, ability, and other particular embodied identities? Is the blend of biblical and Enlightenment ideals of freedom, justice, and liberty for all a basis from which to build and critique our common life together? Or is the essential nature of the country so stained from its beginnings by a legacy of racism, slavery, and settler colonialism that the American project is defunct and in need of new apocalyptic, revolutionary transformation? Or, as white Christian nationalists espouse, is the essential nature of the

---

[19]   King, "I've Been to the Mountaintop," Memphis, Tenn., April 3, 1968, quoted on the website of the American Federation of State, County and Municipal Employees, https://www.afscme.org/about/history/mlk/mountaintop.

country in need of rescue from criminalized foreigners, and from liberals who want both to take away individual liberties (like Second Amendment rights to gun possession) and to center those historically marginalized through reparations and redistributions of power?

Notice that these national imaginaries more or less describe the same ideal virtues and values (freedom, justice, liberty), blended with either nostalgia for a pure or mythic time when they shone forth (a past time of national well-being) or with acknowledgment that there is a long, if shifting, history in which those ideals apply more to some persons than to others. Ironically, those drawn to the former imaginary might mix their nostalgia with an assumption that the sins that the national reckoners seek to redress are all sins in the past. In this respect, Christians engaged in both sides of the "culture wars" are in some sense acknowledging that justice-seeking in the Americas works with the legacy of the European Christian colonization of the Americas. The relations of immigrants to indigenous populations, sovereignty over land as property, and enslavement and exploitation of those who work the land: all these frame an American myth of who belongs. The identity questions at the heart of the culture wars enact competing ways of reckoning with this legacy. Whether in selective apologetics, historical denial, or in denunciation of a settler colonialist legacy, ways of imagining (and interrogating) belonging to America intertwine with ways of imagining the shape of justice-seeking.

Consciously Christian identities intersect with these various national imaginaries as held-in-the-heart-and-mind spaces in which to envision and seek justice. In a country with a discourse of freedom of (and from) religion, with no state-mandated religion, the voluntary association of religious and other group affiliations means that US Christians' power in the political sphere is exercised in part through persuading others of the rightness of our own visions of national identity and the meaning of national values like freedom, justice, and liberty. As we saw with King, one avatar of the civil rights movement, we can do this through imagined pictures of national identity and belonging which function as a kind of "sacred canopy"[20] for political justice-seeking, even if those pictures are not explicitly interpreted theologically or fleshed out in detail. But other ways of imagining the essential nature of America (in any of the American

---

[20] Peter L. Berger, *The Sacred Canopy: Elements of a Sociological Theory of Religion* (New York: Anchor Books / Doubleday, 1969).

continents, potentially) are either defensively irenic or apocalyptically critical. We look briefly at the attacks on teaching critical race theory as one window on these respectively more sanitizing and more damning accounts of (US) America.

Anti–Critical Race Theory (CRT) Rhetoric as a Window into Competing National Imaginaries

As we write, some US states have passed laws banning the teaching of CRT and LGBTQ+ awareness in primary and secondary education.[21] Many have noted that few who are suddenly espousing "anti-CRT" rhetoric really know what CRT is: a legal theory that attends to ways that local, state, and federal laws have been used to systematically discriminate on the basis of race. While Jim Crow laws of racial segregation might be discussed in K–12 contexts, rarely are the fine details of—say—zoning laws that redlined neighborhoods and perpetuated low property values in predominantly Black and Brown neighborhoods. Not knowing what exactly CRT means allows it to become a cipher of moral panic about all manner of white fears, from being replaced in numbers and political power by immigrant and BIPOC populations, to white children being taught to think they and their country are essentially racist.

We also write at a time when a religion-averse Black linguist like John McWhorter and a Black evangelical Christian like Voddie Baucham underscore worries about "wokeness" to racism as a "cancel culture."[22] Even if their own critiques are problematic in various ways, they give voice to the sense that if the anti-CRT movement seeks to cancel substantive

---

[21] For example, Daniel Villarreal, "Librarian Resigns after Violent Threats over LGBTQ Books That Aren't Even Available," *LGBTQ Nation*, August 25, 2022, https://www.lgbtqnation.com/2022/08/librarian-resigns-violent-threats-lgbtq-books-arent-even-available/.

[22] For two Black critiques of critical race theory and of anti-racism movements more broadly, see Christian pastor Voddie T. Baucham Jr., *Fault Lines: The Social Justice Movement and Evangelicalism's Looming Catastrophe* (Washington, D.C.: Salem Books, 2021) and linguist John McWhorter, *Woke Racism: How a New Religion Has Betrayed Black America* (New York: Portfolio/Penguin, 2021). While both authors seem to caricature more than listen deeply to those they criticize, they both warn against ways of practicing anti-racism that essentialize Blacks as victims or white individuals as racist, or that violate due process through a "cancel culture" more interested in virtue signaling and scapegoating than in repair and redress. For another important work that dovetails with the claims here, see sociologist Arlie Russell Hochschild, *Strangers in Their Own Land: Anger and Mourning on the American Right* (New York: New Press, 2016).

discussion of racism in education, the anti-racism movement itself can also manifest in ways that bypass due process for persons accused of racism by calling for their resignations or firing, for example, or that condition social acceptance on not challenging or nuancing how a particular person, group, or event is being called racist.

Such identity politics is tied up with imaginaries—ideological and theological—about the nation itself. In both the anti-CRT movement and the anti-racist movement, emphasis can get placed on rightly construing and visibly upholding what we might call theologically the "moral law," such that social belonging can become conditioned upon public expressions of protest against a real or perceived injustice and on rallying around certain attitudes or ideologies about race and US racial history itself. Grievance around the real or perceived experience of being cast out animates both movements. Hence, identity politics gets at the heart of the conditions of social belonging. In the sphere of the state, it is about who has the right to exercise legal and political authority, and with what sorts of laws that govern bodies, lands, and resources. In the cultural realm, the politics of identity can manifest as a hunger for personal purity in a land perceived to have lost its way due to structural racism and/or a seismic shift in who is seen as properly centered and properly marginalized in status and authority. Interestingly, apart from those overtly supporting white supremacy, white persons in both the anti-CRT and the anti-racist movements can be seen as endeavoring to be regarded as not racist, their moral purity in this regard a condition of their continuing to be welcome at decision-making tables as citizens, employees, and community members. Indeed, where worries about leftist cancel culture have the most purchase may be precisely where progressive whites see their own anti-racist "virtue signaling" as a way to preserve their own power and status in a society in which they will soon be a minority (although from another perspective, most Americans have some white ancestry).

Interestingly, the political and religious right's campaign against CRT shares with one strand of Black radicalism a kind of absolutism about the United States as a nation: whereas the former portrays the United States as essentially good, the latter portrays it as essentially racist, a failed project from the start. The debate between Martin Luther King Jr. and Malcolm X was in part a debate about whether integration or separatist Black power was a more effective strategy toward the end of Black flourishing in an unequal society. But at another level, their debate and its trajectories today are about whether or not there is something to work with in the US American political project, period. Is the best path a nonviolent revolution, an apocalypse that envisions collective belonging on colonized indigenous lands of North America with a politics that is free of all taint of a racist construct called the "United States"? Or is it continuing King's path of perceiving racism as America's original sin, which rejects the idea that America itself was created evil from the start (a kind of gnostic vision of nation-state)? Anti-CRT advocates begin with a different theological position, namely, that America has been created good and was not deeply marred by racism. Hence, from their perspective, they see all discussions of systemic racism as invoking a revolutionary rejection of the United States as essentially corrupt. So they seek to erase awareness of racism in the present, if not the past, in the name of not unnecessarily afflicting the comfortable—at least those who seek comfort in their white flesh.

The anti-CRT versus anti-racist debate is a set of responsive readings to the legacy of enslavement and colonization in American history writ broadly—a legacy encompassing both American continents yet situated in the particular idealized history of the US American project. We have no doubt that truly sharing power, including political power, does involve a white reckoning with these inheritances—what Jason Mahn calls navigating away from "the cheap grace of White privilege" and toward "the costly grace of repentant anti-racism."[23] But we also encourage identifying where there *is* a meaningful contestation at play, one in which the decision is not between naming or silencing the empirical history of a country, but—for Christians—about diverse ways of navigating what are in effect ontological questions of national belonging in relation to belonging to the Beloved Community. Toward that end, we consider some of the dreams of an "otherwise" that animate Christian beliefs about justice-seeking within an American context.

Grappling with Diverse Narratives of an "Otherwise" on a Promised Land

In official narratives, the United States was born in a desire to be "otherwise": to be different from Europe by instantiating participatory democracy without the tyranny of a monarchy or official state church. That

---

[23] Jason A. Mahn, "The Cheap Grace of White Privilege and the Costly Grace of Repentant Antiracism," *Currents in Theology and Mission* 47, no. 3 (2020): 8–14, http://www.currentsjournal.org/index.php/currents/article/view/254/282.

otherwise-imaginary was expressed in the rhetoric of the Enlightenment, with its stress on individual liberties and human rights. This Enlightenment vision of an otherwise was enacted in part through violent revolution, an acceptance of the enslavement of those of African descent, a rejection of women's (and many non-white men's) participation in the electoral process, and a continuation of the anti-indigenous policies of Catholic and Protestant European colonizers of the American continents. Despite the commonly known appeal to universal reason rather than religion as the basis for human identity and authority in the Enlightenment, Christian theological ideas have circulated both within and alongside Enlightenment visions.

In the United States, there are at least two qualifiers to the claim that the Enlightenment-born US political sphere is a theology-free zone, either normatively or empirically. The first is stamped into the nation's founding self-articulation. The First Amendment to the US Constitution not only prohibits the establishment of a state church, but also guarantees religious freedom, thus providing a constitutional basis for diverse religious voices entering spaces of political debate and decision.

The First Amendment's tension is debated more commonly and comfortably than the second qualifier: the long Catholic and Protestant colonial history that shaped US attitudes about sovereignty regarding land, property, and belonging. This colonial legacy predates the 1619 events that brought African-born enslaved persons to colonial settlements, which added people-property to the property of place (and of Native lives) claimed by European immigrants and their descendants. Almost three hundred years before the US Constitution, the two swords of ecclesial and state authority (an inherited notion from Europe's Middle Ages) set in motion an insidious American theological-political relationship through an explicitly Christian justification for the conquest and colonization of indigenous American lands. On the eve of the Protestant Reformation, Pope Alexander VI's 1493 papal bull *Inter Caetera* initiated the Doctrine of Discovery, which stated that any lands not inhabited by Christians could be claimed by whatever Christian nation first discovered them. That initially meant Christian Spaniards could lay claim to the Americas, west of a line of demarcation (and east of that line, Christian Portuguese, settling in what is now Brazil). Under the ostensibly different jurisdiction of a Protestant-dominated US government, the Doctrine of Discovery was treated as an inherited European Christian common law to justify US colonization of Native lands as the United States expanded westward over North America. This was formalized through the US Supreme Court in the 1823 case *Johnson v. McIntosh*, in which Chief Justice John Marshall's opinion in the unanimous decision held "that the principle of discovery gave European nations an absolute right to New World lands."[24] Even before this legal decision, Protestant colonial attitudes to American lands had found a Protestant scriptural justification in the seventeenth- to eighteenth-century Protestant colonial period, when Puritans narratively identified with Israel's conquest of Canaan. Even if Puritans were not of one accord about whether or not to regard the indigenous inhabitants as the Canaanites to be killed or displaced, they thought of themselves as the New Israelites who had found the promised land.[25]

American Christian churches began in the late twentieth and twenty-first centuries to voice repentance for this shared Catholic and Protestant theological-political imaginary of the Americas. To take one example, the Evangelical Lutheran Church of America repudiated the Doctrine of Discovery in 2016.[26] Although many European Lutheran immigrants appeared after both the 1493 and 1823 decisions, early twentieth-century US immigration policies directly favored northern European migrations, including those from predominantly Lutheran Nordic countries. Such repudiation implies that Christian imperialism is a sinful way of theologically legitimating governmental authority, and that Christian tradition can be appropriated not only for imperialism and anti-Semitism, but also for consequence-owning, justice-seeking ways of relating church and state, theology and politics. Just as post-Holocaust Lutheran-Jewish dialogue has included Lutheran repentance for the sins of Christian anti-Judaism

---

[24]   "The Doctrine of Discovery, 1493: A Spotlight on a Primary Source by Pope Alexander VI," The Gilder Lehrman Institute of American History, History Resources, https://www.gilderlehrman.org/history-resources/spotlight-primary-source/doctrine-discovery-1493. We are grateful to an anonymous reviewer for noting that the phrase "the doctrine of discovery" is not in Justice Marshall's opinion itself. Rather, it was the background to a point about transferring indigenous lands to US citizens. The 1823 decision clarified that the federal government had to mediate this transfer by itself first purchasing Native lands. See https://supreme.justia.com/cases/federal/us/21/543/#tab-opinion-1922743.

[25]   Alfred A. Cave, "Canaanites in a Promised Land: The American Indian and the Providential Theory of Empire," *American Indian Quarterly* 12, no. 4 (1988): 277–97, https://doi.org/10.2307/1184402.

[26]   Evangelical Lutheran Church in America, *Repudiation of the Doctrine of Discovery, Social Policy Resolution CA16.02.04*, August 2016, https://download.elca.org/ELCA%20Resource%20Repository/Repudiation_Doctrine_of_DiscoverySPR16.pdf.

and anti-Semitism (including Luther's anti-Jewish texts that were utilized in support of Nazism's own anti-Semitism)[27] and soul-searching reflection on how the two kingdoms doctrine was interpreted in a way that co-opted the German Lutheran church into supporting National Socialism's racialized anti-Semitism, so, too, the Evangelical Lutheran Church in America's (ELCA) repudiation of the Doctrine of Discovery emphasizes repentance, reconciliation, and the claim that the Doctrine of Discovery reflects an "improper mixing of the power of the church and the power of the sword" (Augsburg Confession, Article XXVIII, Latin text).[28] The ELCA document does not itself spell out *what* the proper relationship is, short of pulling back from either a theocracy or a theological legitimation of colonialism and its legacy.

Those of us raised in the United States may not yet learn very often about the Doctrine of Discovery in our schooling. All the same, race-related culture wars in the United States reflect a complex mix of efforts to come to terms with the mixed "freedom-from and freedom-for religion" legacy of the US brand of Enlightenment formation in the context of the deeper, longer history of Christian-supported colonialism in both its exploitative conquest and settler modes. Some seek to name and understand that history; some to essentially deny or look away from it. Others work with the ambiguous deployment of the Enlightenment idea of "universal" human rights (and its biblical roots in the idea of all persons as made in God's image), to interrupt the way an ideology of Christian superiority initially stamped the political imagination of European-descent Christians in a way that confined the more egalitarian impulses of the Enlightenment era to "white" men—"white" being a status to which some European immigrant communities (WASP, northern, Protestant) could assimilate more readily than others (Irish, Eastern,

---

27 For more details, see Christine Helmer, "Modernity and Its Contradictions," in *How Luther Became the Reformer* (Louisville: Westminster John Knox, 2019), 63–82. For two examples, see *A Shift in Jewish-Lutheran Relations? A Lutheran Contribution to Christian-Jewish Dialogue with a Focus on Antisemitism and Anti-Judaism Today*, LWF Documentation 48 (Geneva: Lutheran World Federation, 2003), https://lutheranworld.org/sites/default/files/dts-doc48-jewish-full.pdf; and "Declaration of the Evangelical Lutheran Church in America to the Jewish Community [1994]," in *Guidelines for Lutheran-Jewish Relations*, 1998, http://download.elca.org/ELCA%20Resource%20Repository/Guidelines_For_Lutheran_Jewish_Relations_1998.pdf.

28 Evangelical Lutheran Church in America, *Repudiation of the Doctrine of Discovery*.

Southern, Catholic), although in the end, they did. In addition to displacing indigenous peoples from their lands, the United States took nearly a century to end the legal practice of owning people of African descent as property. They took even longer to count most males (1870 with the Fifteenth Amendment) and all females (1920 with the Nineteenth Amendment) as capable of full citizenship in the sense of having the right to vote (Native Americans were not guaranteed voting rights until the Snyder Act of 1924). Theological voices were heard in both support of and opposition to the expansion of full citizenship rights to non-white and female persons.

Some attempt to pacify by declaring that the realities of racism, sexism, and colonial conquest are long past, at least as structural problems. This suggests that in our personal identities and public politics we can live free from such complications on the other side of the First Amendment's resistance to an official authoritative theological voice, the end of slavery with the civil war (despite the betrayal of the Reconstruction project after 1877), and the 1960s' dismantling of many Jim Crow–era forms of legal racial segregation. Some believe these developments collectively redeem and purify the American dream of itself. A chorus of voices protest this narrative, from the American Indian Movement to the Black Lives Matter movement, from the prison abolition movement (highlighting how Jim Crow persists in the disproportionate numbers of arrests and prison sentences among people of color) to the current effort in all sectors of society to develop policies promoting equity, inclusion, and diversity. Still others affirm the legacy of white supremacy and openly or subtly pursue a white Christian nationalism, as if this in particular will "make America great again."

Navigated in relation to Enlightenment ideals of liberty and human rights, justice-seeking as an "otherwise" imaginary is at play in both the Christian right and the Christian left, each seeking to end (or ward off) some particular form of oppression or tyranny. To be sure, the discourse of "otherwise" is most often voiced by those seeking to name and unsettle the settler colonial foundations of the American political project. Theirs is the language of the prophetic, speaking for the marginalized whose access to the promised land has been hindered. But a nostalgia for "making America great again" involves a kind of otherwise imaginary as well. In any case, political energy emerges in a hunger for something perceived to be lost or newly emerging, under threat of ruin or long overdue in fulfillment.

Theologically Assessing Imaginaries of the Nation and the Political Groups that Mediate Them

A vision or imaginary of a nation and its "otherwise"—its flourishing justly—takes form within the context of what functions as politically expressive groups within a nation. For Christians, and for any global religious community, owning and grappling with the consequences of our respective visions of a just nation includes theologically analyzing the perspective on sin and redemption within a particular imaginary about the nation, as well as the means of production of that vision. For instance, if we view a country as morally bankrupt, we might be more drawn to declaring a state of exception to democratic processes and justifying any means to secure power to enact our vision of justice. Later we consider ways that some in the Christian right use Bonhoeffer to justify such a turn to a state of exception. First, though, we ponder an otherwise-vision that perceives the US project as essentially marred by the sin of whiteness.

Any student of the civil rights movement knows that Martin Luther King Jr.'s legacy was contested by other justice-seeking Black Americans who invested instead in the Black Power movement. Preferring Black power to integration with whites, Malcolm X and those in the later Black Power movement had a hermeneutic of suspicion about the likelihood that white Americans would ever truly share power, or reverse patterns of disinvestment in Black communities. Ending legal segregation did not go far enough. Black liberation theology emerged through James Cone[29] as a way to synthesize the insights of both movements, as well as providing a Christian framing for the Black Power movement itself—a framing that drew on the transcendent power of God to call forth something new, to call into question every oppressive earthly political ordering. Here there is more tension than harmony between a vision of the Beloved Community and a vision of the United States.

Afro-pessimism is one familiar name in scholarly circles for the legacy of the Black Power movement's profound skepticism about the US American political project, an attitude amplified and caricatured by anti-CRT activists who perceive in such despair of the American dream a teaching that the United States is founded on racism and white privilege in an ontological way. Some call thus for an apocalypse, a revelation of alternative values that those on the underside of history have been surviving on

---

[29]   James H. Cone, *A Black Theology of Liberation*, 50th anniversary ed. (Maryknoll, N.Y.: Orbis Books, 2020).

all along—values that affirm the full humanity of Black persons.[30] That apocalypse is envisioned in various forms, from anarchist disengagement from the electoral political process and the creation of alternative economies to an awakening among white-identified persons of the need for their own ontological conversion away from whiteness. These radical, to-the-root-of-the-problem approaches have been construed by white conservatives as essentializing white persons as oppressors and the US project as inherently and irredeemably bankrupt.

The Black radical tradition can be a call to despair or to a born-again conversion of the nation. Theologically speaking, it invites us to ask metaphysical questions about our country: what *is* the United States, as a collectively produced and sustained nation-state? Far from being a "city on the hill" or a "light to the nations," as its founders had hoped, is the United States akin instead to the great beast in the book of Revelation—an imperial power that is two-dimensionally drawn as the villain in a dualistic struggle between good and evil? Is the very notion of a promised land tainted by virtue of its appropriation by European-descent Christians who perceived themselves as the covenant people—the new Israelites—free to dispossess indigenous "Canaanites" from their ancestral lands?[31] Is it possible to distinguish between an essential and a fallen nature of that human social construction we call a *country*? Can we rightly take our bearings from the selective ideals

---

[30] For one example, see J. Kameron Carter, "How a Courtroom Ritual of Forgiveness Absolves White America," *Religion News Service*, October 4, 2019, https://religionnews.com/2019/10/04/how-a-courtroom-ritual-of-forgiveness-absolves-white-america/. Reflecting on how the brother of Botham Jean hugged his brother's killer, Dallas police officer Amber Guyger, Carter suggests that "Black forgiveness is part of the ritual work of absolving or extending salvation to America. It is part of the work of re-cohering or saving whiteness in a moment of crisis. Should such black forgiveness be withheld, whiteness or the American religious project would face a potential collapse. It might suffer a 'white out,' a possible end of the world or an end of *its* world." He adds, "But could the end of the world, a white out, be an alternative understanding of forgiveness, perhaps even an alternative religious orientation? Can there be a forgiveness that does not absolve guilt but brings the antiblack world to an end? Could there be a poetics of forgiveness that pressures forgiveness as we know it? Could there be a forgiveness that ends forgiveness, a forgiveness at the end of the world? Let's hope so."

[31] Sylvester A. Johnson, *The Myth of Ham in Nineteenth-Century American Christianity: Race, Heathens, and the People of God*, Black Religion / Womanist Thought / Social Justice (New York: Palgrave Macmillan 2004); and *African American Religions, 1500–2000: Colonialism, Democracy, and Freedom* (Cambridge: Cambridge University Press, 2015).

of a country, like liberty, justice, freedom for all, or democratic participation in political decision-making? Can we do this even if we acknowledge that the country from its infancy has been warped by the original sins of racism, patriarchy, and the Doctrine of Discovery in combination with chattel slavery? What is the path of redemption from such original sin, if the country is not to be read in a Manichean way—a way that suggests it is essentially evil to *be* the United States (or any colonizer-produced American state, for that matter)? Does an ontological anti-Blackness define the premise and practice of the United States? If so, what is the path to justice-seeking within its geographical borders?

Our own instinct is for an Augustinian reading of human political history that resists conflating any vision or practice of a nation-state with the Beloved Community or kingdom of God itself. Yet our finite political forms of organizing human life inevitably remain ways in which we exercise our search for "a more perfect union," an earth in which God's will might be (as Reinhold Niebuhr put it) approximated. All collective human projects can be stamped by both human fallenness and a prophetic imagination that, for Christians, enables critique and a justice-seeking transformation of society through the exercise of political power. An ordinary faith neither ignores nor idolizes the various political orderings of belonging in which we are held and hold one another accountable.

But the abstract ontological question about a nation's very being (imagined and enacted) is answered within what are effectively social and political kinship groupings within a nation—places that meet our affective need to belong in tangible ways to one another within a shared perspective. So our debates about the nature of our country (whatever our country) are bound up with discursive communities with which we relate *within* a nation (and, consequently, in relation to the Beloved Community as well). Those discursive communities might be political party affiliations, issue-oriented activist communities, or ideologically conscious movements like Marxism, anarchism, libertarianism, white nationalism, Black Lives Matter, or any of various conservative or progressive coalitions or think tanks. They might also be local or translocal communities that form around a sense of place or a shared pursuit. Our beliefs about our nation-state are informed by our value-laden ways of envisioning a just society more broadly, but also by our kinship networks that may ally in various ways with visions of local, state, and national belonging. Belonging is always multifaceted.

Because of our affective ties in local or "team-affiliated" communities of belonging, we may not feel a need to think through all the implications of our attitudes about a country's ontological status before God. So we might find it sufficient to identify with those who emphasize the democratic process as worthwhile and with the United States as something fundamentally good in its idealized form, in a way that precludes our attention to the history of structural racism (or: we see this particular history, but only as something accidental rather than essential, and applicable in the past more than the present). Or we may feel free to define US democracy as a fundamentally racist project because our sense of belonging comes from a kinship group formed around Afro-pessimism, and that is enough to sustain us in our daily lives; we do not need to think through the implications for whether or not we vote, or whether or not (or how) to press for an alternative political structure. Barring a unifying national crisis—like invasion by a foreign power—it is our local kinship groups with which we identify for our everyday sense of belonging within the larger imaginary of a nation.

Perhaps because we can avoid being held to account for all the implications of how we regard the ontology of a nation—as essentially or accidentally sinful—we can also be tempted to work through a particular affiliation with our own team (an advocacy movement or political party) to call for moral purity with regard to the nation, and to hunger for it for ourselves. Whether we regard the nation as in need of apocalyptic replacement or repentant reformation, we might be drawn to turning away from the messiness of working toward the common good across our various kinships or affective affiliations and into trying to justify *ourselves* as morally pure. Through our positionality as marginalized, or through our learning a right way of speaking and posturing as privileged, we can turn the search for justice into a search for cultivating our own image of being just. Out of that space, we can also be tempted to practice inquisitorial denunciation as an exercise of moral (if not also coercive) power, by showing we are on the right team and scoring points against our real or perceived enemies. This is one way of describing the practices colloquially known as "virtue signaling" and "cancel culture."

In his own day, Augustine worried about Donatist Christians who made moral purity *the* mark of Christian belonging. Donatists practiced virtue signaling and cancel culture in their criticisms of Christian leaders who tried to avoid persecution by the Roman state. They believed that sacraments performed by any clergyperson ordained by (or in a lineage traceable back to) a bishop who had in some way accommodated a demand made by the pagan Roman authorities—like handing over scriptures or a chalice or pretending to offer sacrifice to the gods—was illegitimate (even if those offending clergy had later repented). Donatists formed their own churches, conditioning Christian belonging—at least for leaders—on being sin-free in relation to an anti-Christian state. Augustine's response was that it was Christ's holiness, not that of Christians (even the clergy), that makes the church holy, including the clergy-led sacraments of baptism and communion. Augustine also justified the violent suppression of Donatist troublemakers by imploring the power of the state, a key moment in the history of early Christianity. But his theological argument for Christian belonging was based on justification by faith in Christ's own purity.

An ordinary faith, rooted in justification by faith, avoids a Donatist-like tendency to condition Christian belonging on extraordinary displays of moral purity. But it also moves Christians to actively practice justice-seeking with/in the various lived communities of belonging from which we draw parts of our identities—and that includes working creatively and critically with the inherited imaginaries of our national levels of belonging. In the United States, we both assume and debate with Enlightenment values (from human rights to freedom from tyranny) that have been historically practiced in both tension and cooperation with settler colonialism.

Hence while Christians' local "team" identities can provide affective ties that enable us to essentially idealize or problematize a nation-state without thinking through the consequences of doing so, those same comfort-providing spaces can foster collective conversation and self-critical otherwise-thinking. In her conversations with Wisconsin residents who supported ultra-conservative Scott Walker for governor, Katherine Cramer discovered that a "politics of resentment" against liberal elites was associated with a sense of cultural and socioeconomic displacement, accompanied by feelings of being invisible or belittled; this was especially so for people living in declining rural places that have lost well-paying manufacturing jobs.[32] Cramer's readers may be part of that liberal elite, open to hearing and pondering these narratives with fresh empathy if they lack such a cultural background. Moreover, if one kinship identity collapses or proves inadequate, other senses of belonging may emerge. Amy knows of someone from her hometown who, after Trump's election loss, pulled back from polarizing conversations and, without disowning their

[32] Cramer, *Politics of Resentment*.

political views, simply rooted more fully in a love of land and place, of Lake Superior, of hiking, hunting, fishing, and four-wheeling. Loyalty to family, friends, and those with whom one grew up can override an attachment to a compromised political leader or movement and interrupt the addictive habit of polarized political discourse.

Whether we are fanning or tempering the flames of our respective grievances, we do so in relation to various identities of belonging and to a national space into which we project our respective visions of a just society. This is an anthropological observation that takes on theological dimensions for Christians wherever we relate all our intersectional identities and communities of belonging to the Beloved Community. Whether or not they are explicitly Christian organizations, our intermediary "kinship affiliations"—including political parties and movements—are the spaces in which we form perspectives about a nation's ontological status before God or a notion of the good. Martin Luther King Jr. voiced a Christian perspective that finds the nation faulty but not rotten to the core, and that called for national redemption from within the framework of broadly shared US values. Other progressive movements envision a radical participatory democracy with varied attitudes to participation in electoral politics. We turn now to an example of a Christian criticism of a nation-state that invokes the state of exception, prompting an explicit effort to interrupt and replace the current political or economic order: Dietrich Bonhoeffer's theology of political action under a fascist regime. The ironic reception history of Bonhoeffer by conservative Christians is a stark reminder that Christian political engagement benefits from being mindfully responsible about how we live out our ontological assumptions about the nations and political systems to which we belong.

Dietrich Bonhoeffer: A Critical Reflection on States of Exception in Pursuit of an Otherwise

Christians on both right and left agree that Dietrich Bonhoeffer's political decision to break the law in the circumstance of a political dictatorship was theologically and politically the right thing to do. Bonhoeffer has come to represent the idea that a Christian can commit a crime if the political situation is deemed so extreme that no other action can be imagined under that political regime that would bring about change. Yet his example resonates today in a very different historical and political context than Nazi Germany. What Bonhoeffer can say to us constructively is important, although careful analysis is needed to evaluate its relevance.

How does Bonhoeffer offer a theological rationale for political action? Bonhoeffer's proposal is one that differs from King's. In the previous section on King, we wanted to show how King's vision was capacious from a theological perspective, based on a fundamental belonging to the Beloved Community that also advocated trust in national belonging while admitting its constitutive flaws. Bonhoeffer makes a very different case, namely, how to imagine (and then enact) political resistance in a "state of exception."

The state of exception was a term used in 1921 by the German political philosopher Carl Schmitt to identify a political emergency that called for a significant intervention when the normal course of political action proved insufficient. Democracies have this tool in their arsenal, such as martial law to restrict freedom in a situation deemed to be a dire political emergency. Schmitt wrote during the Weimar Republic in Germany, a time of democratic precarity given the growing financial crisis and the intensifying polarization of German society.[33] This accounted for his interest in when and how a leader can resort to imposing his will, rather than obeying the rule of law. In Schmitt's Germany, the state of exception was declared by Hitler in the period following his election in 1932. Hitler's party was only one among others, yet by manufacturing a series of political crises, such as the burning of the Reichstag on February 27, 1933, he was able to blame his opponents and seize ultimate power.[34] While it is difficult to analogize Germany in the 1930s to contemporary American politics, it is useful to invoke the concept of the state of exception in order to discern particular intrusions into the public political process as threats to the rule of law, possibly even to American democracy itself.

Bonhoeffer and the State of Exception

Bonhoeffer's story is well-known. The conservative evangelical author and Trump advocate, Eric Metaxas, the author of a biography of Bonhoeffer, claims him as his intellectual inspiration.[35] Charles Marsh, a politically

---

[33] Carl Schmitt, *Dictatorship: From the Origin of the Modern Concept of Sovereignty to Proletarian Class Struggle*, trans. Michael Hoelzl and Graham Ward (Cambridge: Polity Press, 2014 [1921]); and Carl Schmitt, *Political Theology: Four Chapters on the Concept of Sovereignty*, ed. and trans. George Schwab (Chicago: University of Chicago Press, 2005 [1922]).

[34] Mary Fulbrook, *A Concise History of Germany*, 2nd ed. (Cambridge: Cambridge University Press, 2004).

[35] Eric Metaxas, *Bonhoeffer: Pastor, Martyr, Prophet, Spy* (Nashville: Nelson, 2011).

liberal Christian theologian and professor at the University of Virginia, also published an admiring biography of Bonhoeffer.[36] Two contemporary American theologians who are Bonhoeffer scholars, Lisa Dahill and Reggie Williams, develop their positions of resistance to anti-Black racism in the theological terms they learned from Bonhoeffer.[37] Dahill and Williams draw on the work of South African theologian John de Gruchy, who decades earlier made use of Bonhoeffer's awareness of racism in order to argue against apartheid. And contemporary American writer Diane Reynolds appropriates Bonhoeffer's witness for still another argument, in favor of a capacious view of sexual orientation.[38] It attests to the remarkable generativity of Bonhoeffer's thought that contemporary theologians think with him in order to inspire their different political aims. The common element among these different accounts of Christian justice-seeking together is Bonhoeffer as icon of prophetic truth in an evil age. The differences concern how one configures the present age and identifies the cause of injustice.

Bonhoeffer was a young Lutheran pastor and theologian, living in the 1930s in Germany under the Nazi terror. He discerned the threat early on, unlike many of the educated elite who would only later come to regret their slowness to see and resist. Bonhoeffer's early recognition of the racist, totalitarian regime was in part due to a yearlong stay from 1930 to 1931 at Union Theological Seminary in New York. He had already completed the two dissertations required for entrance into the German professoriate (*Sanctorum Communio* in 1927 and *Act and Being* in 1930) before spending one year in New York. There, he studied with John Baillie; listened to Harry Emerson Fosdick at Riverside Church; and worshiped at Abyssinian Baptist Church with fellow seminarian, Albert Fischer, who was African American.[39] In these contexts, Bonhoeffer learned about

[36]   Charles Marsh, *Strange Glory: A Life of Dietrich Bonhoeffer* (New York: Vintage Books, 2015).

[37]   Lisa E. Dahill, *Reading from the Underside of Selfhood: Bonhoeffer and Spiritual Formation*, Princeton Theological Monograph Series 95 (Eugene, Ore.: Pickwick / Wipf & Stock, 2015); and Reggie L. Williams, *Bonhoeffer's Black Jesus: Harlem Renaissance Theology and an Ethic of Resistance* (Waco: Baylor University Press, 2014).

[38]   Diane Reynolds, *The Doubled Life of Dietrich Bonhoeffer: Women, Sexuality, and Nazi Germany* (Eugene, Ore.: Cascade, 2016).

[39]   For writings at the time of his New York tenure, see Dietrich Bonhoeffer, *Barcelona, Berlin, New York 1928–1931*, trans. Douglas W. Stott, ed. Clifford J. Green, Dietrich Bonhoeffer Works 10 (Minneapolis: Fortress, 2008).

racism. As Reggie Williams argues, Bonhoeffer used this awareness to identify the centrality of anti-Semitism to Nazi ideology. On his return to Germany—and even insisting against Reinhold Niebuhr that he was obligated to return in order to show posterity that there were some Germans who resisted—Bonhoeffer dedicated his work to the Confessing Church, the "alternative" Christian community that resisted the overtaking of the German Lutheran state church by the Nazis. At some point in his political work, Bonhoeffer was involved, together with Claus von Stauffenberg and Bonhoeffer's own brother-in-law, Hans von Dohnanyi, in a plot to assassinate Hitler. This came to be known as the failed Officers' Plot of July 20, 1944. It proved fatal for its protagonists. Bonhoeffer, arrested and detained in Tegel prison, was implicated in the assassination attempt. He was hastily transported from the Secret State prison at Prinz Albrecht Strasse 8 in Berlin to Flossenberg, and hanged on April 9, 1945, just days before the Allied victory.

The question that concerned Bonhoeffer was the following: if some thought that the public sphere was so corrupt that the ordinary political process could not assert justice, then could they declare a state of exception in order to justify inserting political will by force? Bonhoeffer thought so. He lived under the reality of Nazi totalitarianism with its explicit racist and anti-Semitic agenda. It was a regime founded on terror; concentration camps were built to imprison, enslave, and kill political dissidents, homosexuals, captured persons from the eastern front, and finally to realize the genocide of European Jews. This was a "state of exception," in which the rule of law (the democracy of the Weimar Republic) had been suspended and the law of the dictator was upheld by violence. While most political systems are an Augustinian mixture of good and evil, the Nazi regime must be acknowledged for what it was: evil. The Nazi state was exceptional because its fundamental rule was injustice.

In an essay titled "History and Good [2]" written before his imprisonment, Bonhoeffer wrestles with the kind of justice-seeking required in a situation that must be identified as evil.[40] His main opponents were other Lutheran theologians, particularly those who were affiliated with the Nazis, who advocated a political attitude of obedience to the state. This position is a traditional Christian one, whose biblical warrant is

---

[40] Dietrich Bonhoeffer, "History and Good [2]," in *Ethics*, trans. Reinhard Krauss, Charles C. West, and Douglas W. Stott, ed. Ilse Tödt, Heinz Eduard Tödt, Ernst Feil, and Clifford Green, Dietrich Bonhoeffer Works 6 (Minneapolis: Fortress, 2004), 245–98.

Romans 13 in which Paul advocates obedience to the state authorities because those authorities are put in place by God: "Let every person be subject to the governing authorities; for there is no authority except from God, and those authorities that exist have been instituted by God" (Rom 13:1). Yet Bonhoeffer insists that obedience to a rogue state is a crisis of conscience. While Romans 13 might hold for many political rules, it is inadmissible to apply this mandate to the Nazi regime.

The essay attests to Bonhoeffer's wrestling with his conscience. As a Lutheran, he had learned that the Ten Commandments were a *Beichtspiegel*, a "penance-mirror" to hold up in order to examine one's conscience. The fifth commandment according to Lutheran enumeration prohibits murder: "Thou shalt not kill." Yet Bonhoeffer found that the only solution to free the nation from the Nazi injustice was to kill the tyrant. The following lengthy passage from Bonhoeffer's essay articulates his theological conflict:

> Extraordinary necessity appeals to the freedom of those who act responsibly. In this case there is no law behind which they could take cover. Therefore there is also no law that, in the face of such necessity, could force them to make this rather than that particular decision. Instead, in such a situation, one must completely let go of any law, knowing that here one must decide as a free venture. This must also include the open acknowledgment that here the law is being broken, violated; that the commandment is broken out of dire necessity, thereby affirming the legitimacy of the law in the very act of violating it. In thus giving up the appeal to any law, indeed only so, is there finally a surrender of one's own decision and action to the divine guidance of history.[41]

This passage offers a fascinating glimpse into Bonhoeffer's struggle with an ethical decision of extraordinary proportions—namely, the killing of the tyrant. While this decision might seem to us, in retrospect, an obvious one of political expedience in light of Nazi horrors, it is, in Bonhoeffer's text, the result of careful theological analysis. Bonhoeffer is fully aware that this act is an extraordinary measure that entails breaking the law of God. Murder of another renders one guilty before the fifth commandment. Yet Bonhoeffer deems the decision "necessary." It is the only viable political solution because no other political process can be imagined to

<hr />

[41]   Bonhoeffer, "History and Good [2]," 274.

rectify deficient justice. This is a decision made during a "state of exception," when the law must be broken in order to effect political change.

As the saying goes, "desperate times call for desperate measures." Yet Bonhoeffer does not take his decision lightly. As a theological ethicist, he knows that any moral action is based on a free decision. Freedom is the reason why moral decision-making is even possible. Freedom entails responsibility both as culpability for one's own guilt if the decision is an evil one and in accepting the consequences for how the decision will impact others. Responsibility is not just personal; it has social ramifications and assumes decision-making within the social reality of human guilt.[42]

Bonhoeffer admits to freely taking on the responsibility of breaking the law, not knowing if the plot to assassinate Hitler was going to be successful in rectifying the regime's injustice. Bonhoeffer concludes his essay with a move of "surrendering" the decision to divine guidance. How can he claim that a free decision, imposed by necessity of the historical situation, replete with implication of guilt, be assigned to divine providence? Bonhoeffer makes this point with recourse to Christ. "Responsibility in a vocation follows the call of Christ alone."[43] By insisting on Christological seriousness, Bonhoeffer explains that a decision of this weight must be made in view of the reality of Jesus Christ. Only then can such a decision that brings about personal and social culpability be conceptualized within Jesus' redemptive scope. Through Christ, actions are "sanctified," as divinity guides history to its goal.[44] There is no standpoint outside of history from which to evaluate whether a moral decision is justified. Rather, from under the conditions of history, one takes on the risk of a moral decision that is unethical, and in view of Christ, surrenders that decision to divine providence.

Bonhoeffer's story is so inspiring because it draws on the powerful imaginary of an individual risking martyrdom by acting from a place of deep ethical conviction against insurmountable odds. Yet its relevance today to Christians of opposite political leanings shows that something else is at stake, namely, the work of justice-seeking in a political context that one deems to be evil.

The danger with Bonhoeffer's example is that it can be appropriated to prematurely demonize the state. The Nazi regime was evil. The global war

---

[42] Bonhoeffer, "History and Good [2]," 275.
[43] Bonhoeffer, "History and Good [2]," 292.
[44] Bonhoeffer, "History and Good [2]," 297.

it perpetrated resulted in the loss of millions of lives. The racist genocide it realized was of unfathomable magnitude. Any recourse to Bonhoeffer cannot be made as a simple analogue between the regime under which he came to his political calculation and—say—contemporary US democracy, fraught as it is. This should prompt a thoughtful pause before any attempt at extraordinary faith. Heroic action in a dire political time must be seriously balanced against the possibilities of working through democratic processes and contributing to conversations and decisions about the shape of justice. There is danger in feeling the electric current, the affective hold, of the idea that the contemporary moment is a "state of exception."

Bonhoeffer's example is different from King's. While both used theological and ethical reasoning in order to denounce the political regime as unjust, King identified injustice in terms of inadequate and deficient justice under the conditions of the American Constitution, whose terms were not realized for all its citizens. The American Constitution set the ground rules for democracy in which justice is assigned to all citizens as rights and freedoms. Yet democracy, while framed as an ideal good, fails some of its citizens who are deprived of their rights and freedoms by virtue of race, gender, and sexual orientation. Thus justice work is needed to fulfill the democratic ideals through the realm of real politics. Justice-seeking modeled on King's approach presupposes that an existing democratic political process (where it exists) is at least ideally a good. In a US context, such politically engaged justice-seeking works within the democratic process to achieve that "more perfect union," one that seeks to realize rights and freedoms for all citizens as stipulated by the Constitution.

By contrast, the use of Bonhoeffer in expedient conditions invests Christian engagement in the political sphere with a spirit of apocalyptic ultimacy. By making participation in the movement a condition of Christian identity, a justice-seeking movement becomes idolized in the name of a state of exception. How does this happen? Instead of trusting a democratic political process (where it exists) and organizing to cultivate leaders through it, Bonhoeffer might be cited to portray the current moment as one of urgent necessity that warrants interruption of the status quo and its institutions. Those who are allies but do not seem on board with the movement's aims or ways are considered to be sellouts, insufficiently radical—not able to see the core of the problem and to mobilize to root it out. In a Christian context, those who hold to a different vision of justice are cast as heretics, and one's own political movement becomes idolized—felt to be so bound up with the ultimate as to be indistinguishable from the hand of providence itself, a hand read plainly by the movement's leaders. This is idolatry, for it confuses finite nation-states, political movements, or their leaders with the infinite God.

Such idolatrous fervor for participating in a state of exception is out of step with a Christian faith grounded on baptismal belonging. Political engagement cannot substitute for Christian belonging because that belonging depends on our participation in Christ, who names and claims us as children of God. Non-idolatrous Christian freedom thus entails justice-seeking in a capacious way that can imagine new commitments based on dialogue and hearken to stories that show other aspects of a need for justice, as well as unintended consequences of one's own justice-seeking vision or pathway. Christian freedom entails recognizing idolatry in our own commitments—being self-critical so that we can own any unsought consequences of our own visions of justice-seeking, and remain open to revising their features and how we pursue them.

Bonhoeffer's example is thus relevant as an extreme case, a warning about what occurs should Christians seize their freedom to insert their political alliances in a public square that is founded on democratic ideals. Pondering the limit case of Bonhoeffer's own example of anti-totalitarian resistance invites us to take stock of how and when our own political action might be corrosive to democracy, even if it is done with "good intention." We might be wary—as Bonhoeffer himself was—about too eagerly rushing to the state of exception that involves demonizing the barriers, including democratic processes, to realizing one's vision of justice. Until a totalitarian regime occurs, we need ordinary faith to resist demonizing those who disagree with us and to guard against idolatrously construing our own political decisions as extraordinary necessities.

Holding Open the Question for "Otherwise"-Seeking Movements

Bonhoeffer is an example of Christian theological argumentation about an "otherwise" that is cognizant of its dangers, yet insisting on its necessity in a highly specific totalitarian context. It presents the extreme view—one that seemingly resonates with some contemporary US thinkers, yet one that in our view must be understood in light of the dangers of heresy and idolatry that it presents, particularly when imposed upon the current US political context.

In addition to Bonhoeffer's anti-Nazi resistance and the civil rights movement in which King participated, there are many "otherwise" movements our readers might explore within the framework of Christian freedom to discern the shape of justice-seeking in relation to our various communities of belonging, local to national to transnational. As with the legacy of Bonhoeffer's thought, a theological assessment of our participation in justice-seeking movements is not merely about deciding whether that movement is inherently "right" or "wrong," but rather about asking how we are engaging with it in a given time and place. Our premise is that Christian participation in justice-seeking movements of all sorts benefits from our being mindfully responsible about our assumptions about the countries and the political and economic systems to which we belong.

For example, like Bonhoeffer, late twentieth-century liberation theologians wrestled with questions about a state of exception to the status quo. These theologians, mostly Roman Catholics living with particular local communities in Central and South America that they called "comunidades de base" (base or grassroots communities), were interested in developing a mode of theological knowledge that stemmed from the work of political justice-seeking on the part of the poor. Their justice-seeking at the local level was cognizant of the national and transnational institutions that secured wealth for those in power, while subjugating most others through exploitation and poverty. Thus liberation theologians also took up the issue of transnational capitalism bound up with neocolonial control of natural resources. Their justice-seeking allied with the left—sometimes (and usually unfairly) labeled "communist" or "Marxist"[45]—such that their proposals aimed to secure political liberation through economic and social reform, and sometimes even revolution. Those advocating land reforms and other structural changes sought to reverse some of the effects of European colonialism on indigenous populations and enact a more participatory form of democracy—one beginning in base Christian communities that interpreted their own community's needs in light of a reading of the prophets and the gospels (and a selective use of Marx's account of the conditions of production).

Other proposals by liberation theologians were more revolutionary, inspiring utopic hopes elsewhere, as among North American leftists who identified with the success of the Sandinista revolution in

---

[45] Right-wing Christian think tanks demonized liberation theology as violent and communist, dubbing it "LT." There is continuity between right-identified Christian caricatures of "LT" in the 1980s and of "CRT" today. Well-funded right-wing efforts to discredit liberation theology have striking parallels with today's propaganda-driven efforts to demonize as anti-Christian both "Critical Race Theory" and the evangelical left's advocacy of public policies that interrupt economic inequality.

Nicaragua in 1979. There, base Christian communities, such as the one in Solentiname, opted to participate in the Marxist Sandinista revolution, which overthrew the oppressive Somoza regime and instituted land reform, while also improving literacy rates, health care access, and other quality-of-life measures. But the United States covertly supported the Contra opposition to the Sandinistas, which forced the Nicaraguan government to direct resources to ongoing military struggle. Over time, after the movement overthrew an authoritarian government on the basis of good intentions—à la Bonhoeffer—the new government under President Daniel Ortega began undermining due process for its political adversaries. President much of the time since the Sandinista revolution, Ortega has been creating his own family dynasty and arresting, silencing, and killing critics and opposition leaders. Many invested in liberation theology broke with Ortega as his authoritarian tendencies began to surface. One was the poet-priest Ernesto Cardenal, an inspired voice of liberation theology, for whom "Christ had led him to Marx, and the Gospels, with their message of social justice, had led him to communism."[46] Famous for his work with the base Christian community at Solentiname, and for cultivating the arts and poetry as Nicaragua's minister of culture from 1979 to 1987, Cardenal and Solentiname were icons of liberation theology's vision and potential. But as Ortega and his wife, Rosario Murillo, began to create their own family dynasty, and leaders like Cardenal were removed by both the church and the state, Cardenal's artistic focus shifted to nature and the cosmos. His disillusionment would be shared with others who might be arrested or worse for their own efforts at democratic participation in the public sphere, wherever they are openly critical of Ortega's policies or corruption.

How do we live rightly and well with our deepest dreams for a more just world when ousting one regime might bring into political power a new regime that might misappropriate our ideals only so long as they preserve a strong person in power? The widespread hunger for a king or monarch persists. We see it in the idea that voting for one person will make all the difference, as if agency for change is most readily imaginable if we perceive it in one person who—like Joseph in Genesis—has all a nation's resources at its disposal. And monarchy-like authoritarianism

[46]   "Ernest Cardenal Died on March 1st: Nicaragua's Revolutionary Priest-Poet Was 95," *The Economist*, March 5, 2020, https://www.economist.com/obituary/2020/03/05/ernesto-cardenal-died-on-march-1st.

may be tolerated where people feel able to live their everyday lives, have their material needs met, and pursue avenues to increase their economic success. Affordable grain and fuel matter before democracy does. Preservation of status and a longing for physical security can compete with a commitment to democracy when those who might challenge an authoritarian turn in society risk losing both status and security. This could happen whether that authoritarianism is propped up by a pro-capitalist prosperity gospel or by a social justice-seeking liberation theology.

Christian liberation theologies maintained a critical relation (rather than identity) between any particular ideological orderings and a Christian vision of the Beloved Community. Amy learned this while working for the Chicago Religious Leadership on Central America in 1989–1990, and in subsequent Central American human rights advocacy. Jews and Christians in Central and North America involved in liberation, solidarity, and sanctuary movements were less shaken by the loss of a particular election (e.g., of Ortega in 1980). They were centered in a faith that transcended any instantiation of power relations, even as they participated in shaping and speaking to them. In this vein, Argentinian liberation theologian Enrique Dussel proffers a vision of social ethics in which the praxis of the reign of God involves a process of ongoing analysis, critique, and revision.[47] He envisions a liberation-minded community ethics guided by the "Jerusalem principle," modeled on the early church in Acts and on Jesus' kingdom of God movement, and at odds with the "Babylonian principle" or any "prevailing social morality" that fosters oppression or injustice. These principles are not concrete or static; the Jerusalem principle is guided by the gospel vision of the reign of God as that which always transcends any current concretization of social relations. Justice-seeking is in this sense a never-ending process, as new forms of oppression come into focus, and we contemplate together how to create new social orderings to address them.

In the name of a dangerous, two-dimensional enemy, we can cultivate an extraordinary faith to keep company with a state-of-exception sensibility in which due process and democratic norms take a back seat to eliminating a perceived threat to the entire social order. Here an "otherwise" vision is perceived through a dualistic or apocalyptic lens. Indeed, a closer look at the recent history of Central and Latin American countries

---

[47] Enrique Dussel, *Ethics and Community*, trans. Robert R. Barr (Maryknoll, N.Y.: Orbis, 1988), 27, 47.

would reveal that authoritarianism can don itself in the discourse of both the right and the left, of anti-crime law and order and of anti-colonialist socialism.[48] Those of us committed to social justice—be we secular or religious—should not presume to be more immune than those with a more conservative vision of a just society (and vice versa).

An ordinary faith is thus attentive to *process* as well as to a vision of justice in the Beloved Community, as we reckon together with the legacies of racist settler colonialism. As the US Civil War that ended slavery (whatever that war's mixed motives) and as the Confessing Church movement in Nazi Germany remind us, there can be a time for a state of exception, for actively challenging the legitimacy of an entire political system or nation. But discernment is required during these times. We must be cautious about hungering to experience for ourselves the rush of a divinely sanctioned adrenaline that we might think is part of what a prophet feels when they speak truth to power against seemingly implacable evil forces. An ordinary faith reminds us we already belong to the Beloved Community, both eschatologically and in local manifestations or glimmers. We do not need to condition our own sense of personal power on exhibiting a self-righteous, self-enhancing rhetoric of opposition—much less delight in naming and destroying enemies of the good. That is to grasp at our own sanctification (if not prophetic anointing), rather than to trust in our right-alignment with God through faith in Christ and thus be freed to love our neighbors as ourselves, including through the untidy collective labor of political engagement.

Exercising Christian Freedom in Politics: Redux

By highlighting some of the voices and movements that have questioned the legitimacy of national projects so compromised by sin, we hope to encourage self-awareness about when our condemnations of sin invite a state-of-exception sensibility that inspires revolutionary war in the name of justice itself. This is part of the exercise of Christian freedom in the political sphere: not only freely debating with one another the nature of the moral law itself (what is right, what is wrong, and why), but also taking responsibility for the consequences of *how* we seek to advocate for the instantiation of our respective visions of the good.

---

[48]   "A New Group of Left-Wing Presidents Takes Over in Latin America; They Have More Differences than Similarities," *The Economist*, March 12, 2022, https://www.economist.com/the-americas/2022/03/12/a-new-group-of-left-wing-presidents-takes-over-in-latin-america.

The premise behind this generous but demanding understanding of Christian freedom we have voiced repeatedly: ecclesially speaking, our belonging to the Beloved Community as viewed through a Christian lens depends upon our baptismal justification by faith in Christ—*not* upon our adhering to a particular vision of justice within the Beloved Community when our own conscience directs us elsewhere. Far from implying that our passionate visions for justice do not matter, this theological conviction means that we do not condition Christian identity *itself* on everyone else adhering to our own current vision of right relations. Rather, we belong to one another *within* the space of debate about how we envision an ideal church and world. The space of debate is the ecclesial space, or rather, the ecclesial space is a space of ongoing debate about what matters among us. As Kathryn Tanner has pointed out, Christians, like Jews, share a tradition of lively debate about scriptural interpretation and what our interpretations mean for our collective lives together, which includes social justice.[49]

Surely some of our readers have found themselves thinking, *But wait, do we not want to focus first on identifying the* limits *to what Christians consider morally acceptable, in order to prevent a slippery slope toward accepting what is morally repugnant? Does the gospel then erase the moral law? Is the belonging of those ostensibly baptized into Christ without any conditions?* We have tried to address these concerns throughout our book, notably by emphasizing that the perspectives worth listening to are those that are themselves earnestly held and defensible with arguments that can endure criticism and take into account the faces and voices of all affected by them. As we noted from the outset, our foray here is also openly gappy, not airtight; our aim has been less to articulate and defend *the* singularly right position on justice-seeking matters (though we certainly do have our perspectives on them), and more to invite a theological and spiritual pause in an era when Christians spend far more time debating the nature of the moral law than on recollecting our baptismal belonging to one another in Christ. That such a pause is difficult to sustain tells us just how much getting justice right really matters to us. This anxious concern for ensuring that our own convictions about justice get to shape the public sphere and the laws and norms we govern by—surely this is one mark of the Holy Spirit stirring among us. But it is our wager that Christians can better listen together to the witness of the Spirit in our day by recalling the

[49] Tanner, *Politics of God.*

old-fashioned yet unnerving gospel claim that our covenantal belonging is established by our faith in Christ.

Even when we find ourselves inhabiting local congregations and denominations that share our respective justice-seeking visions, the theological fact that we are grounded by Christ's grace should suffice to remind us (over and over, as needed) not to think we belong to the broader body of Christ on the basis of *our own* subgroup's take on political party affiliation, abortion, gender norms, immigration, the specific relationship of "law and order" to racial justice, or any other fraught ethical or political contestation. The "consensus of the faithful" might take centuries to appear, and might arise only through the forced loss of a specific privilege that has narrowed and shadowed a vision of the just society—such as the loss of the evil privilege of enslaving others. But as the old and new "Adam," a human orientation as "flesh" and as "spirit," coexist in this life within each member of the body of Christ (Rom 7:14–8:12), and as the wheat and the weeds grow together in the same plot of ground (Matt 13:24–30, 36–43), so too Christians belong to one another even as we are sorting out which visions of justice hold over time and which do not. This vision of mutual belonging coexists alongside the persistent temptation to collapse the Beloved Community into our own vision of a just society that includes only those who think like ourselves.

The next chapter meditates on some of the spiritual practices we recognize as central to a justice-seeking that flows from—rather than displaces—justification by faith in Christ as the heart of Christian belonging. We conclude here by pointing to some theological observations about how Christian freedom is practiced in politics, mindful that we practice Christian freedom in and across many communities of belonging to which we have affective ties.

Orthodoxy/Heresy and Belonging

In a context in which the Christian right has painted liberal Christians as heretics and the Christian left accuses the right of being irrational, we note the irony of both gestures: each conditions Christian identity on something other than justification by faith in Christ—in this case, on naming and living the moral law in a particular way, even amid Christian contestation about it. Yet as we have suggested, in the history of the church, heresy is that which narrows and restricts what counts as relevant in a substantive theological debate. This can be accompanied by an obsession with a purity of heart itself, especially in a polarized context, whether by

Machiavellian design, or simply by practicing a piety of standing on one pure particular truth that shines so brightly in our eyes that it eclipses all else in the landscape. Recall the log in one's own eye that prohibits seeing any other position (Matt 7:3). Myopic rationalizations of our beliefs specialize in some form of selective purity-seeking, some point of moral clarity from which we view all else. *In this sense, a heretic is one who actually cuts off discussion with fellow Christians who think differently about a matter of justice.* Denouncing fellow Christians while insisting on one's own sole belonging injures the body of Christ. Or to use a phrase from the Reformers, heresy is sin insofar as it indicates a self (or community) curved in upon itself. Heresy dishonors others by refusing to listen to what is at stake in the debate for them, thereby monopolizing Christian freedom only for oneself and one's own position. Heresy, in other words, is a sin against the freedom of fellow Christians to deliberate with integrity about the shape of justice in the church and in the world.

To illustrate this concretely, let's briefly revisit the political debates about abortion in relation to the exercise of Christian freedom. Here the substantive debates about the legality or constitutionality of abortion are bound up theologically for Christians with ontological questions regarding gender and the beginnings of personhood, both tied to human reproductive capacities. We have argued that the exercise of Christian freedom to debate in the political realm about the shape of reproductive justice holds open a space that refuses to condition Christian belonging *itself* on landing upon polemical answers to ontological questions about gender and human beginnings.

The divide in the debate is such that especially abortion opponents tend to construe opposition to abortion's legality as a mark of who is to be considered a true Christian. An anti-abortion posture thus takes on the features of a *status confessionis*, which means an issue so significant to Christian faith that it requires articulation as a confession of faith. As evangelical D. Gareth Jones notes in his preface to a book withdrawn under pressure (later republished) in the mid-1980s because it supported "therapeutic abortion":

> The heresy of which I appear to be guilty is that I cannot state categorically that human/personal life commences at day 1 of gestation. This, it seems, is being made a basic affirmation of evangelicalism, from which there can be no deviation. . . . No longer is it sufficient to hold to classic evangelical affirmations on the nature of biblical

revelation, the person and work of Christ, or justification by faith alone. In order to be labelled an evangelical, it is now essential to hold a particular view of the status of the embryo and fetus.[50]

Those who support the legality of abortion are treated as if they have rejected their baptism, ought to be excommunicated (as with the denial of communion to Speaker of the House Nancy Pelosi as well as some Roman Catholic efforts to excommunicate President Biden), or are simply beyond the pale of a Christian identity unless they repent of their ways.

Christians who support abortion's legality, on the other hand, are less inclined to regard abortion opponents as non-Christian than to regard them as practicing an unpalatable form of Christianity that harms and paternalizes women and disregards the complexity of their lives. Pro-life feminist Christians would push back and insist they do indeed honor the complexity of women's lives, or at least have a vision of how to do so that makes sense to them (with normative framings about what constitutes women's flourishing). But many liberal Christians defend a vision of Christian life that centers the agency and equality of women, not least with regard to their reproductive choices.

Part of the challenge in the debate about abortion's legality is that the antagonists rest on competing visions of an "otherwise"—of a more just world—that in turn motivate different understandings of gender and the beginnings of human personhood. For example, when an "otherwise" vision of a just world assigns to every fetus the necessary opportunity to become a born child, then the opposing perspective—a fluid view of a prenate's moral value—looks to them like a rationalization for calling a fetus "not human" for the sake of avoiding moral queasiness about having an abortion. But let us switch perspectives. If a vision of justice is held to be one in which women are given the opportunity for investing life energy in a career or calling in addition to (or instead of) mothering, and/or in having sufficient resources for the children they do bear, then the "otherwise" vision is one in which pregnant women's reproductive choices are enabled and respected as means to her own and her children's flourishing. From this perspective, denying abortion as a reproductive choice implies

[50]   D. Gareth Jones, *Brave New People: Ethical Issues at the Commencement of Life*, rev. ed. (Grand Rapids: Eerdmans, 1985). See also Fred Clark, "The 'Biblical View' That's Younger than the Happy Meal," *Patheos*, February 18, 2012, https://www.patheos.com/blogs/slacktivist/2012/02/18/the-biblical-view-thats-younger-than-the-happy-meal/.

that women lack moral agency with regard to their bodily integrity and ways of valuing their own lives. Instead, women who seek to control their fertility appear to be in ontological violation of their essential female nature unless they sacrifice every other purpose in their lives to the altar of reproduction (if not also of parenting).

It seems impossible to disentangle the abortion debate from assumptions about gendered existence. Whether or not one perceives every human conception as morally equivalent to a born child factors into whether one perceives women in more essentialist or in more fluidly egalitarian ways. These questions are as difficult to answer as questions about the Son's relationship to the Father seemed to be in the fourth century. For this reason, the exercise of Christian freedom that was at play in the creedal controversies can analogically inform Christian participation in public debates about access to safe, legal abortions.

What might we see if we frame Christian orthodoxy in terms of a processual dynamics, in this case the *process* of Christian debating about abortion? How do creedal affirmations and debates provide a heuristic model for a divisive contemporary *ethical* debate that could not have existed before technology and genetics allowed us to gaze with such penetration into the body of a pregnant woman before the time of quickening? Can we regard the competing intuitions at play in the abortion debate—the contested but real moral values of a prenate *and* of a pregnant woman—as elements we might integrate into a still-emerging synthesis? Is there a possibility of something analogically akin to a creedal orthodoxy that can take the measure of the moral intuitions of both those who support and those who oppose the legality of abortion?

Even if we take time for collective discernment in the body of Christ, we may never in this case find anything analogical (albeit in an ethical or theologically anthropological vein) to a new creed that synthesizes the moral intuitions of those for and against the legal right of women to abort a prenate, or of those who do or do not share the perception that abortion is a criminal act of murder. Yet as Christians we ought to be able to affirm that what unites us to one another in the body of Christ is *not* our coming to agree about when full human personhood begins, but our already belonging to one another through our baptism and faith as Christians. We belong together to the church—the Beloved Community—even when we are in the throes of fundamental but reasoned (justified) moral and theological-anthropological disagreements about the shape of justice for pregnant women and their potential offspring.

On *this* basis of Christian belonging, Christians can frame the process of discernment amid ethical disagreement, as we have discussed, on the model of the generations-long search for orthodox belief about Christology and the Trinity. Moreover, listening to one another's justifications of our beliefs regarding abortion is one expression of our living by the third article of the Apostles' Creed: being one holy catholic (universal) church, attentive to the voice of the Spirit in our midst. Within the orbit of individual Christians' lives, this could include accepting that, amid moral complexity, the freedom of the Christian involves trusting women to discern their most responsible choice regarding a particular pregnancy and their reproductive decisions overall.[51] This claim marks where we ourselves stand with regard to the legality of abortion. Here, however, we underscore that listening to one another across the abortion debate is one of our obligations as confessors of the Apostles' and Nicene Creeds (whether that confession is explicit, marked by corporate recitation in worship, or implicit, in an affirmation of the creedal teachings conveyed about God and the church).

This approach to the creeds—an approach that is grounded in the history of their production and their synthetic genius—differs from the approach of those who perceive within them a set of static absolutes. As we pointed out in chapter 3, the creeds were hammered out amid contention that continued until a way was found to combine competing theological intuitions about Jesus as the Son's (and later the Holy Spirit's) status in relation to God. In this respect, the creeds crystallize a generous, not a narrow, orthodoxy. Some positions were indeed ruled out, particularly those that denied all the insights of those holding opposing views. At the same time, creedal formulations opened the door to a kaleidoscope of ways to continue to nuance the doctrine of God, as Christians have persisted over the centuries in working out different ways of interpreting and relating the person and the two natures (divine and human) of Christ. The creeds thus do not mark the end of all Christian debate, nor ward off an ongoing exercise of our powers of reason and observation concerning the features of creation, including human nature. Rather, the creeds create a space in which we bear witness to the reality of a creative, redeeming God who makes us a church, a communion of forgiven and forgiving saints-in-the-making, who journey together both now and into our resurrections. We are held together less by consensus on everything

---

[51]   Amy Carr and Christine Helmer, "Claiming Christian Freedom to Discuss Abortion *Together*," *Lutheran Forum* 53, no. 2 (Summer 2019): 48–51.

than by a commitment to asking—which often means debating—what our participation in Christ means for our common life together, for the kingdom of God, the Beloved Community.

Attentive as we are to the *process* of creedal formation, we emphasize thus as orthodoxy's mark an openness to continuing to listen to one another amid all the contested ethical issues that divide the present-day body of Christ as everyone earnestly articulates their convictions about what justice and flourishing can or ought to look like among us. Can those who disagree with us about the legality of abortion recognize that we are grasping their own best arguments and taking account of what is morally at stake for them—even if we ultimately redescribe or recontextualize what we hear from one another in the process of justifying our own beliefs, our own ontological perceptions of the nature of being a person and of respecting human lives? Orthodoxy as a heuristic process of discerning the larger truth of things invites this practice of mutual listening—not a closed-minded, defensive rationalization of our own beliefs, in this case about abortion's legality and morality.[52] Orthodoxy thus integrates insights from a long span of conversation, which includes taking responsibility for the consequences of our own positions on a matter at hand—tacking a way forward that heeds those consequences with new measures, new formulations.

In this heuristic context, we are tempted to accuse others of heresy whenever we stand on a particular truth while closing our ears and eyes to the voices, faces, and moral intuitions of those who perceive additional or other truths. Perhaps, over time, our mutual listening will bring more Christians to a particular position about the legality of abortion and about reproductive justice—as, over time, Jews, Christians, and Muslims have almost universally discerned that slavery has no place in a just society, regardless of Scripture verses assuming and legislating it. Minimally, though, mutual listening precludes the practice we are here calling heresy: clinging to a particular belief about abortion we have justified in our minds, in such a way that we foreclose the opportunity to see and hear the

---

[52]   For the distinction among the moral, legal, and constitutional questions regarding abortion in the United States, see Michael J. Perry, "McElroy Lecture: Religion, Politics, and Abortion," *University of Detroit Mercy Law Review* 79 (2001): 1–37, http://ssrn.com/abstract=294506. We do not focus here on the constitutionality of abortion, although we are aware that the July 2022 *Dobbs v. Jackson* decision of the Supreme Court has ended a federal constitutional right to abortion in the United States.

testimonies, stories, and ethical insights of fellow members of the body of Christ that disrupt or complicate that particular pure truth to which we hold. When we close up that way, we are further driven to such lack of charity that we cannot behold one another across this debate as fellow members of the body of Christ. This may be one dimension of blasphemy against the Holy Spirit, who (as the third article of the Creed testifies) blows in and through the church, the corporate body of Christ.

Idolatry and an Ontology of Belonging

Those theologically minded among our readership will discern that we are presupposing a kind of Augustinian criticism of a self-righteous pre-occupation with one's own group having articulated, and then achieved, moral purity. Like Augustine in his struggle with the Donatists, we are convinced that Christian and other forms of belonging depend on Christ's purity, not our own.[53] What do we mean by this? With Paul, we center belonging to the Beloved Community (the church, the kingdom of God) on justification by faith in Christ, which creates freedom from both sin and its effect of affectively curving us in upon ourselves—freeing us also to attend to the common good of our neighbors and ourselves. Yet Paul himself observed that in this lifetime, we are still being formed into the body of Christ, still experiencing the self-centered orientation of the flesh (a worldview, not a body) while also experiencing the lively presence of the Spirit enabling faith, hope, and love. It is on this Pauline basis that we have an Augustinian understanding of belonging to teams, communities, and affinity groups that each claim different visions of a justice-seeking "otherwise," yet which are each predicated on belonging to a still sin-soaked world. The inheritances of the sinful world mark the particular "ontology" of belonging to any kinship group, from local to virtual to national and global. In the United States, as we discussed above, some of the specific sinful inheritances have to do with the his-torical legacy of slavery that perpetuates racism, and with the broader evil of a misogynous patriarchy whose hierarchical patterns from many religions and cultures are infused into the contemporary US context. Our group belongings as such are never free from these insidious evils; their ontology takes structural and systemic form. Yet they are not so acute that they prevent the freedom for justice-seeking that is part and

---

[53]   Augustine, *On Baptism against the Donatists*, trans. J. R. King (London: Aeterna Press, 2014).

parcel of affinity-group belonging, even when that justice-seeking is restricted to seeking benefits for one's own group.

It is at this point that we invoke a theological category that goes back to ancient Israel, which we think is helpful for reflecting on justice-seeking from the perspective of one's particular communities of belonging. Even when justice-seeking is grounded first and foremost in the freedom created by Christ, justice-seeking is also situated within belonging to our various kinship or affinity groups. It is thus inevitably marred and informed by the ontology structuring this belonging. An Augustinian ontology admits the prevalence of sinful dimensions of person and community, but in this age of grace (not yet age of glory), that sinful dimension need not monopolize persons and communities. Rather, reason, will, and the imagination can and do work out an "otherwise." Freedom and responsibility are, as we learned from Bonhoeffer, part of what it means to be human in the world as it is, and as such, to orient sinful selves and structures to visions of justice—and to do so within particular affinity groups or political movements that interact within a greater whole.

Idolatry is often thought of as worshiping false gods, in keeping with the commandment, "you shall have no other gods before me" (Exod 20:3). Yet Luther in his inimitable way reformulated this commandment as he did the others in the positive sense.[54] Rather than a prohibition, he reconstructs the commandment as one having to do with the god to whom one runs in all kinds of joy and trouble, in whom one places a heartfelt trust: the primary orientation of the heart, mind, body. Yet this orientation has a danger, which Tillich made clear when he depicted faith as the state of being ultimately concerned, and when he added the observation that finite symbols participate in the infinite itself.[55] Because anything can be an idol when one makes it one's ultimate concern, everyone has this temptation to idolatry by mistaking the finite for the infinite, thereby rendering a created reality into the sole object of trust. Idols can be money, as in Jesus' binary between God and mammon (Luke 16:13), or a guru who demands obedience even to one's death, or a value (such as freedom above all), or even one's own kinship group to the detriment of others.

---

[54]   "You are to have no other gods. What is this? Answer: We are to fear, love, and trust God above all things." Martin Luther, "Small Catechism," in *The Book of Concord: The Confessions of the Evangelical Lutheran Church*, trans. Charles Arand et al., ed. Robert Kolb and Timothy J. Wengert (Minneapolis: Fortress, 2000), 351.

[55]   Tillich, *Dynamics of Faith*.

An Augustinian perspective is one that recognizes that idolatry is a persistent risk. It cannot be avoided: the double belonging that constitutes the Christian in two dimensions, so to speak—the ultimate belonging to the Beloved Community and the belonging in an ontology marked by the prevalence of sin and evil—are always at risk of confusion. Indeed, there are temptations that insinuate themselves into even the most altruistic person that can draw one into substituting the penultimate for the ultimate, sometimes without even knowing it. We can convince ourselves of our highest integrity and most altruistic justice-seeking. We can be certain that we are motivated by the best of intentions, in the name of equity or moral purity. We can raise our values to causes of ultimate concern—and in the name of equity or moral purity think that we are above criticism. Such is the risk of personal self-deception; we substitute the values of equity or moral purity for God. And why would we not be right? Equity and moral purity are of course to be lauded—who would disagree that these are values intrinsic to imagining "otherwise"? Yet they can become idols, especially when our particular take on a value (like equity) we hold is itself seen to be the only way of holding that value, such that in its name we lose perspective on other dimensions of justice that the promotion of this value entails. In the name of moral purity we can disavow the reality of experiences that might call that abstract purity into question. An idolatry of identity itself can plague us.

Affective orientations inevitably infuse our tendencies toward idolatry. Justice-seeking is about care; we care enough about particular issues that we are willing to go to the mat for them. Yet care can be parsed into other affective moments. We care because we fear that there will be no place for white guys; we fear that our "people" will not have access to the opportunities afforded to others; we fear for the safety of our neighborhoods. We care because of our own grievances and resentments. The groups we fear threaten our access to power and so we are angry. Yes there is righteous indignation, certainly in the Bible. But does being angry and holding resentments affect our capacity to discern? Our grievances in particular can shield us from consideration of others, especially those we perceive as responsible for or benefiting from our grievances. And as such the epithets we hurl at the perceived objects of our uncomfortable feelings give voice to idolatrous inclinations: those bitches, those hooligans, those nutjobs. We have thus turned our grievances into idols, assigning responsibility onto others who may have nothing to do with our feelings. Yet we do so, in righteous indignation.

Individual fear mirrors in personal and group psychology how fear at the national level amplifies polarization. One fears that the other will not recognize one's grievances, and one then takes them up into a worldview. Here the worry about not being heard resonates with the deep personal need for recognition by the other. When this is transferred into the political arena, then the fear of being left behind by the politics of the elite—as is the case with rural small towns in America—lends itself to the fear of being quashed, and thus to the rise in polarization between rural and urban, town and gown, red and blue. But the bottom line of idolatry is the insertion of power at any cost into justice-seeking. This can be so even if we or our group are in a position of powerlessness, with no perceived opportunities to participate in common justice-seeking. Those marginalized or bullied can also precipitate destructive tendencies, exacerbated by grievances out of which one calls out corrections and critiques without paying attention to how one arrived at them, or whether they respect due process for others.

What then are we to do with our vulnerability to idolatry, its risks, tendencies, and desire for power? How do we practice justice-seeking while navigating the prohibition against idolatry and remembering to critically reflect on our personal and corporate commitments and our own capacity for self-delusion? We need to get back (over and over) to our centering in obedience to a Christian understanding of the first commandment—our grounding in Christ as that which sets us free from the sins of idolatry and works us out of them. This is the freedom of ordinary faith, to which we now return.

Ordinary Faith and Trust in Each Other

Our Augustinianism insists that we are thrown into institutions we are complicit in. From there, we can choose to transfer membership. But we do not really have a choice in abdicating from all kinships. We exist in and are supported by them if not thrive in them, as we support them and work out visions of justice from within them and for others. What ordinary faith requires, then, is a process of justice-seeking that retains flexible connections to the kinships in which we find ourselves. Whereas extraordinary faith is an exercise of individual heroism outside institutions, we advocate (wherever possible) ordinary faith from within and in relation to these institutions. Belonging is central; justice-seeking is social. Thus any moves of ordinary faith must be oriented by this centrality.

Key here is a theology of trust. While trust is sometimes reduced to an affective disposition, it is more than this. It is a commitment that can but does not necessarily include *feeling* trust in the institutions that have primacy because of our belonging. While trust invoked by the Reformers aspires to heartfelt trust or faith in God (and Luther himself struggled to maintain trust in God), it can also be a practice of imagining and working toward the "otherwise" while taking care to steward the institutions in which justice-seeking can be carried out.

Trust is of particular significance in today's political times that are characterized by distrust of authority and institutions, even of truth itself. QAnon as a contemporary phenomenon stems from distrust of elected officials and buying into a theory that erodes public confidence in their legitimacy and honor.[56] But distrust does not need to take such extreme conspiratorial forms. The politicization of "science" as a worldview, and distrust of truth-telling expertise—such as empirically based evidence, academic authority, and legal authority—reflect what we have construed theologically as tendencies toward heresy and idolatry that themselves are based on our personal and group-affiliated capacities for self-delusion.[57]

Trust in democratic political institutions and our neighbors offers resistance to these sorts of contemporary conspiratorial affinities that undermine institutions. Such trust presupposes shared values on the

---

[56] On QAnon and other new religious movements that distrust authority and expertise, see Katelyn Beaty, "QAnon: The Alternative Religion That's Coming to Your Church," *Religion News Service*, August 17, 2020, https://religionnews.com/2020/08/17/qanon-the-alternative-religion-thats-coming-to-your-church/. See also Caroline Mimbs Nyce, "*The Atlantic Daily*: QAnon Is a New American Religion," *The Atlantic*, May 14, 2020, https://www.theatlantic.com/newsletters/archive/2020/05/qanon-q-pro-trump-conspiracy/611722/: both these articles highlight how the "heresy" of QAnon is gnostic-like; also Jen Butler, "6 Ways to Protect Your Church from Conspiracy Theories," *Patheos*, September 18, 2020, https://www.patheos.com/blogs/faithinpubliclife/2020/09/protecting-your-church-from-conspiracy-theories/?utm_source=Newsletter&utm_medium=email&utm_campaign=Christians+For+a+Better+Christianity&utm_content=43.

[57] Adam Kinzinger (@AdamKinzinger), "As a Christian, I have read the words of Christ many times. Nowhere have I seen him say or imply that it's ok to lie, so long as you own the Libs. I believe our open lies are an absolute abdication of our duty, and it is shameful," Twitter, May 12, 2021, 1:18 p.m., https://twitter.com/AdamKinzinger/status/1392439102633562114?.

basis of which justice-seeking as mutual belonging can take place. Values such as fairness, due process, and the nature of empirical truth form the basis on which we can develop moral reflection. These are criteria for having conversations that promote democracy even if one's theological theories about democracy or one's democratic contexts differ. Trust includes a fight for recognition of a common truth that serves as a basis for conversation. All conversation must have some common reason that holds things together.

Trust is the antidote to fear. Trust builds bridges; fear builds walls. The reason why fear is the basis of authoritarianism is because fear is needed to assert or submit to domination. When a democracy signals distress it does so on the basis of fear. Hence self-preservation requires suppressing the other whose position is feared as a detriment to one's own. The antidote to a politics of fear is a political commitment to trust. This is why Christian freedom insists on an aural spaciousness that is available for receiving grievances and stories, for recounting losses and being heard.

In the political sphere, trust is an orientation, a basis for shared debate and deliberation in which everyone knows where one's interlocutors stand and why. Interpersonal trust may be felt to varying degrees, but trust in democracy as a norm and in the value of one's continuing to contribute (if like the persistent widow in Jesus' parable [Luke 18:1–8]) to civic engagement—this sort of trust is as much (if not more) a vow and a commitment as it is also an affective state. Significant is the creation of a space of attunement to one another that intersects with the commitment to democracy as a political institution and enables nuance and moral reflection. While such a political democracy might serve only as an ideal, the work of justice-seeking that presupposes spaciousness for shared deliberation can coax the practice of democracy in this direction.

When Christian engagement in the political sphere takes its bearings from ordinary faith, we are both freed and obligated to love our neighbors as ourselves in a way that is curious, attentive, and nimble about how laws and public policies enhance or diminish neighbor-love. Remembering that we are baptized into an eternal covenant with the body of Christ, we act with the trust or knowledge of our belonging—our having a seat at the dinner table (ultimately at the feast of the Lamb), as well as a seat at the table of decision-making about the common good. In a democratic context, the latter means we are free to sit down and deliberate with one another about the best means to create a more just society (and contend with legacies of injustice) through our voting and our public policy advocacy.

Another gift and command of Christian freedom with regard to justice-seeking in the political sphere is one we can turn to even when we are feeling distrust in our political opponents and in political institutions themselves: precisely out of the pain of knowing fellow members of the body of Christ can disagree with us so fiercely, we are reminded that no small part of Christian discipleship involves the spirit of humility that accompanies repentance, including owning the consequences—intended and unintended—of the particular visions of justice which we hold. With regard to abortion, for instance, that might mean pro-abortion activists acknowledging that a potential human life is ended by the choice to abort; for anti-abortion activists, that means owning the consequences of making abortion illegal: from an inherently patriarchal (if not misogynistic) coercion of women's life options and reproductive capacities to the impoverishment, imprisonment, or death of women with unwanted pregnancies. More broadly, it is when we are intoxicated by a particular justice-seeking movement that we might most face a temptation to resist being receptive to noticing unintended consequences of *how* we are going about our justice-seeking, or to minimize them (as in personal conversation an Iranian-born Marxist once did when he was praising communist states and Amy asked him, "What about the human rights violations in the former USSR?" and he replied, "*What* human rights violations? Those were [against] reactionaries"). Remembering that we are justified by our faith in Christ and belong to the body of Christ whose rightly related contours we are still discerning, we can be more open to repentance whenever self-protective attitudes and certainty about the rightness of a cause block our receptivity to both noticing and owning the consequences of any movement for justice-seeking in which we are invested.

Such investment remains part of our vocation as Christians engaging the world. God's Spirit drives us to connect our belonging to the body of Christ with justice-seeking. The path of safety and caution is the path of the servant who hid his talent in the ground, fearing an investment that might prove risky (Matt 25:14–30). The safe path is not to avoid conflict, nor to seek personal purity or comfort as ends in themselves. For again, our belonging to Christ is not conditioned upon our own perfection, but upon a baptismal belonging to one another in Christ that frees and moves us to imagine what loving our neighbors as ourselves looks like, in our respective times and places. This includes participating in shaping neighbor-affecting public policies through electoral politics, engaged citizenship, and civic or social movements. Participating in the politics of the state is one dimension of responsible service to our neighbors. The Beloved Community is never less than local, with congregational and virtual spaces of interpersonal connection, even as it is global and eschatological; so too the Beloved Community or kingdom of God is always at play in this world, expressed in part through our agency as citizens and voters in nation-states that seek to pursue a vision of "liberty and justice for all."

6

The Spiritual Discipline of Ordinary Faith and a Life of Decentering and Recentering

But be encouraged, because even in the throes of tragedy and heart-break, the good news persists. There is no circumstance that can negate our baptismal reality. Jesus has made a way for us. Therefore, our gratitude—our thankfulness—doesn't come from the way our life is unfolding. Rather, our gratitude comes from the life that was laid down for us in Christ Jesus.[1]

—Rev. Angela T. Khabeb

Toward a Theology of Beloved Community

In this book we chose two particularly virulent examples of contention amid justice-seeking—abortion and Christian participation in politics—in order to draw attention to a contemporary rift in the body of Christ. Certainly we could have mentioned other divisive concerns, not least how to interpret and respond to the climate crisis, which is coming into focus as the most grave apocalyptic threat to life on our planet, short of nuclear war or asteroid collision. We trust our fellow Christian readers can pursue this and other questions within a similar overarching framework of remembering our baptism into the body of Christ as the basis for our belonging to God and to one another. We are justified—aligned with God and each other—not by holding this or that political or ethical view when people genuinely, earnestly disagree, but by our faith in the One whose incarnation, dying, rising, and sending of the Spirit makes possible a communion of saints that crisscrosses centuries and intersects time and eternity. In this final chapter, we gather up and add to the theological lenses

[1]   Angela T. Khabeb, "Grateful Ground," *Living Lutheran*, November 22, 2021, https://www.livinglutheran.org/2021/11/48338/.

we have employed thus far, bringing them to bear upon the process—at once personal and communal—of journeying through controversy about justice-seeking within the Beloved Community.

This orientation to the Beloved Community strikes us as especially important today. With this insistence, we resist a common individualistic attitude that gives up on participation in civil society—including investment in a congregation or community—for the reason that available group options do not fit with what one wants or expects them to be. So many of us are tempted to retreat to the private sphere of family and friends, of shared activities that do not ask us to worship together, or that challenge us to think beyond the intimate in order to act together for the common good. It is easier to belong to the church universal than to any of one's available local congregations. The COVID-19 pandemic has made it easier to find social media groups from anywhere in the country or world than to connect with the perhaps less-than-agreeable people in one's home churches. It is also easier to identify as spiritual but not religious, and thereby avoid gathering in visible churches that include familiar problematic characters, such as the lay member who wants to be the pastor and the council member who laments about deferred building maintenance. It is also easy to write off an entire church or denomination if it fails to be woke enough, or too woke for one's tastes, or insufficiently Bible-believing or not political enough. How often do we take our own lives so seriously that we become the measuring rule, such that denominations and/or particular churches have to justify themselves in our sight?

The question of the Beloved Community has to do with the real-life challenges of "life together." How can we bring our full selves to a congregation unless we can feel willing to risk sharing there what we see, feel, believe, wonder—feeling we are heard and that our values are at least significantly shared? But insofar as we understand Christian faith to be rooted in a knitted-together reality—the body of Christ, the Beloved Community—that catches us up in the learning to love God and neighbor that begins with our baptism and continues to and beyond our deaths, we might consider more closely what theological resources we have at hand with regard to interpreting the *process* of debate in the Beloved Community—local to national to transnational—and the spiritual effects on ourselves and others along the way.

We begin by noting that our tendency to polarize over justice-seeking issues is actually an expression of the human capacity for play, especially for competitive play. What are the dangers of one-sided love for one's team?

What theological metaphors and what spiritual resources can facilitate our playing the game that recognizes the dynamic between the tussle of justice-seeking and holding the conviction that all game-players belong to the Beloved Community? This chapter focuses on the spirituality of moving from the secure recognition of our belonging to the Beloved Community into the contentious space of justice-seeking in politics and then back again. This reciprocal movement informs the lifelong process of coming to terms with participation in real communities and the constant need for expanding one's vision, healing one's injuries, and being reminded that the game belongs ultimately to the Spirit. By focusing on this reciprocity, we follow Jesus' own rhythm of moving into the crowds (or *polis*) where he taught those gathered around him, healed the sick, exorcized demons, and disputed with the lawyers, and then his retreat into the wilderness where he was strengthened by communing with his beloved Abba. As we follow Jesus from the wilderness into the crowds and then back again, we offer theological reflections and spiritual resources that facilitate awareness of why this movement is important and how it can be practiced amid the real challenges of ordinary faith. "Life together" is difficult, maddening, frustrating. Yet we take theological courage and spiritual comfort in knowing that it is grounded in the Beloved Community in which Christ heals and forgives, exorcizes the demons of constriction, and creates the space for expanding our moral imaginary.

Homo Ludens (Not the *ecclesia militans!*)

If Dutch historian Johan Huizinga was right in his 1938 book *Homo Ludens*, human nature is expressed through play.[2] We create miniature worlds with their own rules, worlds we enter with earnest vigor. Huizinga focused in part on the play of competitive sports. Sports is about winning and losing. One team is pitted against another, each recognizable by its own color of jersey, mascot, and cheer.

We live our lives in various places of "play." Human society is structured around various spaces that each have their distinctive kind of "play": the sports field, the performance stage, the classroom, the political arena. Each has its own rules for interaction. Soccer regulates offsides and penalties; at a classical music performance one will get shushed if one unwraps a particularly crinkly throat lozenge or be given the stink eye when one

---

[2]   Johan Huizinga, *Homo Ludens: A Study of the Play-Element in Culture* (Boston: Beacon, 1971).

claps between movements. In a classroom, students follow the teacher's guidance for when to listen and when to discuss. The political arena has its own etiquette, some of it rather bawdy and disruptive as anyone who has seen the House of Commons in London can attest. Today many lament the coarsening of political discourse, the vulgarity that has replaced respect, and the outrageous claims of a stolen election when all evidence points to the contrary.

How Christians think and act in the political realm (broadly construed) has been a focus of this book. We have pondered the theological "rules" governing this play. We have set forth a theological paradigm, grounded in justification by faith and oriented to constructing a generous space of mutual listening. We have proposed that the play of Christian faith in politics must be expanded beyond the myopic focus on one's home team. We have sketched a theological path that showed up the heresy of winning at all costs: all who play fundamentally belong to the same larger league—the league of the Beloved Community. Belonging to that league is more primary than the jersey one wears as one cheers on one's own team and prays for the other team to lose. Belonging grounds the quest for justice, enabling justice-seeking as a mutual task among players on different teams. How the teams play, or in other words, how Christians live out their ordinary faith while trying to work out justice in relation to others—other Christians, non-Christians, and secular persons—is a practice that incorporates theological and spiritual tools: identifying when one forecloses someone else's position; reflecting on the propensity to idolatry when one insists on a position of moral purity; and recognizing when one does not own the real-life consequences of one's position, or is drawn to demonizing another. Our starting point, as we have emphasized throughout the book, is the whole "game" even as we each contribute to the plays of one particular team.

The Spirit of Play

We have been calling out how Christians often deem Christian identity for their team alone. And we have called *for* a theological grounding regarding belonging in the Beloved Community, in which one's particular political identity—that is, which team one plays on—is actually rooted in a more fundamental Christian identity—that of being justified by faith in Christ. Justification by faith means that Christ sets one free from obsession with one's own team and frees one to be a team player in the Spirit's league. Justification by faith theologically opens a communal space that is larger than one's own team. Here Christ calls each person into community. Christ sets persons free *from* one-sided obsessions and sets them free *for* recognizing mutual belonging across spirited team differences in the body of Christ.

This is a theological model that has purchase on the reality of how Christians belong to each other through our belonging in Christ. The significance of this is theological, but more. The theological recognition of being grounded in Christ also involves reflecting on how one has perpetuated harm to the body of Christ. Freedom from sin presupposes an awareness of how our each playing on one team is a forgetting that the other team is also important. Such sin includes shutting down discussion by presuming one's own team has the right answers; the sin of not recognizing the consequences of one's position; the sin of presuming that the Spirit is only on *my* side.

But theology does more than just analyze the idea of justification. Theology has to do with realities—the reality of justification by faith that creates Christian subjectivity by grounding it in Christ. While this subjectivity is hidden in Christ (Col 3:3), it is nevertheless real, and as real, initiates the adoption of spiritual practices that shape affect, imagination, and thought. Freedom in Christ is an expansion of mind and heart. The liturgy invokes the "sursum corda"—"lift up your hearts"—intoned at the beginning of the eucharistic prayer in order to imagine and project new spaces and recollected realities for living, thinking, and acting.

Are we giving theology too much credit for justification's transformative potential, especially when addressing such intractable debates between Christian teams as those about abortion and how to live out one's Christian commitments in the public square? Can our introduction of the doctrine of justification by faith into the divisiveness of contemporary politics with its winner-take-all and zero-sum game mentality have any traction? Does justification's insistence on mutual belonging have the power to offer another way of communicating that is not poisoned by the inflammatory rhetoric of denunciation? Does theology really hold out the possibility of moving past our deeply held team identifications and into a sense of spaciousness with one another?

A theology of justification by faith witnesses to a renewing reality in Christ. It includes a theology of the practice of ordinary faith, reflecting on how the faith that is justified by Christ can work out, embody, and live out the Spirit of Christ in our thinking, speaking, writing, and acting. Here theology converges with spirituality, namely, how the theological idea of grounding in the Beloved Community is a practice of ordinary faith, and how faith lives out that reality. Of course, there is no direct line from grounding to everyday life—in fact Christian living falters often, as our Augustinianism tells us. But this inevitable failing should not entail cynicism or despair or resignation. Rather it is an invitation to spiritually practice attunement to faith's original grounding as our source of ever new reality in Christ, and to daily orient heart, body, and mind to the practice of Christian freedom for others in the various communities of justice-seeking into which one is called.

In other words: We live in the radiance of the Christ story, but also in the world of messy tragedy. We struggle with what it means to strive for justice in the world as it is, even as we seek to work toward the world as we think it ought to be.

The Play of Ordinary Faith in the Beloved Community: A Re-Centering Rhythm of Wilderness and *Polis*

We now suggest a guiding metaphor that will accompany us through the rest of the chapter: decentering and recentering and then back again. We will see how "decentering" and "recentering" characterize how Christians live out their grounding in the Beloved Community in their quest for justice in the political realm. That work requires practicing the freedom and spaciousness afforded those in Christ—but it also involves real-world exchanges, emotional flare-ups, diminishments, and dehumanizations that so readily accompany our rallying behind our own team in a game when the shape of shared life is at stake. Yet we can pay attention to the sorts of ingrained habits that do an injustice to the life that Christ has created for us. How a "recentering" takes place, and why it is constitutive of Christian "life together," is the focus of this section; in the next, we will look more deeply at the "decentering" aspect.

We observe first (and once more!) that being centered in one's faith in Christ is an ordinary thing, not an extraordinary display of self-assertion in an "I stand up to evil powers" moment. One's position on abortion is not proof of Christian identity; one's faith as small as a mustard seed does not have to move mountains (cf. Matt 17:20). What we have been insisting on is that faith is *ordinary* because of a basic belonging to the Beloved Community that is the work of Christ. The center of the Christian life is not the ego, but "Christ" who lives in me and in each Christian. A centered life in the Beloved Community is a justified-by-faith life in which the "I" is already decentered from the place of control by being gifted with the place of belonging. This is one of those fantastic theological paradoxes:

a centered life is really a life that decenters the ego from a place of primacy and centers personal existence on Christ: "and it is no longer I who live, but it is Christ who lives in me" (Gal 2:20).

Belonging in this sense of an "I" justified by Christ takes precedence in Christian existence. Justification by faith grounds a life that decenters justice-seeking from being the focal point of Christian identity. Justification frees justice-seeking from standing on its own ground, so to speak. The basis for identity located in God's justifying activity involves a shift away from absolutizing any justice-seeking claim. Justification thus relativizes justice-seeking; the former, not the latter, defines the Christian shape of the Beloved Community. This does not make justice-seeking less important. Rather it centers justice-seeking on the practice of ordinary faith that lives out Christian belonging in the world. Here, in the world, ordinary faith centers one without self-centeredness; we are each informed by a central belonging that includes being informed by others as we navigate the complexities of decision-making about the shape of justice with others.

Yet the mystery is that the center is not there as such, but becomes central when we learn to pay attention to it. We actually learn from Jesus how to become aware of its capacity to recenter us when we become lost in the game and constricted by the desire to win. In the New Testament, Jesus consistently teaches his followers to see the *basileia tou Theou*—the kingdom or kin-dom (referring to the kinships constituting the community) of God. This kin-dom can be recognized by its signs, signs that Jesus embodies: "the kingdom of God is [within] you" (Luke 17:21). "You are not far from the kingdom of God" (Mark 12:34). Jesus proclaims the presence of the *basileia tou Theou*.

The kin-dom is also imminent. It breaks forth in the midst of the Beloved Community in ways that are recognizable, but not complete. This is a paradox—the presence of and the imminent arrival of the kin-dom. The paradox is personified in Jesus, present to his friends and the crowds, yet also not complete in his mission. The imminence of the kin-dom is intimated in its recognition by those who are not part of his band of followers: in a centurion who knows that Jesus' word from afar will be enough to heal his servant (Matt 8:5–13); in a Syro-Phoenician woman who speaks back against Jesus' own ethnic insults and claims a right to his healing power for her daughter (Mark 7:24–30); in a child taken from the crowd and placed on the lap of Jesus, who says one must be like that child to enter the kingdom of God (Mark 10:15). It is very hard for a rich person to enter the kingdom of heaven (Matt 19:23), but the kingdom is near and trespasses borders of Jew and Gentile, oppressor and oppressed. Where there is insight into loving God first and loving one's neighbor as oneself, there the *basileia tou Theou* is arriving.

The difficulty of recognizing the Beloved Community has to do with its setting within a *polis*, within a series of social relations that stretch from the local to the national and international, from the congregational to the denominational, ecumenical, and interfaith, and from the familial to the various political and affinity groups in which we feel at home. Christians have long had various ways of construing the relationship between the kingdom of God and the kingdoms, empires, and nation-states that structure decision-making by or for the collective: from the Puritans embracing theocracy, to the medievals wielding the two swords of spiritual and political authority, to late-twentieth-century anti-colonial liberationists who portrayed the United States as an apocalyptic beast in whose heart the church tries to survive. We can even think of the *polis* in the contemporary term of "culture." And it is this Christ/culture divide that for many complicates the clear distinction between the Beloved Community and the *polis*. We can see the clear divide, but not see how our own assumptions about Christ are continuous with culture, or how we confuse justice-seeking with the Beloved Community's goals of justice-seeking.[3] Christians live in the *polis*, regardless. They must contend with the world that has its own way of running things. In medieval terminology, this means discerning how the "temporal sword" intersects and overlaps with the "spiritual sword."

Let's follow Jesus a bit more to figure out how to recenter on the Beloved Community. The New Testament gospels show Jesus distinguishing between *polis* and wilderness. The Gospel of Mark emphasizes Jesus' own need for respite after teaching the multitudes and healing individuals. Exhausted, he withdraws for quiet into the wilderness—sometimes with his disciples, but often to be alone with the One who sustains him. In this respect, Jesus resembles his cousin and predecessor, John the Baptist, who was "the voice of one crying out in the wilderness" (John 1:23; cf. Isa 40:3). Jesus' retiring to the wilderness also evokes the prophets, especially Elijah and Moses, who departed to a mountain or cave or a solitary place apart

---

[3]   H. Richard Niebuhr, *Christ and Culture*, 50th anniversary ed., foreword by Martin E. Marty and preface by James M. Gustafson (New York: HarperCollins, 2001).

from other people. There, in lonely places, they listened for the voice of God, or would encounter it unexpectedly. The gospel writers depict Jesus traversing back and forth between solitude and public life, returning to the wilderness as a recentering of his focus on his beloved Abba. Even the stories of the devil's tempting Jesus in the wilderness have a recentering effect on Jesus. Jesus declares, against the devil's demonstration of worldly wealth and power, that one lives from "every word that comes from the mouth of God" (Matt 4:4). Jesus' recentering efforts should give us pause. We too should follow him into the wilderness in order to rightly perceive the *basileia tou Theou*.

In the prophetic tradition of the Hebrew scriptures, solitary sojourning in the wilderness means dwelling in a place-time not defined by human culture, human-lived norms and expectations—away from family, from work, even from friendships. Jesus' leadership *began* with a departure to the wilderness for "forty days" after his baptism (Matt 4:1–11). This story marks Jesus' own death to his prior way of life in a temporal and spatial way. Jesus resists the demonic claim that a kind of political authority might meet people's material needs. Like Jonah, Jesus is tempted to run from his vocation. The devil voices this dare: "If you are the Son of God, throw yourself down [off the pinnacle of the temple]" (Matt 4:6). Jesus shows us that the reign of God takes hold in our mind's eye and our heart's work when we take recourse in the wilderness, when we recenter by moving from the public space of human engagement into the solitude of time to listen for the voice of God. Hence Jesus keeps returning regularly to the liminal space of the wilderness. There he fortifies himself with perspective to counter temptations to use his spiritual charisma to his advantage.

Some might be tempted to perceive the reign of God *only* in the wilderness—apart from the demands and expectations of other human beings, apart from the tensions of debating with others. This may be the draw for many who identify as spiritual but not religious, who are uncomfortable with institutional religion because there is usually something that troubles one about the values, worship style, or people in a living congregation. Even Paul was slow to find his way into a public ministry after leaving behind his contentious relationship with Jesus' followers when Jesus confronted him on the road to Damascus (Acts 9:4–5). But such long-term solitude is not the vocation of most Christians. Rather, time in retreat from others is part of the rhythm of ordinary faith.

Indeed, formation in the gospel—and fortitude for the noisy world of justice-seeking—includes time spent in solitude *and* with small circles of others. As Amy tells her students: we all need to find our people, or our various peoples, in order to be and become ourselves. Then we can brave the larger world, or find the particular courage it takes to go out into the world on terms other than the expectations of families or communities of origin. The pioneers of Christian faith lived in remote regions; the desert fathers and mothers and early monastics practiced solitude sometimes in the company of close-knit friendship circles. Saint Jerome relied on his entourage of brilliant female biblical translators and interpreters (like Marcella of Rome); Saint Augustine was persistently followed by his mother Monica and he shared fellowship with many friends, including the famous Alypius; and Saint Francis of Assisi was accompanied by Saint Clare. Sometimes Jesus retreated into the wilderness with his three closest friends, Peter, James, and John (e.g., Luke 9:28; Mark 14:32–33). The Beloved Community is found in the solitude of seeking out God's voice in the wilderness, as well as alongside mutual formation with fellow human beings.

With regard to justice-seeking, then, gospel stories invite us to see the Beloved Community not as a settled place that has all the answers ready-to-hand, but as a space of life together before God in which to hold and carry and debate the questions whose answers at times are truly contested among us. Jesus' passage between perspective-seeking in the wilderness and engaging with the interhuman energy of the multitudes is a model for us as individuals, and also points to and blesses a pattern of ongoing repentant reconfiguration in the Beloved Community as a whole. The wilderness-multitudes rhythm is one in which we practice repentance and renewal not only as individuals, but in and for the Beloved Community as a whole.

The Movement of Ordinary Faith: Decentering to Recentering

How can Christians live out a theology based on justification by faith that is oriented to justice-seeking? Can a theology grounded in justification by faith be lived out in the daily rough-and-tumble of life? Faith is ordinary because it is lived in the day-to-day. The Christian life is not for extraordinary faith-athletes alone. It is meant to be lived in the ordinary ways in which Christians go about their lives, navigating relationships and working toward what they think is the aim of a better life for all. It involves the daily recognition that we are justified by faith in Christ—a profoundly ordinary fact that can order our everyday lives by regulating our orientation to God and one another. Justification by faith is not an abstract idea to be pulled out when we are forced to read Paul's epistles, but a daily practice of becoming attuned to the life-giving and sustaining reality of Christ while engaged in the working out of justice in relationships and communities. In other words, it is the practice of being committed to a team while also recognizing that one's team is part of the league.

One analogy of daily practice can also be taken from athletics. Basketball players practice every day in order to perfect their throws; runners stretch every day in order to keep muscles limber and thus prevent injury. Paul appeals to daily athletic practice when he admonishes the Corinthians in their faith. The athlete trains daily in order to win the prize, Paul writes: "Athletes exercise self-control in all things; they do it to receive a perishable wreath, but we an imperishable one" (1 Cor 9:25). Daily athletic regimen is aimed at winning. Training is goal-oriented, as Paul also notes: "So I do not run aimlessly, nor do I box as though beating the air" (1 Cor 9:26). Practice makes perfect, as the saying goes. One practices in order to become better at the skill. Christian faith, in Paul's conception, is a practice that implies gaining competence—one gets better at it so that one can win the prize.

Paul admonishes the Corinthians with a goal-oriented image of motion. Here ordinary faith is oriented to the finish line. This could be taken to mean running the race so that a particular view of justice will transpire as the prize.

Yet movement in faith can be understood in another way. Ordinary faith, as we have been discussing, is founded on Christ. From that place of belonging, we move out into the world. Ordinary faith moves from an interiorly sensed space of belonging into a place of negotiation and struggle. This movement is inevitably decentering. One can use the image of a discus thrower who makes one and a half turns on the circle before launching the discus as far as possible. Such a propulsion decenters the athlete. The forces used in throwing the discus propel the athlete toward the edge of the circle. She fights hard to stay within the circle. Any step outside will result in a disqualification. She has practiced this movement countless times in order to reach this level of athletic excellence. Yet every time she propels the discus, forces invariably act on her body in destabilizing ways.

Decentering is part of how ordinary faith moves in the world. There are forces—some external, some internal—that are destabilizing. They are part and parcel of moving in the world as a Christian. Decentering is an inevitability when moving from a vision of the Beloved Community into the world. Yet a more insidious decentering occurs where that movement involves sinning and being sinned against. In playing the game, we do not always embody, and sometimes actively resist embodying, the capacious sense of life for and with others that Christ imagines for Christian freedom. We practice justice-seeking in the midst of polarized forms of group belonging that distort our exchanges. As part of collective actions, we often take up unjust means to achieve our goals. This sort of decentering is grounded in ego and our identification with a particular affinity group, not on the central rock, which is Christ. Decentering knocks us off-kilter.

Thus recentering comes into play to correct for the decentering that puts one off balance. Recentering involves spiritual practices that move Christians to see ways in which our thinking and action have caused decentering. In recentering, we call out for divine aid to rectify the injustice of our own self-quarantined thinking and action. Recognition of sin, as Luther always knew, is the precursor to the gospel.

Regaining one's balance is a return to grounding. How might the process of justice-seeking embed a constant return to justification by faith in Christ? How might we navigate the process of justice-seeking within the baptized body of Christ in a capacious orthodox-seeking way, rather than a heretical way of demonizing those with whom we disagree within the body of Christ? And how do we live with the tilt and whirl of being decentered in good ways—as we acknowledge what we had missed seeing or hearing, as we are called to account for the *how* as well as the *what* of our justice-seeking team-playing?

Moved to love our neighbor as ourselves (and thus to love ourselves as well, to listen to our own as well as others' concerns), we find ourselves challenged to move from one moment of identification with a particular configuration of a just community to that identification's breaking and reconfiguring. We can meet that challenge precisely because we are centered in and by our baptism into the body of Christ, and so, like a spinning top that is centered in place but able to move in every direction, we can join with Jesus in our own journeying into the wilderness spaces where we might be undone and redone as we ponder what we have seen and heard from one another and ask: where is the Spirit speaking?

The wilderness-crowd rhythm of Jesus' life can thus inform the kind of piety we might practice as we approach justice-seeking in light of our justification by faith, our baptism into the corporate body of Christ.

The spatial metaphor of decentering and recentering gets at the movement between these two aspects of Christian existence, as well as a dynamic at play in the Beloved Community as it contends with the shape of justice in a given time and place. This metaphor speaks to how justification by faith decenters justice-seeking wherever it bears a proclivity to presumptuous self-identification, to seeing some particular version of justice as *the* mark of Christian identity; it recenters justice-seeking by insisting on the primacy of divine gift in determining Christian existence. Justification grounds Christian identity in the divine act of justifying. This grounding in turn frees Christian existence to pursue justice-seeking together with others. The metaphor of decentering and recentering also comes into play with regard to the nitty-gritty of Christians debating the shape of justice that we envision within and for the Beloved Community. In this second sense, we might find ourselves decentered from an earlier understanding of what right relations look like among us, and recentered in new ways.

Ordinary Faith, Ordinary Repentance

Ordinary faith is a movement back to the place of belonging. We return when we realize how we have strayed or where we feel alienated from others in the struggle to feel heard and be seen in the body of Christ. Martin Luther beautifully captures this return in his *Ninety-Five Theses* from 1517 on indulgences. The first thesis headlines the remaining ninety-five: "Our Lord and Master Jesus Christ, in saying 'Do penance . . .' [Matt 4:17], wanted the entire life of the faithful to be one of penitence."[4] The fact that Luther organizes the entirety of the *Ninety-Five Theses* around the theme of repentance is significant. The entire Christian life, Luther insists, is oriented to repentance. Repentance (in Greek, *metanoia*) should inform every moment of the Christian life. At every point, the Christian should be engaged in a change of heart or understanding. Luther knows all too well the reason for this perpetual attunement of the Christian life to repentance. The Christian is always mired in sin, either through participation in sinful acts or being sinned-against in some way. There is no point—outside of Christ—at which the Christian can claim freedom from sin. Christian repentance is the flipside of sin. Just as every moment is informed by sin, in each moment we can likewise be alert to the need for

---

4   Martin Luther, "[The Ninety-Five Theses or] Disputation for Clarifying the Power of Indulgences, 1517," trans. Charles M. Jacobs, rev. trans. Harold J. Grimm, newly rev. Timothy J. Wengert, in *The Annotated Luther*, vol. 1, *The Roots of Reform*, ed. Timothy J. Wengert (Minneapolis: Fortress, 2015), 34.

a turn away from sin (be it enacted by us, against us, or pervade the atmosphere itself). Just as the Christian life is marked by sin, so too it requires a recentering on Christ. The movement of "change of heart" (*metanoia*) is not a once and for all; it is the persistence in a change of mind that tracks throughout the Christian life.

What does a life of repentance look like? In part it entails identifying all the ways in which we participate in justice-seeking that deny justice in the process. We break connections with people; say things that alienate; do things that harm. We feel cast adrift by what others say and do. Walls go up. We react with biting polemic. We stubbornly insist that we are right and others wrong.

Justice-seeking takes place in the tangled reality of life in the world. It involves a struggle to discern the meaning of neighbor love for the shape of justice. The Beloved Community does not emerge only when we or those around us perfectly keep the law or ways of God; it is not equated simply with a realized just society. The Beloved Community is that which calls out sin, provides a home for repentance to be practiced and for the lost to be found, and Spirit-drives us to discern how to live out love of God and neighbor. From Paul's time to our own, this discernment has involved debate wherever our fears and dreams for ourselves and one another seem to be at odds.

It may be that one of the hardest things of all is for Christians to repent of their ways of practicing their faith, especially as it concerns notions of what is just and right. Lutheran theologian Denise Rector writes about a particular spiritual practice that opens the door for repentance. She advocates that lament be taken seriously as a precursor to repentance. Lament is a liturgical collective cry that puts mourning even before confession of guilt:

> Distinguishing between lament and confession can ease the tension inherent in conversations about race. Defensiveness and accusations resulting from questions of guilt, fault, and responsibility are difficult to avoid when African Americans and whites talk about race relations and racial equity; the very word "racism" engenders much emotional response.[5]

Rector notes that "public and corporate lament" can offer "an entry point to the complexities of racism, making space to consider and mourn the effects

---

5   Denise Rector, "Race and the Gift of Lament," *Dialog* 60, no. 1 (2021): 25.

of racism while temporarily setting aside the varied historical and structural causes." Lament is "a way to call a thing what it is, even a regrettable and hurtful thing, without allowing questions of guilt, fault, or responsibility become a barrier to conversation. It is an act of grief that can take place without assigning blame." Precisely by recognizing with pain that the sin of racism has prevented full belonging of African Americans in her denomination, the Evangelical Lutheran Church of America, Rector notes: "Lament builds the relationship scaffolding and community in Christ necessary to move *through* lament into examination of deeper issues that may exist (including guilt and misunderstanding)." While a fuller repentance calls for analysis and an address of the causes of systemic injustice—a move to confession and redress—lament allows us to begin by seeing and feeling the injustice itself. Like the Psalmist who cries out to God in a desperate situation (i.e., "How long, O Lord?" Ps 13:1), a collective lament allows us to *share* in the brokenness of a sin that directly affects some more than others. The conditions of our Christian life are so often permeated by injustice: white privilege structures anti-Black injustice; patriarchy shapes our diminishment of women in thought, word, and deed; ableism denies the full humanity of the other-abled. Lament about these and many other sinful social conditions draws us into a sense of belonging together to a common humanity that is broken, complicit, and unjust. The lament that is first expressed by those experiencing injustice is also taken up in collective, ecclesial lament by those who may have benefited from that injustice. Thus, suffering becomes *ours* rather than *yours*.

Lament is a sign or first fruits (1 Cor 15:20, 23) of repentance. Luther calls Christians to inhabit repentance like a second skin. Repentance is to be practiced, over and over again, until it becomes second nature. It is a perennial "change of mind and heart," of sensing when to tack in another direction.

Luther sees repentance as a recentering on justification by faith. He invokes baptism in this context of persistent repentance. He writes about the daily remembering of baptism as a symbol of dying and rising with Christ.[6] Luther's call to "remember your baptism" is a reminder that we are daily and regularly in need of repentance, renewal of vision, and an

---

[6]   Martin Luther, "The Small Catechism (1529)," section on "The Sacrament of Holy Baptism," in *The Book of Concord: The Confessions of the Evangelical Lutheran Church*, trans. Charles Arand et al., ed. Robert Kolb and Timothy J. Wengert (Minneapolis: Fortress, 2000), 359–62.

accompanying openness to listening and journeying with ourselves and one another. By returning to baptism, we remember that we have died to sin and are risen in Christ. Baptism is, in effect, the pronouncement of one's sin-defeating, life-affirming identity in Christ. This identity is, by another name, the justification that faith in Christ effects. Repentance is, in other words, a recentering on justification by faith that baptism creates.

The call to daily repentance recenters our limited perspective back to the wider Beloved Community. The recentering of repentance can involve affective dimensions: turning one's heart to those whose voice is eliminated from the algorithm documenting one's search engine. It can also involve enlarging one's mind to provide a space for critical independent thought. Participation in justice-seeking can be influenced by the restricted company we keep, or by our circle of social media "friends." A recalling of our baptism is an acknowledgment that our motivated reasoning and sophism, even in the name of the ideals that center our lives, require forgiveness.

It is common to look at spiritual practices in individualistic terms. Spiritual guidance is one-on-one; individuals read books to help them on their respective spiritual pathways. The individual makes spiritual progress—or backslides—on their own terms.

Yet humans are social creatures. The Christian life is also social, as is systemic sin. When Luther stresses repentance as that which drives the entirety of the Christian life, he also includes a social dimension to repentance—as we saw with Rector's call for collective lament for the sin of racism. To recall the Beloved Community is to return to a social reality, Christians who each and together are justified by faith in Christ. Worship together is one way in which this remembering is enacted. There are concrete liturgical ways in which repentance is rehearsed together. Public (and private) confession comes to mind as the most obvious liturgical instance of repentance. But homilies can also track the movement from decentered existence to recentering in Christ. The classic Lutheran structure for a sermon is to move from law to gospel, from recognition of sin to forgiveness of sin. Hymns, like "Amazing Grace," narrate the shift from being "lost" to being "found" and thereby track the movement from decenteredness to being recentered by grace. Gathering for communion with bread and wine gathers us together again in Christ—those who think like us politically and those who do not. Luther constantly insists that a recalling of baptism is central to the Christian life in its recentering action. Of course, some may have vexed relations to actual churches. But the communal dimension of spiritual practices focused on repentance traces its recentering in the community of saints.

Individual and corporate repentance is a lifelong practice because it needs to be practiced. We might get better at it; practice promises improved adeptness. But like yoga or floor exercises for some of us, the more we stretch our tight hamstrings, the more we might experience the same inflexibility that inspired us to start practicing yoga in the first place!

Key though is that we come to appreciate the rhythm of recentering, alone and with the community of saints. This is the practice of living out our baptism, together. Repentance is a liturgical tracking of the movement from decentering to recentering, from sin to grace, from fiercely held narrowness to spaciousness of heart and mind, from captivity to freedom. As such, this movement is a recollection of baptismal belonging, as Luther loved to say. Repentance recalls baptismal belonging as a present-tense reality. While one cannot easily remember one's experience of baptism if baptized as an infant, all Christians can make present in the imagination our centering in the Beloved Community as an achievement of baptism, performed by Christ. We acknowledge that it is not possible to recenter with every individual Christian, especially perhaps with those who have harmed us deeply. But all of us can keep justification by faith as the larger landscape and horizon around the set patterns we have inherited.

Presumption and Despair as Ways of Naming the Sins of Christian Partisanship

As we noted above, and as Luther succinctly claimed in his catechetical teachings for all Christians, repentance is a lifelong practice, one that accompanies life in the Beloved Community. It is a daily recollection of Christian belonging by virtue of one's baptism. Repentance involves recognition of sinning and being sinned against. There are cognitive and linguistic dimensions to this practice. It also involves becoming aware of particular affective states infusing sinning and being sinned against. Luther will serve as guide in this section for naming the psychological dynamics in sin as "presumption" and "despair," a classic way of identifying sin that long predates Luther and was especially developed among soul-attentive monastics. While we discussed presumption and despair—and idolatry—in an earlier chapter, we revisit this dynamic here for two reasons: first, to emphasize our overarching theme that recollection of confession of sin and grace is a dynamic deeper than our particular contested views of justice; and to retrieve attention to presumption and despair

236 | Ordinary Faith in Polarized Times

within ourselves (and one another) as a fruitful spiritual practice amid the rock and roll of justice-seeking together.

As we noted earlier, as a friar in the rigorous branch of the Augustinians, Luther was accustomed to introspection of mind and heart. He became particularly attuned to two states that he discerned were exacerbated by the divine imperatives of the Ten Commandments. One state is presumption, the feeling that one can fulfill the divine law and thereby merit eternal grace. The other is its opposite, the despair that arises after an awakening to one's own sin: the temptation to believe one is essentially damned, that one can never earn good standing with God and neighbor. While presumption names a psychological state of obliviousness to one's sin, despair amplifies a sense of the insurmountability of sin.

Both states have their concomitant dangers. Presumption is dangerous insofar as it denies the need for repentance. We assume all is well with us, that we are righteous or righteous enough; we are satisfied with what we have achieved and how we have achieved. Our exulting closes us off from God and neighbor. But despair too is dangerous. Despair prevents us from experiencing the reality and power of the gospel. Because the gospel preaches that our orientation to God is not based on becoming personally worthy to stand before God, the gospel is the antidote to despair. But despair's affective state, as Luther experienced for many years in the monastery before his so-called Reformation breakthrough, was a deterrent to even hearing this good news. We need the moral law proclaimed to us when we are caught up in presumption, and the gospel proclaimed to us when we are vulnerable to despair.

In the context of debates within the contemporary body of Christ about the shape of justice, presumption and despair name temptations that arise when we experience cognitive dissonance as we encounter fellow Christians who disagree with us about what justice looks like. Presumption names the temptation to condition Christian identity upon holding one's own position in a debate about the shape of justice—or, to use Pauline language, the nature of the moral law. Despair names the temptation to believe the worst of ourselves, our opponents, or the condition of the world's receptivity to redemption, namely its capacity for justice. Both presumption and despair also reflect a mode of decentering: presumption by our identifying with one side, one team, and thinking this makes us righteous; despair by the feeling of being decentered, unmoored, as if righteousness does not exist for us or for creation itself.

On one hand we can be tempted to a presumptuous spirit of self-righteousness about our own position in a particular debate about ethics or justice. One expression of this is in the rhetoric of a polarity between a "Christian" and a "secular" worldview, common among culturally conservative evangelicals who feel their "traditional" views on gender and society are no longer mainstream, but instead considered unjust and even potentially illegal. Here there is a presumption that any contrary view about gender or other contested matters (like abortion) is by definition *not Christian*. Presumption thus names the temptation to define Christian identity around one's own team's position in a debate about proper Christian living—a debate that is actually *in-house*. Presumption is here the sinful assumption that Christians who hold a contrary view cannot *really* be Christians and thus should be excommunicated. While excommunication can be an intervention that bears witness to an injustice that has been normalized—as when Spanish missionary Bartolomé de las Casas (1484–1566) excommunicated landowners who enslaved indigenous persons in Chiapas—it can also be a way of refusing to listen to those who have arguably enduring and compelling reasons for a contrary view of what justice entails. In this case, presumption involves denying the complexity of truths at play with regard to a specific ethical or justice-related issue, and instead equating purity with a selective truth within the larger spectrum of truths.

Likewise, those who identify on a progressive team within the body of Christ might be tempted presumptuously to declare not truly Christian those who hold a contrary view of justice, or to deny due process and voice for those who are called out as complicit in the sins of racism, sexism, heterosexism, and other sins that sustain patterns of wrongful privilege and hierarchy. Those on the Christian or secular left can—in the name of justice—ignore, silence, or denounce those who feel left behind by cultural or political changes. Here presumption names what some have called virtue signaling, especially by those with privilege seeking to be allies of those with less privilege: when our own verbal performance of being in the right is more important than righteousness itself being made possible. This form of presumption is easier than the hard, mundane collective work of creating more just policies and truly sharing power with the marginalized in whose name we speak. Such collective labor entails a more demanding conversion than that of a shift in perspective alone.

Despair, on the other hand, is a risk when we enter a repentant mode. Repentance extends to conversions of perspective, as we find the ways we formerly understood ourselves or the world to be profoundly challenged—as when the depth and persistence of racism dawns upon those with white privilege, or when we realize the ways we have internalized notions of female inferiority. Despair can then lurk within the presumption of our own efforts at compensating by demonstrating righteous views, especially on the other side of getting converted or "woke" to a particular justice perspective. We can become attached to the idea that a particular pattern of sin is so implacable that we center our identity upon constantly naming and denouncing that sin. More broadly, though, when our presumption is interrupted and we realize the enormity of a problem we had ignored—in ourselves or in the world at large (such as the extent of the climate crisis)—we become vulnerable to despairing that all can *ever* be made well, for ourselves or for creation as a whole. So we might abdicate the space of politics to others, perhaps by not voting in primaries or general elections, perhaps by not feeling up to spending time researching the issues that are addressed through legislative decision-making at state and federal levels. Here we are tempted to an escapist use of Christian freedom, to focus solely on our inter/personal or professional lives, or on wishing for the world to come. Moreover, insofar as presumption about one's own rightness can be a way of warding off despair of an ability to trust others to share one's own view of justice, Christian freedom to deliberate together about the shape of justice can also be replaced in practice with a Christian will to power—a willingness to cynically use any political means necessary to enact one's own Christian vision of justice. Here a vision of justice is corrupted by a will to power that either ignores or abuses democratic processes.

Both presumption and despair are forms of decentering. Presumption names the habit of denying our decentering from the truth of justification by faith in Christ. In presumption, we instead condition Christian identity upon identifying with one team, one vision of justice in a way that closes us to the humanity of those who seem to (or really do) hold a different vision of justice, a vision we might regard as truly unjust. Resentment and grievance can fester when we condition belonging on holding a particular morally freighted point of view, or on participating in cultural norms or spaces in which others do not feel at home.

Despair names the experience of being decentered from a sense of belonging to the body of Christ because of our own complicity in sin.

Despair can also name the sense that there is no divine justice at all, that creation is and will remain unredeemed, that the forces of destruction will only intensify for all of us. This form of despair may hold us most ferociously in its spell when we realize the degree to which we have damaged the earth and one another, and do not believe our species can collectively course-correct—at least in time to preserve life on our planet. But just as the mustard seed can grow into a large tree (cf. Matt 13:32), so our seeds of investment in using our Christian freedom to understand the concerns of our neighbors and our planet can nourish our growth beyond despair. The tree bears fruit when we participate in public conversation and political decision-making about justice on various concrete issues.

Here remembering our baptism amid daily repentance is a profound act of ordinary faith in the face of our temptations to both presumption and despair. We need this catechesis, for so much invites us to forget it. In a world saturated by social media memes that amplify our fears and righteous grievances and that draw us readily to acts of denunciation and virtue signaling, remembering our baptism into Christ nudges us to notice and navigate our temptations to presumption and despair. Together, repentance and remembering our baptism form part of the ongoing rhythms of faith. It is normal in ordinary faith to find ourselves decentered from old views or senses of self when we are exposed to ethical/political debates and social change movements, and recentered again and again through a piety of wider perspective-seeking that imitates Jesus and the prophets' own sojourns away from—then back toward—all humanly constructed habitations. Remembering our baptism amid repentance orients and reorients us in the wilderness of our private prayer, and in the communal space of gathering to hear the Word of God and share in the sacramental meal that expresses our belonging to one another in Christ. Recalling our baptism is a perspective-forging habit that helps us not only to continue to reflect on the shape of justice and our accountability for it, but also to find hope in an "otherwise"—a world of peace and righteousness—that is ultimately of God's making, and ours by participation.

But the aim of remembering our baptism is never simply holding an eschatological vision of hope in mind. Baptismal recollection also involves recognizing our own sins of presumption and despair. Doing so ought not prevent us from risking participation in justice-seeking. We have sought to illuminate how Christian freedom interrupts self-righteous or cynical practices that foreclose the genuine conversation constitutive of a healthy political process—within and beyond the church. Christian freedom in the political sphere construes politics as a space of figuring out together how discrepant positions and complexities can be negotiated. By contrast, in self-righteous presumption (with its undercurrent of despair about our opponents' capacity to change), we can be drawn to manipulative tugs on our values, and reactively signal our allegiance to them. Yet Christian freedom means breaking these restrictive cycles of manipulation and response, and instead infusing an ethos of Christian freedom into religiously and politically multivalent spaces—the world in its many configurations of political decision-making.

Idolatry and Mutual Belonging

Christian liturgy concludes with the imperative, "Go out into the world." Going out into the world is the way that Christians live out faith in the day-to-day. The liturgy pronounces forgiveness of sin, Christ gives the gift of bread and wine, and the ordinary priesthood orients believers to their central identity in Christ. Yet believers must come down from the mountaintop. They must go out into the world to share the gospel message and seek justice and well-being in their communities.

Going out into the world invariably involves the risks of disagreement. In the examples we have held up—abortion and the role of Christian faith in politics—going out into the world means genuinely disagreeing because of differing (and often incommensurable) visions of justice. All too often we go out into the world and double down within our various affinity groups as we regard the other team as mortal enemy. Sometimes we denounce our "opponents" as anti-Christian. "Abortion is demonic" is one tweet we have seen. One Christian demonizes the other, denying that they share a common identity in the Beloved Community and refusing to see the face of Christ in a neighbor.

Going out into the world is a decentering movement. We become vulnerable to new input. We encounter Christians who hold different visions of justice-seeking. In response, we might hold tenaciously on to what we think is true and just, afraid of the other who might also be right. When we are in danger of regarding the other as not centered with us in the Beloved Community, we are also in danger of elevating our own advocacy for a position of justice to ultimacy.

This, in theological terms, is the danger of idolatry. When the team represents the league; when the play is a winner-takes-all; when one decides that one's own position is right and the other "demonic"—this is when idolatry happens. It is *the* risk of justice-seeking in our current climate. It is the risk of one side co-opting the center amid the decentering that occurs when going out into the world.

Why do we face this problem (one we also noted in chapter 5)? Idolatry in traditional terms means mistaking the part for the whole, elevating one side to represent all sides, or taking what is penultimate to be ultimate. It means confusing creature for creator, and thus worshiping that which is falsely deified. The biblical prohibition of idolatry is represented by the first commandment, "you shall have no other gods before me" (Exod 20:3). When this prohibition is translated into theological vocabulary it can be formulated as mistaking the part for the whole in such a way that obeisance to the part detracts from a purview of the whole. Idolatry can thus consist in our viscerally holding on to partial truths. It can be the refusal to honor the other; it can be the erecting of walls, the doubling-down in the name of justice. And it is this idolatry that all too readily haunts the movement of "going out into the world."

The decentering of "going out into the world" is unavoidable. Idolatry is not. But as we explored in chapter 3, as a species, we are prone to self-delusion, believing in what can foster optimism—even if based on a falsehood—when we might otherwise feel overwhelmed by harsh realities. Our defense mechanisms include affective tenacities that intensify when we feel our position is threatened by another. On such occasions we can fall into elevating our own perspective as ultimate, and then impose the power of our own position onto others.

As we have noted in previous chapters, there is a Reformation emphasis on what has been called the Protestant principle, or being aware that we are vulnerable to idolatry precisely where we risk investing in our particular moral and justice-seeking commitments. Here the Protestant Reformers entreat us to regularly recenter in the Beloved Community that offers us the capaciousness of belonging to Christ as the One who sets free from the sins of presumption, despair, and idolatry. Ordinary faith is a life of repentance, specifically of the sins that so easily accompany the decentering that happens when we walk into the world to live the gospel. Such repentance includes fostering self-awareness about when we are tempted to perceive others as cast out from fundamental belonging because we so disagree with them. Repentance includes owning such tendencies to dehumanize—owning our complicity, our my-team fandom, our ways of using social media to "like" one side of a moral debate with a relish that over-emphasizes our grievances. Repentance is a recentering and becoming aware of the idolatries involved in "going out into the world."

Repentance of our ongoing pulls to idolatry is also a living-into a sense of the ampleness of the Beloved Community as a spiritual practice, through a reminder of our belonging to it with others. In this sense, repentance is a metacognitive practice of widening (not shrinking) our empathy—a widening that has intellectual, imaginative and affective dimensions, all elements at play when we are attuned to the complexity of justice-seeking in the presence of the Beloved Community.

One practice for metacognitive attention to our inner lives as we navigate justice-seeking can be regular time-outs. As Sarah Semmler Smith put it in a sermon on Mark 7 and James 1, we can be aware of all the raw emotion and first judgments stirring in our hearts. It is then up to us to

> pause, and ask Christ to put a filter on our words, our thoughts—that any words we utter might be used to build up the world around us instead of just cut it down. Because even the most divinely right position, if ushered with violence of judgement, will not be heard, it will only be deflected; it will only deepen division.
>
> So we can pause and choose our filters—to let some things through but not others. The filter of Compassion, which asks, instead of 'What is wrong with this person': 'What story from their life explains their position on this?' The filter of Time—taking as many minutes as your age to respond, instead of react. Perhaps? Or, never sending or posting that first draft. And the filter of Christ, to whom we can pray that most simple but profound prayer: *Lord help me love them.*[7]

Pausing is one basic strategy for recognizing and resisting ways we restrict others. It offers us moments to reflect on the truth that there are different and relevant sides to a story—as we discussed in chapter 4 on abortion. To be sure, truth as multifaceted does not mean that all positions are equally valid for moral consideration or for policymaking. The challenge, regardless, is to recognize the multiple truths and affective dimensions for all that are at play as we journey with others in the lifelong process of recentering in the body of Christ and decentering as we go out into the world again and again.

The first commandment and its related double love commandment enjoin us to put no other gods before the God whom we must love with all our hearts, souls, mind, and strength (cf. Deut 6:5; Matt 22:37). Keeping

[7]   Rev. Sarah Semmler Smith, sermon at Good Shepherd Lutheran Church, Houghton, Mich., August 29, 2021.

the first commandment is not a one-time accomplishment, as the Reformers knew. It is a disposition of the heart, a perpetual orientation, a calling to tend toward our own "dynamics of faith." Keeping the first commandment is the most enduring, viable expression of our ultimate faith and trust, a way that Jesus illuminates for Christians through his life, death, resurrection, and sending of the Holy Spirit, who makes us children of God in our baptism. Its opposite is idolatry, the perennial temptation to trust in what is penultimate, to mistake God for a moral position, to confuse the living God with the idol that damages the body of Christ. How can one resist this temptation and become more attuned to God? In the next section we consider a piety of theocentrism with regard to practices of justice-seeking.

The Piety of Theocentrism as Orthopraxy: Ways of Acknowledging Divine Sovereignty in Relation to Justice-Seeking

Theocentrism means being single-heartedly centered on God. This is the implied posture of faith among those who are children of God within the Beloved Community. Theocentrism has long been understood to imply perspectives about the nature of justice as well: if God is sovereign in our lives, does that not imply we will live according to the will of God? Some have appealed to the rhetoric of divine sovereignty to shore up views of justice that silence and oppress others: "It is God's will!" Yet theocentrism can be understood as a spiritual practice of recognizing divine sovereignty that ultimately draws us ever more deeply into the mystery of shared justice-seeking, as we explore here.

We ought first to acknowledge, though, that many Christians feel ambivalent (at best) about directly connecting the political, historical realm to the idea of divine sovereignty. It is used to underscore partisanship: our team will score theological points because God is on our side. Thus, for example, Calvinists from North America to South Africa wed divine sovereignty with biblical narratives about the promised land to justify their colonial claims to land as well as their acts of genocide and apartheid. But divine sovereignty can also remind us that finitude and partiality characterize *all* efforts to discern and institutionalize particular shapes of justice; no one vision can match the divine will, yet God is ultimately responsible for guiding different visions to unify around more just systems. Black Christians in the United States and South Africa, for example, have trusted that God is God; white supremacists are not God. Racial segregation and a racialized caste system reflect a blasphemous perversion of the will of a sovereign God. The oppressed thus look to a righteous God who will come and who will judge injustices perpetrated by white supremacists. All this is to say that if we are indeed to associate the sovereign will of God with our deepest convictions about the shape of justice, the direction of our ethical judgments matters all the more. Consequently, we need to be vigilant in discerning how we appeal to divine sovereignty, in our species-long dance between a recognition of the finite, creaturely nature of all our human endeavors, and our earnest investment in concrete political projects to perceive and support the common good.

How to discern the will of a sovereign God is thus part of Christian orthopraxis, or the praxis side of Christian orthodoxy: acknowledging God as our creator and redeemer in worship flows into acknowledging God in the ethics of our life together. This premise, of course, lies behind every Christian effort to participate in justice-seeking. But *how* do we connect a recognition of divine sovereignty with making judgments about God-willed approaches to questions of ethics or justice? We briefly engage here two approaches that associate ethics with a non-idolatrous theocentrism as it is expressed in worship and in the God-centered piety it cultivates. But the first option, which we will critique, perceives a direct line between a revealed divine will in Scripture and an ethical prescription. We will suggest that this approach forecloses Christian debate because it conditions Christian identity on adhering to a specific set of ethical perspectives.

Mark Liederbach and Evan Lenow perceive an explicit connection between being theocentric and particular positions on justice-seeking in *Ethics as Worship: The Pursuit of Moral Discipleship*.[8] They argue that worship is not only a ritualized space for acknowledging that God is God and that all of creation depends upon God in Christ for its existence and its redemption. Rather, practicing a particular set of ethical norms is *itself* part of the act of worshiping the sovereign God. Christians can thus espy a "revealed morality," a "normative formulation of ethics as worship":[9] "when understood through a theocentric lens, the pursuit of justice *is* ethics as worship."[10] In their account of ethics as worship, Liederbach and

---

Mark D. Liederbach and Evan Lenow, *Ethics as Worship: The Pursuit of Moral Discipleship* (Phillipsburg, N.J.: P & R Publishing, 2021).

Mark D. Liederbach and Evan Lenow, "Part 3: Revealed Morality: The Normative Formulation of Ethics as Worship," in *Ethics as Worship*, 173–243.

[10]   Liederbach and Lenow, *Ethics as Worship*, 308.

Lenow presuppose biblical inerrancy. They assume that a Christian reading of Scripture yields sufficient access to the divine will on any ethical topic. To be theocentric means to see and follow a clearly revealed way to live rightly, one in which ethics as worship of a sovereign God is tied to notions of biblical infallibility and inerrancy because God has "sovereign control of every word recorded in the Bible."[11] Liederbach and Lenow then apply "ethics as worship" to a range of issues—race, ethnicity, and kingdom diversity; creation care; abortion; biblical and disordered sexuality; war; and so on—making a case for the right Christian perspective on each one. Taking what they term a "humble absolutist" position, they assert that "Scripture contains numerous absolute commands, which never conflict." This means that on such topics, "moral dilemmas are existentially/experientially 'real' to nonbelievers" because of sin, but in Christ "regeneration enables greater epistemological clarity" and a "progressive moral transformation such that believers improve in their ability to see and work out morally complex situations."[12] Moreover, by framing ethics as worship, they seek to inspire Christians to practice ethics not as a set of obligatory rules, but as part of the joy of God-centered discipleship itself. Here a theocentric orthopraxis is also a robust defense—however nuanced—for their own position on ethical debates where broader consensus, in fact, has not been found.

By contrast, our own approach to connecting visions of justice within the Beloved Community to divine sovereignty—or to what Liederbach and Lenow call "the total alignment of all creation with the eternal law of God"[13]—takes its bearings from the historical observation that orthodoxy itself is a normative theological perspective *because* it seeks to integrate the most compelling, abiding insights of competing positions in a debate within the Christian community. This insight extends to discernments about what constitutes orthopraxis, or ethical living, as well. While the creeds were about clarifying the nature of Jesus' relationship to God, contemporary Christian debates focus on the nature of the moral law. Yet just as the creeds distilled hard-fought consensus positions, so we are suggesting that the *process* of discerning orthodoxy is an analogy for engaging ethical sorts of questions, especially where a widely agreed consensus position does not readily emerge. To be sure, ethical debates with

---

[11]   Liederbach and Lenow, *Ethics as Worship*, 139.
[12]   Liederbach and Lenow, *Ethics as Worship*, 270.
[13]   Liederbach and Lenow, *Ethics as Worship*, 308.

political dimensions can and do resolve in a particular team's direction—a direction that names and breaks with structures of oppression that were once normalized in the name of divine sovereignty and providence. For example, despite the persistence of white supremacy and global variants of ethnocentric Christian nationalism, most Christians no longer openly defend racism, slavery, or ethnocentrism.[14] Instead, some might rationalize ethnic and racial hierarchies without overtly claiming to hold to them (as many will still openly do with regard to gendered distinctions and hierarchies), often in the name of a way of life that has implicitly relied upon protected spaces of ethnic or racial homogeneity. The process of discerning our temptations to misusing the name of God persists as we continue to work our way through the legacy of white supremacy and enchanting forms of ethnonationalism that remain institutionalized in various ways. But discernment of an orthodox-forming sort is also vital as we seek to block out the cheers of our own team in order to listen to what we can affirm is genuinely at stake for the other team in a contested ethical debate. As Pope Francis put it in his Christmas 2022 sermon to the Roman Curia, fellow church leaders ought to beware of the "elegant demon" that tempts them to "rigidity and the presumption that they were better than others."[15]

We suggest that orthodoxy is like what Pope Francis called tradition: "a process of understanding Christ's message [that] never ends, but constantly challenges us."[16] Orthodoxy as the right praxis of justifying our beliefs resonates with Christian traditions of theological ethics as a practice of ongoing discernment. These practices draw upon all forms of human knowing, framed within a God-centered worldview. The theological ethicist James Gustafson outlined a vision of the Christian life that we have in mind. In his *Ethics from a Theocentric Perspective*, Gustafson connects a Calvinist emphasis on giving God glory with a process of Christian formation that associates theocentrism not only with Scripture-inspired interpretations

---

[14]   Unlike nineteenth-century slaveholding Christians who appealed to biblical inerrancy to defend slavery, Liederbach and Lenow appeal to biblical authority to construe racism as a sin and to defend a "color-celebratory" form of addressing racism. See Liederbach and Lenow, *Ethics as Worship*, 321–27.

[15]   Pope Francis, "Address of His Holiness Pope Francis to the Roman Curia for the Exchange of Christmas Greetings," December 22, 2022, https://www.vatican.va/content/francesco/en/speeches/2022/december/documents/20221222-curia-romana.html.

[16]   Pope Francis, "Address to the Roman Curia."

of the world in relation to God, but also with attention to more deeply understanding that world itself.[17] Unlike Liederbach and Lenow, Gustafson reads Scripture-as-revelation alongside careful attention to the natural and human worlds. To ignore a rich understanding of the natural and human worlds would be to draw our circles of accountability before God and creation in a nearsighted and arbitrary way. Gustafson perceives that being theocentric entails becoming increasingly cosmocentric. In this way, we become ever more adept together at extending our neighborliness from our immediate kin to the ends of creation.

For Gustafson, the relationship of ethics to worship emerges through worship-cultivated piety as a lived practice of discerning the divine will in the world. God-centered worship cultivates religious affections of awe, wonder, loyalty, and care for creation—affective dispositions that foster attention and accountability to all those with whom we see ourselves in interrelationship. Theological ethics for Gustafson integrates Christian dispositions with insights from empirical scientific and social scientific studies. Gustafson thus depicts the ethical work of theology not as a matter of biblical proof-texting, nor as a matter of heeding a magisterium *per se*, but as a worship-formed practice of attention to God and the world in relation to God. Theological ethics here builds upon a worldview that orients us to attend to our lives in all their complexity, fully informed by human sources of knowledge.

Gustafson relates the piety that arises while pondering divine sovereignty to the search for a justice-seeking orthopraxis in a way that we believe fosters more persuasive, sustainable ethical perspectives over time. This is because they take their bearings from attention to a wide array of truths about creaturely existence before God, rather than highlighting one particular truth as the only relevant one, or as one behind which to hide all other morally inconvenient truths. Being theocentric, acknowledging divine sovereignty, entails more than knowing and defending one's own team's position where earnest debate exists among Christians. Rather, it cautions against too readily assuming that the power of the Almighty can be called upon to defend a straightforward line drawn from biblical principles to "the" Christian ethical perspective on a disputed topic in the public sphere. Practicing ethical discernment in a theocentric vein includes a wide and deep listening to those with

---

[17]   James M. Gustafson, *Ethics from a Theocentric Perspective*, vol. 1, *Theology and Ethics* (Chicago: University of Chicago Press, 1981).

competing intuitions. We each still have to risk picking a team that voices a perspective on justice that we find the most compatible with the will of God. That means selecting the team that we believe best gathers up all the relevant intuitions and observations about human beings and the larger creation. For just as many on the Arian "side" later joined in support of the Nicene Creed, so too can different teams on opposite sides of a debate begin to hear and integrate the insights of their opponents. Orthodoxy is thus a theocentric piety in which Christians continue to ask how we are seeking and holding together all the relevant truths in our picture of justice in and through the Beloved Community.

Whether we can find comparable consensus on all persistent ethical disputes that divide Christians is an open question, even as we seek to practice a theocentric piety attuned to cosmocentric rather than parochial truth-seeking. As Amanda Ripley notes in *High Conflict: Why We Get Trapped and How We Get Out*, a conflict can shift from "high" to "good" when mutual demonization finally gives way to mutual listening.[18] This is, again, one way of understanding what happened among fourth-century Christians with the Arian conflict. Competing theological parties began to hear what was at stake for one another, even amid their having to navigate imperial powers. Then as now with regard to ethical debates that have public policy dimensions worked out in state and federal laws, theological skirmishes are entangled with political ones. It will not do to simply declare that "religion has no place in politics" when the policy options each relate to a theological position of some kind. Indeed, recalling this should prompt the related remembrance that there is freedom among Christians to debate the nature of the moral law, and to bring their various perspectives into the mixed secular, religiously pluralistic space of public policy disputes.

A theocentric piety, then, does not fixate us on a selected, carefully curated truth to stand on passionately as if it alone offered a sufficient point of moral purity for all ethically significant decision-making, individually or politically, on a contested matter. Least of all would a theocentric piety seek to claim the authority of a sovereign God for an ethical or policy perspective that denied the other worthy truths at play in a heated conversation about the shape of justice within the Beloved Community, within our shared world.

---

[18] Amanda Ripley, *High Conflict: Why We Get Trapped and How We Get Out* (New York: Simon & Schuster, 2021).

Nor, however, does a theocentric piety avoid the risk of engaging in conflict out of a legitimately grave fear of idolatry or blasphemy. Any human perspective will always be short-sighted before the grandeur of the living God. Here we agree with Liederbach and Lenow that giving glory to God *does* mean praising God with our whole being, including our ethical and political commitments, even as we remain open to experiencing an ongoing purgation or purification of our vision of justice and our ethical imaginations. Wherever our particular group identities are based (consciously or unconsciously) on artificial boundaries (like whiteness or gender hierarchies), or whenever we are drawn into identifying most with our own team in the justice-seeking endeavor, the Spirit's work in us opens our eyes in ways that create discomfort as our vision shifts and readjusts,[19] triggering a particular season of dying and rising to new life. When we feel pulled to speak prophetically without listening any longer to neighbors we write off as backwards or perverters of the truth, it might be precisely then when we find the Spirit recalibrating us to a more truthful perception of those neighbors.

We suggest that belonging to the Beloved Community has sustained a decentering and recentering all along in Christian history. Indeed, we are vulnerable to the sins of presumption (self-justification) and despair when we try to secure *ourselves* by freezing this movement, by digging our heels into a Christian partisanship that risks idolatry. Being theocentric, being orthodox: these involve being open-minded enough to hear and synthesize the spectrum of truths at play in any given justice-seeking debate. Being decentered and recentered taps into Christian traditions about faith's ongoing purification. Here the metaphor of sight often comes into play: we realize that how we have seen or understood something is false or inadequate. We undergo an iconoclastic moment, a shattering of our old ways of seeing or understanding. Our vision needs correction. The Platonic strain in Christian thought highlights a refining in how we see created beauties in relation to Divine Beauty. The "Protestant principle" involves the recognition that all mediated symbols of faith can become idolatrous. Faith in Christ opens us to a lifetime of iconoclastic breaking open, as we hear the Spirit calling us to see and to do a new thing. We are

---

[19]   On perception-shifting through the ways we attend to one another in relation to a transcendent purity or goodness, see Simone Weil, "Forms of the Implicit Love of God," in *Waiting for God*, trans. Emma Craufurd (New York: Harper Colophon Books, 1973 [1950]), 137–215; Iris Murdoch, *The Sovereignty of Good* (Abingdon, UK: Routledge, 2001 [1970]).

called to live out our faith in the public realm, even as that means tussling with one another about how exactly to do that.

Our debating about what justice looks like is ultimately one expression of praise of God: a doxology. In this sense, doxology is itself a dance of centering, decentering, recentering—sometimes a standing still in adoration, but also a moving about to notice and lift up to God a glint of this or that bit of creation, be it whole or in need of remembrance or repair. It is to the spiritual connection between doxology and the risk of particular, created participation in divine justice that we now turn.

A Christoform Theocentrism: The Freedom to Risk Justice-Seeking Together

We have been articulating a spirituality that attends to the different truths at play in any genuine debate about justice-seeking. By "genuine," we mean a debate in which there are compelling, relevant truths that seem to clash. Along the way, we have problematized rhetoric that casts "Christian" against "secular" positions, as if "*the* Christian position" is simple and clear. There are many Christian proposals, programs, and visions—not just one. We have also insisted that orthopraxy involves more than a direct line from a particular Christian take on revealed divine will to politics. Orthopraxy, as Gustafson suggests, is centered on the God of the cosmos. When our justice-seeking is oriented to God, we are freed from the idolatry of confusing justice proposals *themselves* with God and we can then navigate various resources for ethical reflection regarding justice. A theocentric piety is focused on God, but attends to neighbors, in their remarkable diversity, as well as to the planet as a whole.

Here, in closing, we revisit our overarching theme of justification by faith in Christ as the ground of Christian identity and belonging, a ground from which we dare to risk jumping into the fray of contentious debates about the shape of justice in the Beloved Community. For this spirituality of jumping-in, we turn to another rich theological tradition, one with roots in Jesus' teaching: "And why do you not judge for yourselves what is right?" (Luke 12:57); as well as the writings of the apostle Paul (as interpreted by Luther) on Christian freedom.

Luther famously voiced the dynamic of liberty and obligation, of rights and responsibilities, of gospel and law when he distilled two Pauline statements on Christian freedom (1 Cor 9:19 and Rom 13:8) into the quip, "The Christian individual is a completely free lord of all, subject to none. The Christian individual is a completely dutiful servant of all, subject to all.""[20] In the terms of our book, we can summarize Luther's paradox as that between justification by faith—which frees a Christian from works that aim to secure divine favor—and justice—works of love that establish justice for neighbor. The way Luther solves this paradox is by focusing exclusively on Christ's work. Christ frees the sinner from the obligation of works intended to gain divine favor. Yet this freedom in Christ imposes another obligation on the Christian, that of assuming responsibility for neighbor love. Luther thus connects justification by faith to justice-seeking by gathering both together in Christ. For the Christian, then, becoming formed by Christ is to stand firmly on Christ, whose freedom sets the sinner free from sinning and being sinned against, and sets the sinner free for serving Christ by loving the neighbor.

Luther can also subsume this Christoform orientation into a theocentric perspective. Christ's obedience to the law, even to death, fulfills the first commandment, the prohibition against idolatry. In Christ the imperative against idolatry is fulfilled; in Christ, God is honored above all. Christ orients us to God in a way that precludes our own justice-seeking from bearing ultimacy. Freed by Christ to be oriented to God as object of our ultimate concern, Christians can pursue justice-seeking in ways that honor the neighbor. *Because we are being freed in Christ to love God above all, our ability to serve one another in neighborly love presupposes a freedom to exercise agency—including ethical reflection and decision-making.* As Christians baptized into the body of Christ, our liberty is always mutual and communal; Christ's formation in us is always corporate. To love God in Christ with all our heart, soul, and mind both frees and obligates us to hazard asking what it actually means, in a given time and place, to truly love our neighbors as ourselves.

Why not invoke the metaphor of dancing to illustrate how this Christoform navigation with others in theocentric perspective might look? Justification by faith impels us to seek justice with and among the many members of the corporate body: Christians, non-Christians, nones, and secularists. This is a difficult coordination to figure out, yet the performance can also be beautiful. Learning to dance is not easy; we have to show up for practice, be willing to stumble, be open to getting off balance as we move our muscles. We must furthermore learn to dance in

[20]   Martin Luther, *The Freedom of a Christian, 1520*, trans. W. A. Lambert and Harold J. Grimm, rev. trans. Mark Tranvik, newly rev. Timothy J. Wengert, The Annotated Luther Study Edition, ed. Timothy J. Wengert (Minneapolis: Fortress, 2016), 488.

ensemble. There we learn to be responsive to the movements of other dancers around us. Synchrony is the goal, so that one does not knock the other off-balance or step on their toes.

Or what about the metaphor of debate? As any high school debater learns at summer debate camp, the most persuasive arguments are not those that simply express one point of view over and over, however vociferously. The best arguments are those that *acknowledge the claims of the other team and take account of them* in rebuttals. The aim of debate is showing how one's position best takes account of those very claims. Jonathan Malesic puts it like this, citing Timothy Shenk's critique of "patreon politics" as a "system of commodified tribalism" in which we believe it is only the "bad faith of the other side" that is the obstacle: "If we want a better world, we'll need better arguments. And for that, we'll need to practice them with, and against, our friends."[21] As Christians, we can learn to dance beautifully together; we can practice making arguments that integrate the best claims of our interlocutors. We recognize that our fellow dancers and debaters are also interested in beauty and logic.

Whether our dance is uncontrolled or in synchrony, whether our debate is raucous or dialectical depends on how (and whether) we attend to the fuller spectrum of truths that are multifarious witness-bearers to what we and our neighbors need to flourish. Indeed, feminist and other liberation-minded theologians highlight *flourishing* as a criterion for judging what is and is not harmonious with the gospel. The gospel can only *be* good news if it fosters well-being for our neighbors and ourselves. This fact frames, rather than ends, debate. As we have seen in the debate about abortion, who or what counts as our neighbor remains an urgent question centuries after Jesus' parable about the Good Samaritan. Our freedom and obligation as Christians is to venture into the fray. We are centered by remembering our baptismal belonging; we are decentered by both our own experiences with oppression and our own recognition of ways we ourselves have been partial seers of truth, complicit in dynamics of harm.

[21] Jonathan Malesic, "Nuance Is Not Dead: People Are Having Thoughtful Disagreements about Politics and Intellectual Life. But They're Fighting against Huge Incentives Not To," *Burnout Culture* newsletter, September 7, 2021, https://jonmalesic .substack.com/p/nuance-is-not-dead?fbclid=IwAR2VBbIlNYYo4DpkHw KbQn5xBH59mcZ4mHP7CZ-PpDia-gu3xgAY88WiXQw&s=r. Malesic cites Timothy Shenk, "For Love or Money: The American Political Infotainment Machine Has Turned the Ethics of Conviction into a Source of Profits," *Dissent*, Summer 2021, https://www.dissentmagazine.org/article/for-love-or-money.

A theocentric perspective of Christian freedom means that one stands at the intersection of love of God and love for creation *without a full picture of what justice entails*. Justice-seeking with Christian freedom is a dynamic, contextual process that includes exercising judgment, paying attention to affect, and trying to dance with others. While some might insist that judgment is not required because the divine law is clear, we counter that any particular sense of moral clarity is partial in its sighting, lacking the full God's-eye picture. Our points of moral clarity also stand under the warnings against idolatry, just as any other justice-seeking vision does. Any of us can be tempted to prioritize a certain sort of moral purity while not owning the consequences of our position. Just as one cannot legislate morality, as Kant once said, one group does not ever know the whole lay of the land as to what conforms to the divine will. Claiming to have the whole map in our hands is idolatry—for it does not distinguish between God and creature, and thereby dishonors God and does injustice to our neighbors, especially when we diminish or oppress them in the name of imposing a particular vision of justice upon them.

Justice-seeking is truly "to see in a mirror, dimly" (1 Cor 13:12). As we dance and debate with one another about the moral questions of the day, our answers can only be as good as what we can come up with together. Our answers will often feel penultimate. A moral decision might benefit one neighbor but not another; trying to act might seem as harmful as doing nothing. Christian freedom is the freedom to discern the best path forward amid trying circumstances—and being alert to noticing when following an idealized depiction of neighbor-love (like that of the Virgin Mary) entails destroying some lives.

We exhort our fellow Christians thus to practice the art of robust discussion in the public sphere. If we are right that making space to listen to our opponents within the body of Christ is part and parcel of remembering that our Christian identities depend upon justification by faith in Christ (not by identifying with a specific interpretation of the moral law), then it is an act of neighbor-love to participate in debates about laws and public policies. Once again, this does not mean that moral relativism is the actual norm, or that *all* positions in a debate are acceptable simply by virtue of one's baptism. We are presupposing ethical contestations in which a lack of consensus is due to there being defensible disagreements about what justice looks like within the Beloved Community. In this context, we ask together with all the resources and perspectives at our disposal: *what does it mean to love our neighbors as ourselves on this or that matter at hand?*

As we have suggested with regard to abortion, there are some contested moral debates in which Christian freedom ought to be exercised at an individual level. Abortion is always at heart about the moral decisions made by a particular pregnant person. In some cases, neighbor love means respecting another individual's decisions. In such cases, the best public policy framework may be one that preserves the exercise of Christian freedom to take responsibility for discerning the best path forward, all things considered, knowing that another person in her shoes might interpret the same circumstances—and choose—differently. Here, we suggest, loving one's neighbor as oneself means respecting the irreducible responsibility we each have with regard to our own lives, owning the consequences, confident that we are beheld by the gaze of a discerning God who holds us accountable within the grace of Christ.

Because we are justified by faith in Christ rather than ourselves, in Christian freedom we risk the decentering that can come with discerning how exactly to love our neighbors—and ourselves—in mutually accountable ways. Lurching about, so to speak—feeling or becoming decentered by the heady winds of justice-seeking debate—comes along with claiming our authority as Christians to discern, alone and together, what the Spirit is calling us to be and become within the Beloved Community. As the Spirit calls us into a Christoform reality, the Spirit orients us to a theocentric perspective, so that our dance and debate might truly honor God and serve the justice-needs of ourselves and our fellow human beings.

We write a doxology with our lives when we take this risk with integrity, asking and expressing what it means to love our neighbors as ourselves. We do this in the presence of one another—including others who write that doxology differently—so a dynamic of justice-seeking decentering and faith-borne recentering constitutes Christian life together before God.

Justice in and through the Beloved Community

There is something single-minded about recentering in the life of faith. It involves recollecting our baptism; it is recognizing that our belonging to the Beloved Community endures on the condition of the gift of our participation in the body of Christ—not based on our own having to strive to prove ourselves worthy of it. An orientation toward trust is warranted on the basis of this covenantal belonging to God in Christ "who gave himself for our sins" and "came to seek out and to save the lost" (Gal 1:4; Luke 19:10).

By contrast, decentering in the life of faith can take many forms. We are decentered from a full this-worldly recognition of our belonging—from full equality with other human beings—whenever we are marginalized by systemic or interpersonal sin. Being dislocated from a place of relative privilege is decentering. We get decentered whenever we identify the fullness of the church with our particular team in the pursuit of justice for all. And our proclivities for self-delusion—as well as the one-sided social media posts and false politicians we believe—can exacerbate our fight on behalf of the team. We get thrown off our game—even as we are playing it!—when we identify with our own position in a moral or justice-oriented debate in an idolatrous or heretical way. And we get decentered in yet another way when we have a conversion from one justice-seeking team to another, and have to find our bearings all over again as a particular picture of justice dissolves and comes into focus for us with different features.

In short, decentering in the life of faith inevitably occurs because of our sin and the sins of others. Moreover, acts of repentance are also decentering, as they move us from one way of life to another. Seeking to address sin involves decentering. Ironically perhaps, what centers the project of justice-seeking is remembering that decentering occurs with every risked step toward justice. Decentering occurs even when we name what we believe is right and invest in configuring the world in keeping with that right vision of things. Justice-seeking forms of decentering can blur our eyesight with regard to our own complicity in sin (for we see and practice justice imperfectly); we thus compromise our efforts to mend the world.

The fourteenth-century English anchoress Julian of Norwich speaks perceptively about this way that sin can flow straight out of our earnest efforts to serve God. In her analogy for Adam's fall, she sees Adam as a servant who "starts at once and runs in great haste for love to do his lord's will," then "falls into a ditch and receives very great injury." Unable to get out of the pit by himself, his "greatest mischief . . . was failing of comfort" because of his inability to see "his loving lord," even though his lord was watching "very tenderly" nearby, without casting blame—"for his good will and his great desire only were cause of his falling."[22] In Julian's vision of this story, Jesus goes into the pit to rescue the servant. But her story also illuminates the way that we can err and get disoriented precisely out of our

---

[22] Julian of Norwich, *A Revelation of Love*, ed. with intro. by Elisabeth M. Dutton (Lanham, Md.: Rowman & Littlefield, 2008), ch. 51, citations on 82 and 83.

earnestness in pursuing justice—in a way that causes us to lose touch with our baptismal belonging.

The life of faith is in so many varied ways a search to discover how we are decentered as we try to interpret and join the ethical/political debates and social change movements of our times. When we become aware of our decentering, we need the recentering that comes with being reminded of our primary belonging to the Beloved Community conjured in Christ. Recentering is a perpetual movement, strengthened by practices that imitate Jesus and the prophets' own theocentric sojourns away from—then back toward—humanly constructed habitations. Those sojourns can interrupt the many internal and external pulls that seem to offer a more tangible, immediate sense of belonging and power, including those that urge us to simplify the stories and shapes of justice in ways that fail to "do justice" to the empirical and experiential truths of human and planetary life. It is understandable that we face temptations to both presumption and despair when we experience cognitive dissonance upon encountering fellow Christians who disagree with us about what justice looks like on a matter of common concern. Dancing and debating as forms of theocentric piety take patient practice.

But when we dance and debate while remembering our covenantal belonging in baptism, we do so knowing that we belong to the process of discerning the common good as much as we belong at the communion rail. We can exercise our Christian freedom by sitting down and deliberating with one another about the best way to create a more just society (and contend with legacies of injustice), taking responsibility for our visions of justice and for how we pursue them, and remaining open to beholding the face of God shining in the many faces of the Beloved Community.

As we participate in political justice-seeking, the Christian freedom we exercise is the work of ordinary faith. We exercise our spiritual mnemonics to recall our baptismal belonging to the Beloved Community. We flex and move, pirouette and leap, debate and listen as we practice dancing and debating with others and as we insist on the space-making conditions of the gospel for the work of justice. We "lift up [our] eyes to the hills" (Ps 121:1) to orient all our finite work to the One who alone can claim justice as the content of revelation: "For in it [the gospel] the righteousness of God is revealed through faith for faith" (Rom 1:17).

Bibliography and
Suggested Readings

Chapter 1

Augustine, Saint. *Sermons on the New Testament: Sermon 23*. Translated by R. G. MacMullen. In *Nicene and Post-Nicene Fathers. First Series*, vol. 6. Edited by Philip Schaff. Buffalo, N.Y.: Christian Literature Publishing, 1888. Revised and edited for New Advent by Kevin Knight, http://www.newadvent.org/fathers/160323.htm.

Chaplin, Jonathan. *Faith in Democracy: Framing a Politics of Deep Diversity*. London: SCM Press, 2021.

Chittister, Joan. *The Rule of Benedict: Insights for the Ages*. New York: Crossroad, 2004.

Conference of Benedictine Prioresses. *Wisdom from the Tradition: A Statement of North American Benedictine Women in Response to Our Times*. Atchinson, Kans.: Mount St. Scholastica, 2006.

Helmer, Christine. *How Luther Became the Reformer*. Louisville: Westminster John Knox, 2019.

———. *Theology and the End of Doctrine*. Louisville: Westminster John Knox, 2014.

Herman, Judith Lewis. *Trauma and Recovery: From Domestic Abuse to Political Terror*. New York: Basic Books, 1992.

Imhof, Paul, and Hubert Biallowons, eds. *Karl Rahner in Dialogue: Conversations and Interviews, 1965–1982*. Translated by Harvey D. Egan. New York: Crossroad, 1986.

"Joint Declaration on the Doctrine of Justification." The Lutheran World Federation and the Roman Catholic Church. October 31, 1999. https://www.lutheranworld.org/sites/default/files/Joint%20Declaration%20on%20the%20Doctrine%20of%20Justification.pdf.

King, Martin Luther, Jr. "Read Martin Luther King Jr.'s 'I Have a Dream' Speech [Washington, D.C., August 28, 1963] in Its Entirety." *NPR*, updated January 16, 2023. https://www.npr.org/2010/01/18/122701268/i-have-a-dream-speech-in-its-entirety.

——. "The Power of Nonviolence (1958)." In *A Testament of Hope: The Essential Writings and Speeches of Martin Luther King, Jr.*, edited by James M. Washington, 12–15. New York: HarperOne, 1991.

Klein, Ezra. *Why We're Polarized*. Lakewood, Calif.: Avid Reader Press, 2021.

Luther, Martin. *The Freedom of a Christian, 1520*. Translated by W. A. Lambert and Harold J. Grimm. Revised translation by Mark Tranvik. Newly revised translation by Timothy J. Wengert. The Annotated Luther Study Edition. Edited by Timothy J. Wengert. Minneapolis: Fortress, 2016.

McCord Adams, Marilyn. *Christ and Horrors: The Coherence of Christology*. Current Issues in Theology. Cambridge: Cambridge University Press, 2006.

Moreland-Capuia, Alisha. *The Trauma of Racism: Exploring the Systems and People Fear Built*. Cham, Switzerland: Springer, 2021.

Niebuhr, Richard H. *Christ and Culture*. 50th anniversary ed. Foreword by Martin E. Marty and preface by James M. Gustafson. New York: HarperCollins, 2001.

Parks, Rosa, with Jim Haskins. *My Story*. New York: Puffin Books, 1992.

Ringel, Shoshana, and Jerrold Brandell, eds. *Trauma: Contemporary Directions in Trauma Theory, Research, and Practice*. 2nd ed. New York: Columbia University Press, 2019.

Ripley, Amanda. *High Conflict: Why We Get Trapped and How We Get Out*. New York: Simon & Schuster, 2021.

Stout, Jeffrey. *Ethics after Babel: The Languages of Morals and Their Discontents*. Princeton: Princeton University Press, 2001.

Stoute, Beverly J., and Michael Slevin, eds. *The Trauma of Racism: Lessons from the Therapeutic Encounter*. London: Routledge, 2022.

Chapter 2

Bainton, Roland H. *Here I Stand: A Life of Martin Luther*. New York: Penguin Books, 1977.

Bayer, Oswald. *Living by Faith: Justification and Sanctification*. Translated by Geoffrey W. Bromiley. Lutheran Quarterly Books. Minneapolis: Fortress, 2017.

Burnett, Amy Nelson. *Debating the Sacraments: Print and Authority in the Early Reformation*. Oxford: Oxford University Press, 2019.

Daughrity, Dyron B. *Martin Luther: A Biography for the People*. Abilene, Tex.: Abilene Christian University Press, 2017.

Dieter, Theodor. "Why Does Luther's Doctrine of Justification Matter Today?" In *The Global Luther: A Theologian for Modern Times*, edited by Christine Helmer, 189–209. Minneapolis: Fortress, 2009.

Helmer, Christine, ed. *The Global Luther: A Theologian for Modern Times*. Minneapolis: Fortress, 2009.

—— *How Luther Became the Reformer*. Louisville: Westminster John Knox, 2019.

————, ed. *The Medieval Luther*. Spätmittelalter, Humanismus, Reformation / Studies in the Late Middle Ages, Humanism, and the Reformation 117. Tübingen: Mohr Siebeck, 2020.

Hinlicky, Paul R., and Derek R. Nelson, eds. *The Oxford Encyclopedia of Martin Luther*. Oxford: Oxford University Press, 2017.

Holl, Karl. *What Did Luther Understand by Religion?* Translated by Fred W. Meuser and Walter R. Wietzke. Edited by James Luther Adams and Walter F. Bense. Philadelphia: Fortress, 1977.

Isasi-Díaz, Ada María. *Mujerista Theology: A Theology for the Twenty-First Century*. Maryknoll, N.Y.: Orbis Books, 1996.

Julian of Norwich. *A Revelation of Love*. Edited with introduction by Elisabeth Dutton. Lanham, Md.: Rowman & Littlefield, 2008.

King, Martin Luther, Jr. "The Role of the Church in Facing the Nation's Chief Moral Dilemma. Address Delivered on 25 April 1957 at the Conference on Christian Faith and Human Relations in Nashville." In *The Papers of Martin Luther King, Jr.*, vol. 4, *Symbol of the Movement, January 1957– December 1958*. Berkeley: University of California Press, 2000. Available online through the website of the Martin Luther King Jr. Research and Education Institute at Stanford University, https://kinginstitute.stanford .edu/king-papers/documents/role-church-facing-nation-s-chief-moral -dilemma-address-delivered-25-april.

Leppin, Volker. *Martin Luther: A Late Medieval Life*. Translated by Rhys Bezzant and Karen Roe. Grand Rapids: Baker Academic, 2017.

Lindbeck, George A. *The Nature of Doctrine: Religion and Theology in a Postliberal Age*. 2nd ed. Introduction by Bruce D. Marshall. Louisville: Westminster John Knox, 2009 [1984].

Luther, Martin. *The Freedom of a Christian, 1520*. Translated by W. A. Lambert and Harold J. Grimm. Revised translation by Mark Tranvik. Newly revised translation by Timothy J. Wengert. The Annotated Luther Study Edition. Edited by Timothy J. Wengert. Minneapolis: Fortress, 2016.

————. "The Large Catechism (1529)." In *The Book of Concord: The Confessions of the Evangelical Lutheran Church*, translated by Charles Arand et al., edited by Robert Kolb and Timothy J. Wengert, 461–66. Minneapolis: Fortress, 2000.

————. "Preface to the Complete Edition of Luther's Latin Writings (1545)." In *Luther's Works*, vol. 34, *Career of the Reformer IV*, translated by Lewis W. Spitz Sr., 327–38. Philadelphia: Fortress, 1960.

Mannermaa, Tuomo. *Christ Present in Faith: Luther's View of Justification*. Edited and introduction by Kirsi Stjerna. Minneapolis: Fortress, 2005.

Massing, Michael. *Fatal Discord: Erasmus, Luther, and the Fight for the Western Mind*. New York: HarperCollins, 2018.

Melanchthon, Philip. *Commonplaces: Loci Communes 1521*. Translated with introduction and notes by Christian Preus. St. Louis: Concordia Publishing House, 2014.

Oberman, Heiko A. *Luther: Man between God and the Devil*. Translated by Eileen Walliser-Schwarzbart. New York: Image Books, 1992.

Orsi, Robert A. "Everyday Miracles: The Study of Lived Religion." In *Lived Religion in America: Toward a History of Practice*, edited by David D. Hall, 3–21. Princeton: Princeton University Press, 1998.

Roper, Lyndal. *Living I Was Your Plague: Martin Luther's World and Legacy*. The Lawrence Stone Lectures. Princeton: Princeton University Press, 2021.

———. *Martin Luther: Renegade and Prophet*. New York: Random House, 2017.

Rubenstein, Richard E. *When Jesus Became God: The Epic Fight over Christ's Divinity in the Last Days of Rome*. New York: Harcourt Brace, 1999.

Saarinen, Risto. *Luther and the Gift*. Spätmittelalter, Humanismus, Reformation / Studies in the Late Middle Ages, Humanism, and the Reformation 117. Tübingen: Mohr Siebeck, 2017.

Schüssler Fiorenza, Elisabeth. *Wisdom Ways: Introducing Feminist Biblical Interpretation*. Maryknoll, N.Y.: Orbis Books, 2001.

Stjerna, Kirsi. *Lutheran Theology: A Grammar of Faith*. New York: Bloomsbury Publishing, 2020.

Wandel, Lee Palmer, ed. *A Companion to the Eucharist in the Reformation*. Brill's Companions to the Christian Tradition 46. Boston: Brill, 2013.

Chapter 3

Ayres, Lewis. *Nicaea and Its Legacy: An Approach to Fourth-Century Trinitarian Theology*. Oxford: Oxford University Press, 2004.

Behr, John. *The Formation of Christian Theology*, vol. 2, *The Nicene Faith*. Crestwood, N.Y.: St. Vladimir's Press, 2004.

Caremans, Gregory. *Master Your Brain: Neuroscience for Personal Development*. Brain Academy, Udemy. Online Course. January 2022.

Chadwick, Henry. *The Early Church*. Rev. ed. The Penguin History of the Church. New York: Penguin Books, 1993.

Corrigan, Lisa M. *Black Feelings: Race and Affect in the Long Sixties*. Jackson: University Press of Mississippi, 2020.

Coulter, Dale M., and Amos Yong, eds. *The Spirit, the Affections, and the Christian Tradition*. Notre Dame: University of Notre Dame Press, 2016.

Crossley, Michele L. *Introducing Narrative Psychology: Self, Trauma, and the Construction of Meaning*. Philadelphia: Open University Press, 2000.

Despotis, Athanasios, ed. *Participation, Justification, and Conversion: Eastern Orthodox Interpretation of Paul and the Debate between Old and New*

Perspectives on Paul. Wissenschaftliche Untersuchungen zum Neuen Testament, Second Series 442. Tübingen: Mohr Siebeck, 2017.

Fairbairn, Donald. *Life in the Trinity: An Introduction to Theology with the Help of the Church Fathers*. Downer's Grove, Ill.: InterVarsity Press Academic, 2009.

Gonzáles, Justo L. *The Story of Christianity*, vol. 1, *The Early Church to the Dawn of the Reformation*. 2nd ed. New York: HarperOne, 2010.

———. *The Story of Christianity*, vol. 2, *The Reformation to the Present Day*. 2nd ed. New York: HarperOne, 2014.

Halsall, Paul. "Medieval Sourcebook: Bernard Gui: Inquisitorial Technique (c. 1307–1323)." In *Internet History Sourcebooks Project*. Fordham University. January 1996, https://sourcebooks.fordham.edu/source/heresy2.asp.

Heim, Mark, ed. *Faith to Creed: Ecumenical Perspectives on the Affirmation of the Apostolic Faith in the Fourth Century*. Grand Rapids: Eerdmans, 1991.

Helmer, Christine, and Ruth Jackson Ravenscroft. "Genderealogy: Erasure and Resistance." *Modern Theology*. Published online on Feb. 19, 2023, https://onlinelibrary.wiley.com/doi/pdf/10.1111/moth.12849, DOI: 10.1111/moth.12849.

Jackson, Michael. *Coincidences: Synchronicity, Verisimilitude, and Storytelling*. Oakland: University of California Press, 2021.

Kelly, John N. D. *Early Christian Doctrines: Revised Edition*. 5th rev. ed. London: Bloomsbury Academic, 2000.

Kim, Yung Suk. *A Theological Introduction to Paul's Letters: Exploring a Threefold Theology of Paul*. Eugene, Ore.: Cascade, 2011.

Kohli, Candace L. "The Medieval Luther on *Poenitentia*: Good Works as the Completion of Faith in the Christian Life." In *The Medieval Luther*, edited by Christine Helmer, 127–42. Spätmittelalter, Humanismus, Reformation / Studies in the Late Middle Ages, Humanism, and the Reformation 117. Tübingen: Mohr Siebeck, 2020.

Lázló, János. *The Science of Stories: An Introduction to Narrative Psychology*. New York: Routledge, 2008.

Luther, Martin. *The Freedom of a Christian, 1520*. Translated by W. A. Lambert and Harold J. Grimm. Revised translation by Mark Tranvik. Newly revised translation by Timothy J. Wengert. The Annotated Luther Study Edition. Edited by Timothy J. Wengert. Minneapolis: Fortress, 2016.

———. "Preface to the Book of Psalms." In *Martin Luther's Manual on the Book of Psalms*, translated by Henry Cole, 17–23. London: R. B. Seeley and W. Burnside, 1837. https://www.lutheranlibrary.org/pdf/367-luther-psalms-cole.pdf.

Madsen, Anna M. *I Can Do No Other: The Church's New Here We Stand Moment*. Minneapolis: Fortress, 2019.

Mahn, Jason A. *Neighbor Love through Fearful Days: Finding Purpose and Meaning in a Time of Crisis*. Minneapolis: Fortress, 2021.

Malcolm, Lois. *Holy Spirit: Creative Power in Our Lives.* Lutheran Voices. Minneapolis: Augsburg Fortress, 2009.

Marshall, Taylor R. *Origins of Catholic Christianity Trilogy*, vol. 2, *The Catholic Perspective on Paul: Paul and the Origins of Catholic Christianity.* Dallas: Saint John Press, 2010.

Ngozi Adichie, Chimamanda. "The Danger of a Single Story." *TEDGlobal*, 2009. https://www.ted.com/talks/chimamanda_ngozi_adichie_the_danger_of_a_single_story.

Nirenberg, David. *Anti-Judaism: The Western Tradition.* New York: Norton, 2013.

Plato. *The Republic.* Translated by Benjamin Jowett. The Internet Classics Archive. 1994. http://classics.mit.edu/Plato/republic.html.

Peterson, Cheryl M. *Who Is the Church? An Ecclesiology for the Twenty-First Century.* Minneapolis: Fortress, 2013.

Phillips, Thomas E. *Paul, His Letters, and Acts.* Library of Pauline Studies. Peabody, Mass.: Hendrickson, 2009.

Proust, Joëlle. *The Philosophy of Metacognition: Mental Agency and Self-Awareness.* Reprint ed. Oxford: Oxford University Press, 2016.

Raunio, Antti. "Introduction: Faith as Darkness and Light Active in Love: Luther on Christian Life." In *Darkness Light and Active Love: Studies on Theory and Practice in Luther and Lutheran-Orthodox Ecumenical Theology*, edited by Antti Raunio, 7–38. Schriften der Luther-Agricola-Gesellschaft 74. Helsinki: Luther-Agricola Gesellschaft, 2020.

———. "Luther's Social Theology in the Contemporary World: Searching for the Neighbor's Good." In *The Global Luther: A Theologian for Modern Times*, edited by Christine Helmer, 210–27. Minneapolis: Fortress, 2009.

Rhoads, David M., Joanna Dewey and Donald Michie. *Mark as Story: An Introduction to the Narrative of a Gospel.* 3rd ed. Minneapolis: Fortress, 2012.

Rivera, Robert J., and Michele Saracino, eds. *Enfleshing Theology: Embodiment, Discipleship, and Politics in the Work of M. Shawn Copeland.* Lanham, Md.: Lexington Books/Fortress Academic, 2018.

Rubenstein, Richard E. *When Jesus Became God: The Epic Fight over Christ's Divinity in the Last Days of Rome.* New York: Harcourt Brace, 1999.

Schaefer, Donovan O. *Religious Affects: Animality, Evolution, and Power.* Durham, N.C.: Duke University Press, 2015.

Spufford, Francis. "From Rules to Principles: How My Mind Has Changed." *Christian Century* 138, no. 15 (July 28, 2021): 26–31.

Stolt, Birgit. *Martin Luthers Rhetorik des Herzens.* UTB für Wissenschaft. Tübingen: Mohr Siebeck, 2000.

Thompson, Michael Bruce. *The New Perspective on Paul.* Grove Biblical Series. New York: Grove Press, 2002.

Vedantam, Shankar, and Mesler, Bill. *Useful Delusions: The Power and Paradox of the Self-Deceiving Brain.* New York: Norton, 2021.

Vial, Theodore. *Schleiermacher: A Guide for the Perplexed*. London: T&T Clark, 2013.

Wallace, Cynthia. *Of Women Borne: A Literary Ethics of Suffering*. Gender, Theory, and Religion. New York: Columbia University Press, 2016.

Wesley, John. *A Plain Account of Christian Perfection*. Blacksburg, Va.: Wilder Publications, 2001 [1738].

Westerholm, Stephen. *Perspectives Old and New on Paul: The "Lutheran" Paul and His Critics*. Grand Rapids: Eerdmans, 2003.

Wright, N. T. *Paul: In Fresh Perspective*. Minneapolis: Fortress, 2008.

———. *What Saint Paul Really Said: Was Paul of Tarsus the Real Founder of Christianity?* Reprint ed. Grand Rapids: Eerdmans, 2014.

Yinger, Kent L. *The New Perspective on Paul: An Introduction*. New York: Cascade, 2010.

Chapter 4

Boston Women's Health Collective. *Our Bodies, Ourselves: A Book by and for Women*. New York: Touchstone, 1976.

Cahill, Lisa Sowle. "Abortion, Autonomy, and Community." In *Abortion: Understanding Differences*, edited by Sidney Callahan and Daniel Callahan, 261–76. The Hasting Center Series in Ethics. New York: Plenum Press, 1984.

Carr, Amy, and Helmer, Christine. "Claiming Christian Freedom to Discuss Abortion *Together*." *Lutheran Forum* 53, no. 2 (Summer 2019): 48–51.

"*Dobbs vs. Jackson Women's Health Organization* (2022)." Legal Information Institute, Cornell Law School. https://www.law.cornell.edu/supremecourt/text/19-1392.

Early, Joe, Jr. "From Permissible to Intolerable: Southern Baptists and the Abortion Debate in the 1970s." *Baptist History & Heritage* (Summer 2020): 73–91.

Fienen, Dan. "Can We Talk? Another View of the Abortion Discussion." *Lutheran Forum* 54, no. 1 (2020): 58–61.

Gadamer, Hans-Georg. *Truth and Method*. Translated by Marvin Brown. New York: Crossroad, 1982 [1960].

Gress, Carrie. *The Anti-Mary Exposed: Rescuing the Culture from Toxic Femininity*. Charlotte: TAN Books, 2019.

Gudorf, Christine E. "Contraception and Abortion in Roman Catholicism." In *Sacred Rights: The Case for Contraception and Abortion in World Religions*, edited by Daniel C. Maguire, 55–78. New York: Oxford University Press, 2003.

Gurr, Barbara. *Reproductive Justice: The Politics of Health Care for Native American Women*. New Brunswick, N.J.: Rutgers University Press, 2014.

Helmer, Christine. "Luther Scholarship under the Conditions of Patriarchy." *Journal of Lutheran Ethics* 22, no. 4 (August/September 2022: Gender

Identity, Gender Expression, and Sexuality). https://learn.elca.org/jle/luther-scholarship-under-the-conditions-of-patriarchy/.

Jones, Rachel K., Lori F. Frohwirth, and Ann M. Moore. "More than Poverty: Disruptive Events among Women Having Abortions in the USA." *Journal of Family Planning and Reproductive Health Care* 39 (2013): 36–43.

Jones, Rachel K., and Megan L. Kavanaugh. "Changes in Abortion Rates between 2000 and 2008 and Lifetime Incidence of Abortion." *Obstetrics and Gynecology* 177, no. 6 (June 2011): 1358–66.

Kamitsuka, Margaret D. *Abortion and the Christian Tradition: A Pro-Choice Theological Ethic.* Louisville: Westminster John Knox, 2019.

Kimport, Katrina. *No Real Choice: How Culture and Politics Matter for Reproductive Autonomy.* Families in Focus. New Brunswick, N.J.: Rutgers University Press, 2022.

Luker, Kristin. *Abortion and the Politics of Motherhood.* Berkeley: University of California Press, 1984.

Luther, Martin. *The Babylonian Captivity of the Church, 1520.* Translated by A. T. W. Steinhäuser. Revised translation by Frederick C. Ahrens and Abdel Ross Wentz. Newly revised translation by Erik W. Herrmann. The Annotated Luther Study Edition. Edited by Paul W. Robinson. Minneapolis: Fortress, 2016.

———. *The Bondage of the Will, 1525.* Translated by Philip S. Watson in collaboration with Benjamin Drury. Revised translatin Volker Leppin. The Annotated Luther Study Edition. Edited by Kirsi I. Stjerna. Minneapolis: Fortress, 2016.

Maguire, Daniel C., ed. *Sacred Rights: The Case for Contraception and Abortion in World Religions.* Oxford: Oxford University Press, 2003.

Manne, Kate. *Down Girl: The Logic of Misogyny.* New York: Oxford University Press, 2018.

Mathewes-Green, Frederica. *Real Choices: Listening to Women; Looking for Alternatives to Abortion.* Ben Lomond, Calif.: Conciliar Press, 1994.

Oehlschlaeger, Fritz. *Procreative Ethics: Philosophical and Christian Approaches to Questions at the Beginning of Life.* Eugene, Ore.: Cascade, 2010.

Parker, Willie. *Life's Work: A Moral Argument for Choice.* New York: First 37 Ink/Atria, 2017.

Peters, Rebecca Todd, and Margaret D. Kamitsuka. *T&T Clark Reader in Abortion and Religion: Jewish, Christian, and Muslim Perspectives.* New York: Bloomsbury / T&T Clark, 2023.

Pollitt, Katha. *Pro: Reclaiming Abortion Rights.* New York: Picador, 2014.

Reagan, Leslie J. *When Abortion Was a Crime: Women, Medicine, and Law in the United States, 1867–1973.* Berkeley: University of California Press, 1997.

Scaer, David. Theological Observer review of "Claiming Christian Freedom to Discuss Abortion Together." *Concordia Theological Quarterly* 84, no. 1–2 (2020): 175–76.

Schlesinger, Kira. *Pro-Choice and Christian: Reconciling Faith, Politics, and Justice*. Louisville: Westminster John Knox, 2017.

Schoen, Johanna, ed. *Abortion Care as Moral Work: Ethical Considerations of Maternal and Fetal Bodies*. Critical Issues in Health and Medicine. New Brunswick, N.J.: Rutgers University Press, 2022.

Sherratt, Timothy. *Power Made Perfect? Is There a Christian Politics for the Twenty-First Century?* Eugene, Ore.: Cascade, 2016.

Smith, Bardwell L. *Narratives of Sorrow and Dignity: Japanese Women, Pregnancy Loss, and Modern Rituals of Grieving*. Oxford: Oxford University Press, 2013.

Taylor, Janelle S. *The Public Life of the Fetal Sonogram: Technology, Consumption, and the Politics of Reproduction*. Studies in Medical Anthropology. New Brunswick, N.J.: Rutgers University Press, 2008.

Todd Peters, Rebecca. *Trust Women: A Progressive Christian Argument for Reproductive Justice*. Boston: Beacon, 2018.

Wallace, Cynthia. *Of Women Borne: A Literary Ethics of Suffering*. Gender, Theory, and Religion. New York: Columbia University Press, 2016.

Walsh, Matt. *The Unholy Trinity: Blocking the Left's Assault on Life, Marriage, and Gender*. New York: Image, 2017.

Weingarten, Karen. *Abortion in the American Imagination: Before Life and Choice, 1880–1940*. New Brunswick, N.J.: Rutgers University Press, 2014.

White, Graham. "Modal Logic in Luther's *Enslaved Will*." In *The Medieval Luther*, edited by Christine Helmer, 91–103. Spätmittelalter, Humanismus, Reformation / Studies in the Late Middle Ages, Humanism, and the Reformation 117. Tübingen: Mohr Siebeck, 2020.

Chapter 5

Ahn, Ilsup. *The Church in the Public: A Politics of Engagement for a Cruel and Indifferent Age*. Minneapolis: Fortress, 2022.

Augustine, Saint. *Homilies on the First Epistle of John*. Edited by Daniel E. Doyle and Thomas F. Martin. Translated by Boniface Ramsey. Hyde Park, N.Y.: New City Press, 2008.

———. *On Baptism against the Donatists*. Translated by J. R. King. London: Aeterna Press, 2014.

Baucham, Voddie T., Jr. *Fault Lines: The Social Justice Movement and Evangelicalism's Looming Catastrophe*. Washington, D.C.: Salem Books, 2021.

Benne, Robert. *The Paradoxical Vision: A Public Theology for the Twenty-First Century*. Minneapolis: Fortress, 1995.

Berger, Peter L. *The Sacred Canopy: Elements of a Sociological Theory of Religion*. New York: Anchor Books / Doubleday, 1969.

Bonhoeffer, Dietrich. *Barcelona, Berlin, New York 1928–1931.* Translated by Douglas W. Stott. Edited by Clifford J. Green. Dietrich Bonhoeffer Works 10. Minneapolis: Fortress, 2008.

———. "History and Good [2]." In *Ethics*, translated by Reinhard Krauss, Charles C. West, and Douglas W. Scott, edited by Ilse Tödt, Heinz Eduard Tödt, Ernst Feil, and Clifford Green, 245–98. Dietrich Bonhoeffer Works 6. Minneapolis: Fortress, 2004.

Bretherton, Luke. *Christ and the Common Life: Political Theology and the Case for Democracy.* Grand Rapids: Eerdmans, 2019.

Carr, Amy, and Christine Helmer. "Claiming Christian Freedom to Discuss Abortion *Together.*" *Lutheran Forum* 53, no. 2 (Summer 2019): 48–51.

Cave, Alfred A. "Canaanites in a Promised Land: The American Indian and the Providential Theory of Empire." *American Indian Quarterly* 12, no. 4 (1988): 277–97.

Cone, James H. *A Black Theology of Liberation.* 50th anniversary ed. Maryknoll, N.Y.: Orbis Books, 2020.

Craigo-Snell, Shannon, and Christopher J. Doucot. *No Innocent Bystanders: Becoming an Ally in the Struggle for Justice.* Foreword by Timothy P. Shriver. Louisville: Westminster John Knox, 2017.

Cramer, Katherine J. *The Politics of Resentment: Rural Consciousness in Wisconsin and the Rise of Scott Walker.* Chicago: University of Chicago Press, 2016.

Dahill, Lisa E. *Reading from the Underside of Selfhood: Bonhoeffer and Spiritual Formation.* Princeton Theological Monograph Series 95. Eugene, Ore.: Pickwick / Wipf & Stock, 2015.

Day, Katie. *Difficult Conversations: Taking Risks, Acting with Integrity.* Herndon, Va.: Alban Institute, 2001.

Dionne, E. J. *Souled Out: Reclaiming Faith and Politics after the Religious Right.* Princeton: Princeton University Press, 2008.

Dussel, Enrique. *Ethics and Community.* Translated by Robert R. Barr. Maryknoll, N.Y.: Orbis, 1988.

Eig, Jonathan. *King: A Life.* New York: Farrar, Straus and Giroux, 2023.

Fletcher, Jeannine Hill. *The Sin of White Supremacy: Christianity, Racism, and Religious Diversity in America.* Maryknoll, N.Y.: Orbis Books, 2017.

Fulbrook, Mary. *A Concise History of Germany.* 2nd ed. Cambridge: Cambridge University Press, 2004.

Graves-Fitzsimmons, Guthrie. *Just Faith: Reclaiming Progressive Christianity.* Minneapolis: Broadleaf Books, 2020.

Helmer, Christine. *How Luther Became the Reformer.* Louisville: Westminster John Knox, 2019.

Heschel, Abraham Joshua. "What Manner of Man Is the Prophet?" In *Abraham Joshua Heschel: Essential Writings*, selected and edited by Susannah Heschel, 62–63. Modern Spiritual Masters. Maryknoll, N.Y.: Orbis Books, 2011.

Hochschild, Arlie Russell. *Strangers in Their Own Land: Anger and Mourning on the American Right*. New York: New Press, 2016.

Jenkins, Willis, and Jennifer M. McBride, eds. *Bonhoeffer and King: Their Legacies and Import for Christian Social Thought*. Minneapolis: Fortress, 2010.

Jones, D. Gareth. *Brave New People: Ethical Issues at the Commencement of Life*. Rev. ed. Grand Rapids: Eerdmans, 1985.

Johnson, Sylvester A. *African American Religions, 1500–2000: Colonialism, Democracy, and Freedom*. Cambridge: Cambridge University Press, 2015.

———. *The Myth of Ham in Nineteenth-Century American Christianity: Race, Heathens, and the People of God*. Black Religion / Womanist Thought / Social Justice. New York: Palgrave Macmillan, 2004.

King, Martin Luther, Jr. *A Gift of Love: Sermons from "Strength to Love" and Other Preachings*. Foreword by Coretta Scott King and Raphael G. Warnock. Rev. ed. Boston: Beacon, 2012.

———. "I've Been to the Mountaintop." Memphis, Tenn., April 3, 1968. Website of the American Federation of State, County and Municipal Employees. https://www.afscme.org/about/history/mlk/mountaintop.

———. "Pilgrimage to Nonviolence." In *A Testament of Hope: The Essential Writings and Speeches of Martin Luther King, Jr.*, edited by James Meville Washington. New York: HarperOne, 1991.

———. "Read Martin Luther King Jr.'s 'I Have a Dream' Speech [Washington, D.C., August 28, 1963] in Its Entirety." *NPR*, updated January 16, 2023. https://www.npr.org/2010/01/18/122701268/i-have-a-dream-speech-in-its-entirety.

Lamm, Julia A. *God's Kinde Love: Julian of Norwich's Vernacular Theology of Grace*. New York: Crossroad, 2019.

Lloyd, Vincent W., and Andrew L. Prevot, eds. *Anti-Blackness and Christian Ethics*. Maryknoll, N.Y.: Orbis Books, 2017.

Luther, Martin. *The Babylonian Captivity of the Church, 1520*. Translated by A. T. W. Steinhäuser. Revised translation by Frederick C. Ahrens and Abdel Ross Wentz. Newly revised translation by Erik W. Herrmann. The Annotated Luther Study Edition. Edited by Paul W. Robinson. Minneapolis: Fortress, 2016.

———. "To the Christian Nobility of the German Nation concerning the Improvement of the Christian Estate, 1520." Translated by Charles M. Jacobs. Revised translation by James Atkinson. Newly revised translation by James M. Estes. In *The Annotated Luther*, vol. 1, *The Roots of Reform*, 376–465. Edited by Timothy J. Wengert. Minneapolis: Fortress, 2015.

———. *The Freedom of a Christian, 1520*. Translated by W. A. Lambert and Harold J. Grimm. Revised translation by Mark Tranvik. Newly revised by Timothy J. Wengert. The Annotated Luther Study Edition. Edited by Timothy J. Wengert. Minneapolis: Fortress, 2016.

———. "The Small Catechism (1529)." In *The Book of Concord: The Confessions of the Evangelical Lutheran Church*, translated by Charles Arand et al., edited by Robert Kolb and Timothy J. Wengert, 359–62. Minneapolis: Fortress, 2000.

Madsen, Anna M. *I Can Do No Other: The Church's New Here We Stand Moment*. Minneapolis: Fortress, 2019.

Mahn, Jason A. "The Cheap Grace of White Privilege and the Costly Grace of Repentant Antiracism." *Currents in Theology and Mission* 47, no. 3 (2020): 8–14. http://www.currentsjournal.org/index.php/currents/article/view/254/282.

Marsh, Charles. *Strange Glory: A Life of Dietrich Bonhoeffer*. New York: Vintage Books, 2015.

McWhorter, John. *Woke Racism: How a New Religion Has Betrayed Black America*. New York: Portfolio / Penguin, 2021.

Metaxas, Eric. *Bonhoeffer: Pastor, Martyr, Prophet, Spy*. Nashville: Nelson, 2011.

Müller, Jan-Werner. *Democracy Rules*. New York: Farrar, Straus and Giroux, 2021.

Niebuhr, Reinhold. *Moral Man and Immoral Society: A Study in Ethics and Politics*. Foreword by Cornel West. Reinhold Niebuhr Library. Louisville: Westminster John Knox, 2021.

Niebuhr, Richard H. *Radical Monotheism and Western Culture*. Glasgow: HarperCollins, 1972.

Papanikolaou, Aristotle. *The Mystical as Political: Democracy and Non-Radical Orthodoxy*. Notre Dame: University of Notre Dame Press, 2021.

Perry, Michael J. "McElroy Lecture: Religion, Politics, and Abortion." *University of Detroit Mercy Law Review* 79 (2001): 1–37. http://ssrn.com/abstract=294506.

Phillips, Elizabeth. *Political Theology: A Guide for the Perplexed*. London: T&T Clark, 2012.

Reynolds, Diane. *The Doubled Life of Dietrich Bonhoeffer: Women, Sexuality, and Nazi Germany*. Eugene, Ore.: Cascade, 2016.

Ripley, Amanda. *High Conflict: Why We Get Trapped and How We Get Out*. New York: Simon & Schuster, 2021.

Sample, Tex. *Working Class Rage: A Field Guide to White Anger and Pain*. Nashville: Abingdon, 2018.

Schade, Leah D. *Preaching in the Purple Zone: Ministry in the Red-Blue Divide*. Lanham, Md.: Rowman & Littlefield, 2019.

Schmitt, Carl. *Dictatorship: From the Origin of the Modern Concept of Sovereignty to Proletarian Class Struggle*. Translated by Michael Hoelzl and Graham Ward. Cambridge: Polity Press, 2014 [1921].

———. *Political Theology: Four Chapters on the Concept of Sovereignty*. Edited and translated by George Schwab. Chicago: University of Chicago Press, 2005 [1922].

Smith, James K. A. *Awaiting the King: Reforming Public Theology*. Cultural Liturgies 3. Grand Rapids: Baker Academic, 2017.

Tanner, Kathryn. *The Politics of God: Christian Theologies and Social Justice*. 30th anniversary ed. Minneapolis: Fortress, 2022.

Tillich, Paul. *Dynamics of Faith*. New York: Harper & Brothers, 1957.

Williams, Reggie L. *Bonhoeffer's Black Jesus: Harlem Renaissance Theology and an Ethic of Resistance*. Waco: Baylor University Press, 2014.

Chapter 6

Collins, John J. *What Are Biblical Values? What the Bible Says on Key Ethical Issues*. New Haven: Yale University Press, 2019.

Gench, Roger J. *The Cross Examen: A Spirituality for Activists*. Eugene, Ore.: Cascade, 2020.

Gustafson, James M. *Ethics from a Theocentric Perspective*, vol. 1, *Theology and Ethics*. Chicago: University of Chicago Press, 1981.

Helmer, Christine, and Shannon Craigo-Snell, eds. *Claiming God: Essays in Honor of Marilyn McCord Adams*. Eugene, Ore.: Pickwick, 2022.

Hart, David Bentley. *The Beauty of the Infinite: The Aesthetics of Christian Truth*. Grand Rapids: Eerdmans, 2004.

Huizinga, Johan. *Homo Ludens: A Study of the Play-Element in Culture*. Boston: Beacon, 1971.

Julian of Norwich. *A Revelation of Love*. Edited with introduction by Elisabeth M. Dutton. Lanham, Md.: Rowman & Littlefield, 2008.

Khabeb, Angela T. "Grateful Ground." *Living Lutheran*. November 22, 2021. https://www.livinglutheran.org/2021/11/48338.

Liederbach, Mark D., and Evan Lenow. *Ethics as Worship: The Pursuit of Moral Discipleship*. Phillipsburg, N.Y.: P & R Publishing, 2021.

Luther, Martin. "[The Ninety-Five Theses or] Disputation for Clarifying the Power of Indulgences, 1517." Translated by Charles M. Jacobs. Revised by Harold J. Grimm. Newly revised by Timothy J. Wengert. In *The Annotated Luther*, vol. 1, *The Roots of Reform*, edited by Timothy J. Wengert, 34–46. Minneapolis: Fortress, 2015.

———. *The Freedom of a Christian, 1520*. Translated by W. A. Lambert and Harold J. Grimm. Revised Translation by Mark Tranvik. Newly Revised Translation by. Timothy J. Wengert. The Annotated Luther Study Edition. Edited by Timothy J. Wengert. Minneapolis: Fortress, 2016.

———. "The Small Catechism (1529)." Section on "The Sacrament of Holy Baptism." In *The Book of Concord: The Confessions of the Evangelical Lutheran Church*, translated by Charles Arand et al., edited by Robert Kolb and Timothy J. Wengert. Minneapolis: Fortress, 2000.

McCord Adams, Marilyn. *Christ and Horrors: The Coherence of Christology*. Current Issues in Theology. Cambridge: Cambridge University Press, 2006.

Murdoch, Iris. *The Sovereignty of Good*. Abingdon, UK: Routledge, 2000 [1970].

Nessan, Craig L. *Free in Deed: The Heart of Lutheran Ethics*. Minneapolis: Fortress, 2022.

Niebuhr, H. Richard. *Christ and Culture*. 50th anniversary ed. Foreword by Martin E. Marty and preface by James M. Gustafson. New York: HarperCollins, 2001.

Rector, Denise. "Race and the Gift of Lament." *Dialog* 60, no. 1 (2021): 22–27.

Ripley, Amanda. *High Conflict: Why We Get Trapped and How We Get Out*. New York: Simon & Schuster, 2021.

Schiess, Kaitlyn. *The Liturgy of Politics: Spiritual Formation for the Sake of Our Neighbor*. Foreword by Michael Wear. Downer's Grove, Ill.: InterVarsity Press, 2020.

Springs, Jason A. *Healthy Conflict in Contemporary American Society: From Enemy to Adversary*. Cambridge: Cambridge University Press, 2018.

Trigg, Jonathan D. *Baptism in the Theology of Martin Luther*. Studies in the History of Christian Traditions 56. Boston: Brill, 2001.

Weil, Simone. "Forms of the Implicit Love of God." In *Waiting for God*, translated by Emma Craufurd, 137–215. New York: Harper Colophon Books, 1973 [1950].

Wengert, Timothy J. *Martin Luther's Catechisms: Forming the Faith*. Minneapolis: Fortress, 2009.

Index of Biblical Passages

Index of Names and Subjects

Page numbers in *italics* represent figures.

heresy/heresies, 61, 90–91, 93, 98–99, 138, 142–43, 153, 160, 165–66, 209, 214; and the Christian Right, 204; and debates, 93, 100–101; and states of exception, 198; and winning, 222; *see also* orthodoxy; practices, of orthodoxy or heresy

Herman, Judith Lewis, 23

hero/heroism, 74; actions of, 197; individual (extraordinary faith), 14, 213; and justice-seeking, 64, 67; Luther as modern hero, 15; moral, 14, 18, 24; and ordinary faith, 24, 61; and prophetic speech, 24

Heschel, Abraham Joshua, 176

history: *see* arc

Hitler, Adolf, 192

Holl, Karl, 35

Holy Spirit, 1, 9, 11, 27, 28–29, 34, 44, 45, 50, 52–53, 55, 58, 60, 63, 66, 67, 84, 85, 94, 96, 99, 102, 103, 107, 124–25, 150, 154, 203, 208, 210, 216, 219, 221, 223, 230, 232, 243, 249, 254

hope: *see* emotions, hope

hopelessness, 87

Huizinga, Johan, 221

icon: Bonhoeffer as, 193; female power and authority, 149; "here I stand," 16; the iconic, 141; iconoclasm, 249; of liberation theology, 200; Martin Luther the reformer as, 14–15; Martin Luther King as, 169; maternal, 150; pregnant woman as icon of Mary, 147, 149; solo truth-to-power speaker as icon of modernity, 16; women as, 150

identity politics, 180; *see also* Christian identity

idol(s), 19, 29, 53, 90–91, 175–76, 211–12, 243

idolatry, 148, 175, 198, 210–14, 222, 235, 240–43, 249–50, 253

imaginaries, national, 168–69, 174–75, 177–80, 186

imagination, 15, 20, 26–28, 39, 43–44, 52, 55, 60, 66, 72–74, 78–83, 86, 91, 93, 100–101, 106–7, 112, 134, 139–41, 144, 153, 160–63, 169–70, 174, 177–86, 188, 192, 195–96, 200, 211–12, 214, 216, 223, 230, 235, 249; *see also* stories; storytelling

imago dei (image of God), 130–31

incurvatus in se (curved in upon oneself), 51–52, 54

individualism, and American Christianity, 7, 16

inequality, 39, 49, 169, 199n45; economic, 199n45; of gender, 113n15, 124–25; *see also* racism; injustice

injustice, 9, 24, 39, 48–49, 66, 68, 81, 88, 151, 162, 168, 173, 180, 193–97, 201, 215, 224, 230, 233, 237, 244, 253, 256; church divisions over, 54; *see also* inequality

Inter Caetera (1493 papal bull), 182

introspection, 86, 236

Ireland, 122, 127

Isasi-Díaz, Ada María, 50

Jesus, 3, 9, 11, 24, 37, 49, 81–82, 85, 221, 225–28; *see also* Christ

John the Baptist, 226

Johnson v. McIntosh, 183

Jones, D. Gareth, 205–6

Julian of Norwich, 47–48, 255

just societies, 2, 53, 79, 188, 203, 232

justice, 13, 42, 64–65, 68, 197, 231, 250; divine, 32, 41–42, 239; and divine sovereignty, 245; and freedom, 162–63; vs. justification, 33; naming, 12; structural, 88–89; and a will to power, 238

justice-seeking, 3, 13, 59, 64–65, 68, 107, 156, 159, 178, 196–97, 199, 201, 212, 226, 232, 251; and abortion, 106, 114–15, 131, 153; and Christian faith, 24; and Christian freedom, 165–66, 216,